The Teaching for Social Justice Series

William Ayers
Series Editor

Therese Quinn
Associate Series Editor

Editorial Board: Hal Adams, Barbara Bowman, Lisa Delpit, Michelle Fine,
Maxine Greene, Caroline Heller, Annette Henry, Asa Hilliard, Rashid Khalidi,
Gloria Ladson-Billings, Charles Payne, Mark Perry, Luis Rodriguez,
Jonathan Silin, William Watkins

Refusing Racism:
White Allies and the Struggle for Civil Rights
CYNTHIA STOKES BROWN

A School of Our Own:
Parents, Power, and Community at the East Harlem Block Schools
TOM RODERICK

The White Architects of Black Education:
Ideology and Power in America, 1865–1954
WILLIAM WATKINS

The Public Assault on America's Children:
Poverty, Violence, and Juvenile Injustice
VALERIE POLAKOW, Editor

Construction Sites:
Excavating Race, Class, and Gender Among Urban Youths
LOIS WEIS and MICHELLE FINE, Editors

Walking the Color Line:
The Art and Practice of Anti-Racist Teaching
MARK PERRY

A Simple Justice:
The Challenge of Small Schools
WILLIAM AYERS, MICHAEL KLONSKY, and
GABRIELLE H. LYON, Editors

Holler If You Hear Me:
The Education of a Teacher and His Students
GREGORY MICHIE

REFUSING RACISM

WHITE ALLIES AND THE STRUGGLE FOR CIVIL RIGHTS

Cynthia Stokes Brown

Teachers College, Columbia University
New York and London

Published by Teachers College Press, 1234 Amsterdam Avenue, New York, NY 10027

Excerpts from *Outside the Magic Circle: The Autobiography of Virginia Foster Durr*, by Virginia Durr, reprinted by permission of University of Alabama Press. Copyright © 1985 by University of Alabama Press.

Excerpts from *Reminiscences of Waties Waring* (1955–1957), in the Columbia University Oral History Research Office Collection, reproduced by permission.

Excerpts from *A Passion for Justice: J. Waties Waring and Civil Rights*, by T. E. Yarbrough, reprinted by permission of Oxford University Press. Copyright © 1987 by Oxford University Press.

Excerpts from *Reminiscences of Anne Braden* (July 1979), in the Columbia University Oral History Research Office Collection, reproduced by permission.

Excerpts from *The Wall Between*, by Anne Braden, reprinted by permission of Anne Braden. Copyright © 1999 by Anne Braden.

Excerpts from "You Can't Be Neutral: An Interview by Sue Thrasher and Eliot Wigginton" (interview with Anne Braden) reprinted, by permission, from *Southern Exposure, 12*, pp. 79–85. Copyright © 1984 Southern Exposure.

Excerpts from Herbert Kohl's talk at Cody's Bookstore used by permission of Herbert Kohl.

Library of Congress Cataloging-in-Publication Data

Brown, Cynthia Stokes.
    Refusing racism : white allies and the struggle for civil rights / Cynthia Stokes Brown.
      p.   cm. — (The teaching for social justice series)
    Includes bibliographical references (p.   ) and index.
    ISBN 0-8077-4204-X (pbk. : alk. paper) — ISBN 0-8077-4205-8 (cloth : alk. paper)
    1. Civil rights workers—United States—Biography. 2. Whites—United
States—Biography. 3. African Americans—Civil rights—History—20th century.
4. Civil rights movements—United States—History—20th century. 5. Racism—United
States—History—20th century. 6. United States—Race relations. I. Title. II. Series.

E185.98.A1 B76   2002
323.1'196073'00923034—dc21   2001060356

ISBN 0–8077–4204–X (paper)
ISBN 0–8077–4205–8 (cloth)

In the long run there is no more liberating, no more exhilarating experience than to determine one's position, state it bravely and then *act boldly*. Action brings with it its own courage, its own energy.

—Eleanor Roosevelt, *Tomorrow Is Now*

Contents

Series Foreword

TEACHING FOR SOCIAL JUSTICE might be thought of as a kind of popular education—of, by, and for the people—something that lies at the heart of education in a democracy, education toward a more vital, more muscular democratic society. It can propel us toward action, away from complacency, reminding us of the powerful commitment, persistence, bravery, and triumphs of our justice-seeking forebears—women and men who sought to build a world that worked for us all. Abolitionists, suffragists, labor organizers, civil rights activists: Without them, liberty would today be slighter, poorer, weaker—the American flag wrapped around an empty shell—a democracy of form and symbol over substance.

A teacher for social justice might think of participatory democracy as both a means and an end—a sweet romance to imagine and to work toward; a concrete living commitment to a kind of classroom life. This teacher is interested in solidarity, not service; in justice, not charity—and must work, then, to become fully alert and present to the students as three dimensional and fully human, and at the same time wide awake to a world in need of repair.

Rousseau argues that equality "must not be understood to mean that degrees of power and wealth should be exactly the same," but only that with respect to *power*, equality renders it "incapable of all violence" and only exerted in the interest of a freely developed and participatory law; and that with respect to *wealth*, "no citizen should be so opulent that he can buy another, and none so poor that he or she is constrained to sell himself." The quest for equality and social justice over many centuries is worked out in the open spaces of that proclamation, in the concrete struggles of human beings constructing and contesting all kinds of potential meanings within that ideal. Nothing is settled, surely, once and for all, but a different order of question presents itself: Who should be included? What do we owe one another? What is fair and unfair?

This series gathers together examples of popular education being practiced today, as well as clear and new thinking concerning issues of democracy, social justice, and educational activism. Many contributions will be grounded in practice and will, we hope, focus on the complexities built into popular education: difficulties, setbacks, successes, steps forward—work that reminds us of what Bernice Johnson Reagon calls "the sweetness of struggle." We seek, as well, developing theoretical work that might push us all forward as we look for new meanings of democracy in these changing times, the demands of justice in our imperfect world, and the imperatives, then, of social change. We want to encourage new voices and new ideas, and in all cases to contribute to a serious, grounded, and thoughtful exchange about the enduring questions in education: Education for what? Education for whom? Education toward what kind of social order?

For every human being life is, in part, an experience of suffering and loss and pain. But our living experience also embraces other inescapable facts: that we are all in this together, for example, and that much (but not all) of what we suffer in life is the evil we visit upon one another; that is, it is unjustified suffering, unnatural loss, unnecessary pain—the kinds of things that ought to be avoidable, that we might even imagine eliminating altogether.

In the realm of human agency and choice, we come face to face with some stubborn questions: Can we stop the suffering? Can we alleviate at least some of the pain? Can we repair any of the loss? We lurch, then, toward deeper considerations: Can society be changed at all? Is it remotely possible—not inevitable, certainly, perhaps not even very likely—for people to come together freely, to imagine a more just and peaceful social order, to join hands and organize, to struggle for something better, and to prevail?

If society cannot be changed under any circumstances, if there is nothing to be done, not even small and humble gestures toward something better, well, that about ends all conversation. Our sense of agency shrinks, our choices diminish. What more is there to say? But if a fairer, more sane, more person-oriented (instead of thing-oriented) society is both desirable and possible, that is, if some of us can join one another to imagine and build a participatory movement for justice, a public space for the enactment of democratic dreams, our field opens slightly. There is still much to be done, for nothing is entirely settled. We still need, for example, to find ways to stir ourselves and our neighbors from passivity, cynicism, and despair; to reach beyond the superficial barriers that wall us off from one another; to resist the flattening effects of consumerism and the blinding, mystifying power of the familiar social evils—racism, sexism, and homophobia, for example; to shake off the anesthetizing impact of most classrooms, most research, and the authoritative, official voices that dominate the airwaves, the media, and so much of what we think of as common sense; to, as Maxine Greene says, "release our imaginations" and act on behalf of what the known demands, linking our conduct firmly to our consciousness. We are moving, then, without guarantees, but with purpose and with hope.

Education is, of course, an arena of struggle as well as hope—struggle because it stirs in us the need to reconsider everything we have wrought, to look at the world anew, to question what we have created, to wonder what is worthwhile for human beings to know and experience, to justify or criticize or bombard or maintain or build up or overthrow everything before us—and hope because we gesture toward the future, toward the impending, toward the coming of the new. Education is where we gather to question whether and how we might engage and enlarge and change our lives, and it is, then, where we confront our dreams and fight out notions of the good life, where we try to comprehend, apprehend, or possibly even change the world. James Baldwin reminds us that any real change implies the breakup of the world as we know it, the end of safety. Education is contested space, a natural site of conflict—sometimes restrained, other times in full eruption—over questions of justice.

Even now there are young women in Mexico and the Philippines who must choose between selling their bodies and starving; children in Palestine/Israel who are asked to eat dust and breathe humiliation; young men in American cities who can find a gun and a packet of drugs more easily than a library card, a job, or a decent school to attend; young men whose pathway to prison is already scripted, already paned, even now.

The work, of course, is never done. Democracy is dynamic, a community always in the making. Teaching for social justice continues the difficult task of constructing and reinvigorating a public. It builds on a fundamental message of the teacher—you must change your life—and goes a notch deeper: you can change the world. It broadens the table, so that more may sit together. Clearly, we have a long, long way to go. And we begin.

William Ayers, Series Editor
Therese Quinn, Associate Series Editor

Acknowledgments

I AM INESCAPABLY INDEBTED to the individuals featured in this book—for their lives and, in several cases, for their direct assistance. Herb Kohl and Anne Braden read and reread, helping me clarify the issues and get things straight. Virginia Durr visited me on one of her trips to Berkeley to visit Jessica Mitford. Judge Waring became vivid to me through the late Septima Poinsette Clark, whom I visited in Charleston first in August 1979. I am also indebted to Lucy Hackney, one of Virginia Durr's daughters, for reading her mother's chapter and responding with ideas and corrections.

A book such as this one requires the rigorous self-examination that can occur only with supportive, yet challenging, friends and colleagues. For this I am deeply indebted to Jack Robbins, Daphne Muse, Karen Jorgensen, Francie Kendall, Paul Kivel, Marlene Griffith, and Marianna Eraklis. I also wish to thank Beverly Daniel Tatum, Louise Derman-Sparks, Carol Brunson Phillips, and Gary Howard for their helpful examination of White racial identity development.

I was able to commence this book with the assistance of a one-semester sabbatical granted by the trustees of then Dominican College of San Rafael, now Dominican University of California. I am grateful for their generosity. My colleagues in the Secondary Teaching Program have supported my ideas and my writing and have picked up some slack when necessary; I want to thank Grace Grant, Barry Kaufman, Ed Kujawa, Carol Treasure, Lisa Soll, and the late Paul Bosque. My students, the wonderful people taking up the challenge of public school teaching, provided my most constant incentive.

Finally, this book came into being because Bill Ayers and Therese Quinn, and Catherine Bernard at Teachers College Press, recognized its possibilities and provided the exact support and criticism that was needed. My hat is off to their whole project.

Introduction

THE FIGHT AGAINST RACISM in the United States has always involved not only people of color but also some white allies. These white allies have usually not been portrayed in U.S. history textbooks—one indicator of the unacknowledged racism that has been present in the U.S. school system (Aptheker, 1992).

In this book I tell the stories of four white allies, starting in the 1930s and coming up to the present. I hope my accounts will keep these stories in circulation and reinforce the idea of the white ally. I want to show, in detail, how some of those considered white were able to join unequivocally in the fight for the liberation of those considered other "races," as well as for their own freedom from racism. I do this to provide role models of antiracist white identity and action. In addition, I hope my stories will give readers of all backgrounds a chance to reflect on their lives; grasp the complexity of the idea of the white ally; and come away with increased hope for, and determination to achieve, intercultural cooperation.

Only after we white people work our way through understanding racism, a painful and difficult part of our growth, can we realize how stunted we were before. I hope these stories will contribute to a positive white perspective, to aspects of our culture that we can embrace with pride. One way to be antiracist without seeming to be antiwhite is to know the stories of other white antiracists.

More specifically, this book contains material that teachers, professors, and workshop leaders can add to their curricula, whether by retelling some of these stories in middle and high school or by sharing chapters or the entire book with university and nonuniversity adult groups. In addition, the history of the false idea of race needs to be talked about and discussed, so that everyone, oppressed as well as oppressors, can perform the difficult operation of removing it from our minds. The capsule history in chapter 1 provides material for this.

I have been encouraged to persist with these stories by the observations of two university teachers, Michelle D. Young at the University of Iowa and Jerry Rosiek at the University of Alabama, who wrote in their review of the book *White Reign*:

> One is given the impression that, to date, we have no living and breathing models of fierce anti-racist people who identify as white to whom we can look for inspiration (among other things). No one was identified [in *White Reign*] whose practical struggles with things like cultural disequilibrium, being pathologized by other whites, or dealing with racist family members could at least provide an occasion for these issues to be discussed. Historical figures like John Brown, or civil rights martyr Viola Liuzzo come to mind. Similarly, readers who are interested in meeting the challenges raised by authors [of essays in *White Reign*] are not only left to reinvent themselves with no tangible models, but we are also given no information as to what kinds of supports or resources one might need to make such a transformation. What kinds of communities or resources will individuals with these white identities need in order to practice anti-racism and work for equity and social justice? (Young & Rosiek, 2000, p. 43)

This lack of discussion about the lives of living, breathing white antiracists is the gap I hope my stories will help to fill. By featuring specific details and the development of thought and action, my stories reveal how four white allies figured out how to be effective antiracists in a racist society.

TERMS DEFINED

Before I can begin, there is the complicated matter of how to write about "race." I put the word in quotation marks because I believe the biological evidence is now unequivocal that race does not exist as a biological category, that people cannot be divided into racial groups on any consistent physical traits. This is the conclusion reached after recent decades of theorizing about race by such authors as Stephen Jay Gould (1981); R. C. Lewontin, Steven Rose, and Leon J. Kamin (1984); Audrey Smedley (1993); Eugenia Shanklin, (1994); and John Relethford (1994), a conclusion now confirmed by the Genome Project as it nears completion.

Sociologists and anthropologists today regard the concept of race as a social construct, that is, a label that politically and culturally dominant groups apply to themselves and to other groups. Racial designations and definitions are understood to change over time, reflecting changes in political power and attitudes (Derman-Sparks & Phillips, 1997; Walker, Spohn, & Delone, 2000).

The idea of race was used by European and European American people to explain and to justify their domination of the world and the domination of people of color in their own lands. This is racism, or "white" people's discrimination against people of color based on their belief in the supremacy of the "white race." Another, more specific, term for racism is "white supremacy," which underscores the way in which white people have created entire social, political, economic, and cultural systems that assign people of color to the bottom rungs of the ladder of privilege (Blaut, 1993; Mills, 1997).

Hence the paradox that, even though race does not exist as a biological reality, racism certainly does. Racism exists both in the current manifestations of the white supremacist system that have not yet been dismantled and in the present consequences for people of color of the discrimination that happened in the past under more nearly complete white supremacy. An example of current racism would be the failure of European American teachers to create a positive educational experience for children of color or the failure of European American doctors to offer all available treatment options to people of color. An instance of racism from the past would be living with the effects of policies that ensured that parents and grandparents would have little education and no financial assets to transfer to the present generation.

The goal I envision is for the people of the United States to continue to transform their country from a white supremacist society into one that is antiracist; multicultural; and more democratic, both politically and economically. In such a society, some individuals in each cultural/ethnic group would maintain and elaborate traditional identities, while others would seek exchanges among cultures and create ways to evolve into new, hybrid forms of culture.

To this end, it seems wise to stop using any kind of racial terminology and use only terms that refer to cultural, ethnic, or national origins. Racial terms refer to some physical dimension, whereas ethnic and national ones refer solely to culture and location.

National agreement on terms for groups has certainly not yet been reached, especially since usage has political consequences. Census 2000 thoroughly mixed its usage. It designated three racial categories: white, black–African American–Negro, and American Indian–Alaska native. Then it offered eleven ethnic or national categories for Asian Americans to fit themselves into, plus a catch-all category: "some other race." This confusion demonstrates the disagreements people have regarding what terms should be used and what the reality is.

Because I no longer believe that "race" is a valid category, I am trying to abandon the racial designations "black" and "white," even though they are short and handy. But in writing about the past, I use them, or similar racial labels, because they reflect the terms people used during the times I am writing about. In my final two portraits I switch my terminology to European American and African American to reflect my own view that only ethnicity and nationality make sense, not race.

"White ally" is a term that I learned from Beverly Tatum, dean of Mount Holyoke College. In 1994 Tatum wrote that when she teaches about racism to college students and to teachers, she finds that almost no one can name any white allies, either now or in the past. Tatum defines a white ally as "an antiracist activist, a white man or woman who is clearly identifiable as an ally to people of color in the struggle against racism" (1994, p. 462). I take this to mean taking a public stand against the racist assumptions that surround one, against the prevailing system of white supremacy, when one is the beneficiary of the system. Tatum's plea for the need to honor white allies gave me the idea for this book.

Tatum believes that "teaching about racism needs to shift from an exploration of the experience of victims and victimizers to that of empowered people of color and their white allies, creating the possibility of working together as partners in the establishment of a more just society" (p. 474). She urges that stories of white allies be emphasized because this model of whiteness is not as readily available to European Americans as three other models, which she calls "white supremacist," "what whiteness?" and "guilty white." White people, she says, need "white ally" as a model, since it is the only model by which they can achieve a fully positive white identity. Other theorists agree with Tatum that a positive white identity is possible (Derman-Sparks & Phillips, 1997; Howard, 1999).

Yet some current theorists believe that no positive white identity is possible and advocate renouncing whiteness all together. They prefer the term "race traitor," making proud use of what white supremacists use as a hostile epithet. See, for example, Noel Ignatiev and John Garvey, editors of *Race Traitor* (1996) and of the online journal *Race Traitor*. They argue that whiteness has no content beyond the exclusion of non-whites and therefore the idea of whiteness should be eliminated.

At first I disliked the term *race traitor*. *Traitor* seemed too negative; who would aspire to that? Plus, a traitor has to betray something, which seems to dignify race. But with familiarity I have seen that *race traitor* is a double negative, making a positive, and have come to enjoy the punch of the term. It points in the right direction. Yet the problem remains that, even if some whites manage to abolish whiteness in their minds, other people still perceive them as white. In addition, whites cannot at once abolish the privileges that have accrued from past racism, nor can we abolish the culture we carry as European Americans. Presumably Garvey and Ignatiev hope that if European Americans just stop thinking of ourselves as "white," then we will just stop reproducing racist structures. But the process takes time. Whites need to choose antiracist elements of their culture as the foundation of a new identity and take active responsibility for eliminating racism. Hence, I am sticking with the term "white ally" as referring to a positive European American identity.

To qualify as a white ally in the past demanded a high degree of moral courage, and in some cases it still does. A Caribbean American colleague of mine, Carol Treasure, defines white ally as "one who stands besides you and goes with you, as to war." This suggests the severe consequences often faced by white allies, consequences such as rejection and ostracism by family, friends, and other whites; and loss of job opportunities and upward mobility.

In writing about white allies, I want to focus on the complex reasons European American people would give up some of their racial privilege. What motivated them to act? Were they aware of what they might lose? What did they lose? What did they gain? What did they think as they paused to consider their next decision? At what point in their lives did they begin to act against the system of white supremacy? How did they find or create support? On what systems of morality did they base their moral decisions? Reflecting on the answers to these questions may illuminate the answers to them in our own lives.

Under this layer of questions lies another. Were some white people really able to support people of color? How could they possibly understand oppression that they had not experienced? Could they actually relinquish privilege rather than simply talk as if they would? Not everyone who thinks they want to help dismantle white supremacy succeeds at being effective. These questions often undermine the confidence of white people and the trust of people of color; they need to be brought to the surface as much as possible.

I have chosen four white allies, each of whom I present in a short biography. This is a complicated undertaking. On the one hand, I need to portray a complex inner reality of choices, decisions, values, beliefs, and feelings, which only the protagonists themselves can report. For this reason my accounts rely heavily on oral interviews, many unpublished, and on autobiographical writings. On the other hand, white allies interacted with a tremendously complex outer reality, with which the reader must be familiar to understand the choices made by the allies. Therefore, to provide a background for my biographies, in my first chapter I set out a capsule history of white supremacy in the United States and of resistance to it in the twentieth century. In that chapter I explain more about my understanding of race and racism. In it I tell an extremely short version of a long, complicated story; it is my own interpretation, fashioned to create a big picture of the idea of race and to provide a backdrop for the four stories that follow. We European Americans can only break our silence about these complicated matters if we attempt some coherent summary of them.

The first two portraits in this book are those of white allies who lived in the South and who focused their efforts on ending discrimination against African Americans. In making this choice, I do not mean to insinuate that white supremacy did not, and does not, have an impact on other people of color. I have chosen to focus on black/white relations for a number of interconnected reasons. I believe that African Americans were the primary group enslaved, had the longest way to go, and often led the way in fighting for their rights. I want my portraits to play off one another and build common connections. And I need to draw on my own experience of racism, which has had a black/white focus since I grew up in the 1940s and 1950s under full segregation in a ex-Confederate town in western Kentucky.

My final two portraits extend the struggle against racism beyond the black/white dimension. The third features an ally who began her antiracist work for African Americans, but expanded it to include all people of color, while my fourth portrays a man who, from his adolescence, fought discrimination against all groups of people.

WHICH WHITE ALLIES?

By the time I arrived at adulthood in the early 1960s, legal segregation was cracking open in final defeat. It took great courage then to stand against segregation, but what did it mean to oppose it as a white southerner in the 1930s, 1940s, and 1950s? How could a white person find a way to stay in the South, while rejecting the whole white supremacist social structure?

To answer this question, I chose to start with two white allies in the generation previous to mine who stayed in the South and defied its racist structure. To continue, I chose one southerner and one northerner whose lives extend into the present and reveal the continuing dilemmas of being a white ally. My choices are

Virginia Durr (1903–1999)—housewife and political activist from Birmingham, Alabama, who fought against the poll tax and southern white male domination and for racial equality

Waties Waring (1880–1968)—federal judge from Charleston, South Carolina, who opened white primaries to black voters in his jurisdiction

Anne Braden (born 1924)—journalist and community organizer from Louisville, Kentucky, who defied real estate practices and the House Un-American Activities Committee and organized white southerners to support the civil rights movement

Herbert Kohl (born 1937)—writer and educator from New York City; author of *Thirty-six Children* and 25 other books about education and civil rights

The criteria I used to select these four lives for examination are somewhat arbitrary. I sought people who had a lifetime of sustained dedication to eradicating racism, yet I included one, Judge Waring, whose conversion occurred in his 60s. I looked for people with some historical signficance, yet not so much significance that they could not serve as models for ordinary people. My four choices are little known, except in the subculture of racial equality and social justice activism. Anne Braden calls this group the "other America"—not to be confused with Michael Harrington's use of that phrase for poor Americans.

I chose to tell stories for which documentation already existed—biographies, autobiographies, and oral histories—to provide materials for my work. I was able to personally interview three of the four; Judge Waring I never met, but he left a full oral history at Columbia University. My profiles are based extensively on the words of my protagonists, letting them interpret the way they conceived their own lives, given their chosen objectives.

In addition to these basic requirements, I wanted some balance to the stories I told, a balance of men and women, of northerners and southerners, and of religious and political beliefs. Two are men; two are women whose stories reveal the sexism of the southern ideal of women. Two are southerners, one is northern, while one grew up southern but lived in a border city, Louisville, Kentucky. The first three grew up in Protestant households, the last one in a culturally Jewish but nonreligious family. The first two were liberals—they supported increased democratization within a capitalist framework. The last two can be called radicals—they sought deeper transformations of U.S. society and consistently criticized capitalism.

I also chose allies from across the class spectrum. Judge Waring was an upper-class aristocrat. Virginia Durr and Anne Braden both renounced their upper-class status for working-class lives. Herb Kohl lives as a middle-class person, while retaining allegiance to the working class. Class issues have always been intertwined with race issues; when my narrative of Braden and Kohl's lives brings us to current times, the issues of race seem almost to merge with those of class (hooks, 2000).

   Herb Kohl and I have been friends over 30 years and intermittently colleagues on various projects. My choice of his story as the capstone for this book reveals my belief that schools are a pivotal arena in which issues of race and class clash and are negotiated.

   In choosing four white allies, I have omitted hundreds. Three I particularly wanted to include are Myles Horton, founder of Highlander Folk School; Lillian Smith, north Georgia writer; and Morris Dees, founder of the Southern Poverty Law Center. There have been many white allies, to African Americans and to other people of color, contrary to what our textbooks have led us to believe. The more I have investigated, the more I have found, including refugees from Nazism who taught at black colleges (Goldcomb, 1993). Perhaps what is needed is a granite wall like the Vietnam War Memorial on which to list the names. I have added an appendix as a start. We need all the models we can find—in books, on TV, and in our daily lives. Each of us has to figure out which stones in the wall between us we can personally remove.

1

Racism and Resistance:
A Capsule Sketch

I T SEEMS LIKELY to historians that racist thinking in the West does not extend to earlier than the sixteenth century. Ethnic differences are probably nearly as old as the human species, and so is ethnocentrism, the belief of each group that its customs are superior to all others. But this is different from racist thinking, which holds that cultural attributes correlate with perceived or imagined physical traits such as skin color or skull shape.

An early example of racist thinking in global history occurred in India when a linguistic group called the Aryans migrated there in the middle of the second millenium B.C.E. The Aryans, who spoke a variant of an Indo-European language, were herders in the area between the Caspian and Black seas. They had a warrior culture and, after they arrived in India, pictured themselves as light-skinned conquerors of the indigenous, dark-skinned peoples. Their laws and practices gave rise to a caste system based on skin color, with dark-skinned people assigned to the lowest positions, that has formed the basis of Indian social organization in subsequent history (Stearns, Adas, & Schwartz, 1992).

In Western history, however, early texts in general do not mention much about the physical features of different groups. Their authors seem to have assumed that language and customs were more significant differences than physical traits and that language and customs were not inborn or correlated with physical traits. As the British historian Ivan Hannaford argues in his history of the idea of race in the West, "There is very little evidence of a conscious idea of race until after the Reformation" (1996, p. 187). Even the slavery that had existed for thousands of years in the Mediterranean area was based, not on skin color, but rather on traditions that persons of a different religion, or persons captured in war, could be enslaved for life (Smedley, 1993; Meltzer, 1993).

THE TRAJECTORY OF WHITE RACISM

Racist thinking seems to have developed as Europeans spread out from Europe, subjugating other peoples who were less technologically advanced. Slavery based on skin color developed in the Americas in Spanish, Dutch, and English colonies, between 1492 and 1700. In Spanish colonies it developed in the 1500s; in the Dutch and English colonies it occurred largely from 1650 to 1700. During these years Dutch and English colonists gradually began to think of themselves as "white" rather than as Christians, and to think of Africans as Negroes rather than as heathens, using skin color to mark them as inferior and to justify their enslavement (Wood, 1996).

How did this transformation to enslavement by skin color happen in what would later become the United States? It took hold slowly over many decades. It began in the Caribbean and Latin America, where Spanish and Portuguese colonizers enslaved "infidels," first Indians and then Africans. The colonizers first rationalized that enslaving non-Christians was acceptable, and that those who converted to Christianity would receive their freedom. But gradually, in order not to lose their cheap labor through conversion, the wealthy planters in the tropics changed their rationale for enslaving people to something permanent, to skin color (Jordan, 1974; Wood, 1996).

By 1650, the Dutch, and the English too, had begun to use enslaved Africans to produce sugar in the Caribbean and the tropics. In 1660 the restored English king, Charles II, chartered the Royal African Company to compete in the slave trade; he also chartered a new colony in Carolina to challenge the Spanish colonies. Gradually, the landowners had increasing difficulty obtaining labor for their holdings—a plague reduced the population in England, and Native American captives could easily escape. From about 1660 to 1680, the dominant English gentry, with that of the tobacco colonies of Virginia and Maryland taking the lead, shifted the definition of who could be a slave from someone who was not a Christian to someone not European in appearance, and they made this enslavement hereditary (Jordan, 1974; Wood, 1996).

Thus enslavement based on skin color began in the American colonies before there was any comprehensive formulation of what the so-called races were supposed to be. Such formulations developed in the eighteenth century, as European scientists began to classify human groups. The Swedish botanist Carolus Linneaus was one of the first when, in 1737, he listed four varieties of humans, based on skin color and temperament. In 1775 the German originator of anthropology, Friedrich Blumenbach, introduced the use of skull shape and the term "Caucasian," based on one skull he possessed from the Caucasus Mountains. Blumenbach set up five "racial" categories—Caucasian, Mongolian, Ethiopian, American, and Malay—to classify human beings (Shanklin, 1994).

While the idea of race and white supremacy was becoming more entrenched, the actual enslavement of African people was being abolished in Europe and the Americas. When West Indian planters began to carry their domestic slaves to England, the Anti-Slavery Society was organized there, in 1765. Within 7 years English courts ruled slavery illegal in that country. In 1807 Parliament declared the slave trade illegal. This occurred in part because of moral opposition by Quakers and Methodists, and in part because the new industrial leaders of England no longer responded to the needs of the planters of the West Indies and North America. The new industries had been funded by profits from the slave trade, but once in business industrial leaders needed to find labor at home and markets in Africa. A year later the U.S. Congress declared the slave trade illegal, and European countries followed, so that by 1842 the trade was legally dead. Smuggling continued until slavery itself was abolished, which occurred in the United States in 1862, ended by a civil war (Meltzer, 1993).

But the idea of white supremacy endured, serving as the rationale for European and American imperialism and, internally, for the allocation of wealth and status. Science and social science, especially through the disciplines of anthropology, sociology, and psychology, persisted in supporting the theory that humanity could be categorized into separate "races" and that those races differed in brain capacity as well as skin color. During the nineteenth century anthropologists madly measured skulls, trying to establish the dimensions of each race. Many deluded themselves into believing that they had succeeded. By the end of the nineteenth century a bewildering variety of racial classifications was in use; scientists never agreed even on how many races there were (Banton & Harwood, 1975; Gould, 1981).

In nineteenth-century political and social life, too, the definitions of race were fluid and constructed by the people in power. For example, when the Irish began arriving in the United States in large numbers in the 1840s, they found themselves in a society based on a strict racial hierarchy. To native-born "white" Americans, the Irish seemed of another race, just as Poles or Italians did, based on supposed skull differences and on cultural differences that were seen to be inborn. The Irish were thought to belong to the Celtic "race," and were depicted as apelike in cartoons. They had to struggle for their whiteness; by adopting the white supremacist doctrine of the Democratic Party, the Irish were eventually successful in establishing their identity as white people and overcoming anti-Irish and anti-Catholic attitudes (Sipress, 1997).

After the Civil War, for the period of barely a decade known as Reconstruction, the United States had a chance to overcome White supremacy and transform itself into a multiracial, democratic society. But the promise of Reconstruction tragically failed. The North's commitment to racial equality was partial and weakened steadily after 1870. The Supreme Court made rulings on the 14th Amendment that rendered it meaningless for decades. Congress pardoned former rebels in 1872; the Democratic Party regained control of eight southern states by 1876 and increased its power in the North. The new president elected in 1876 without the popular vote, Rutherford B. Hayes, although Republican, withdrew federal troops from the South and acknowledged that Reconstruction was over. Those defined as white regained economic control of the labor of those defined as black and blocked their access to political representation (Moore & Banfield, 1983; Norton, Katzman, Escott, Chudacoff, Paterson, & Tuttle, 1990).

Republicans in the South tried a race policy of moderation and Populists tried an alliance with Negroes, but by the 1890s white supremacy, through the Democratic Party, prevailed. Between 1890 and 1907, every southern and border state "legally" disenfranchised the vast majority of its African American voters (all male) by closing primaries to them and by instituting poll taxes and literacy requirements, among other devices. These laws reduced, as well, the number of poor European Americans who voted, leaving the South more than ever governed by a small group of wealthy European American men. During this period more than 80% of all African Americans lived in the South. By 1910 Jim Crow laws, segregating them as completely as possible from European American society, were in place across the South (Loewen, 1995).

In the period 1890–1930, the expression of European American racism in the United States against all people of color reached new heights. In 1896 the Supreme Court upheld segregation in *Plessy v. Ferguson*. Both houses of Congress and a succession of presidents of both parties supported segregation in the South. In 1898 the United States embarked on imperialistic conquests in the Caribbean and the Pacific. Minstrel shows grew wildly popular from New England to California. The first masterpiece of American film was the racist epic *Birth of a Nation* (1915), which helped the Ku Klux Klan (KKK) rise to its zenith in the early 1920s with a national membership of more than 4 million. The KKK openly dominated the state government of Indiana for a time and inducted President Warren G. Harding as a member in a ceremony at the White House. European American mobs killed tens of thousands of African Americans across the United States, by hanging, burning, shooting, or torture, with only a tiny fraction of these crimes ever investigated by a grand jury. This is a horrifying story, but its omission from most textbooks leaves student readers of all skin colors unable to understand the systemic racism, upheld by terrorism, that African Americans, and all people of color, continued to face long after the abolition of slavery (Allen, Als, Lewis, & Litwack, 2000; Loewen, 1995; Woodward, 1966).

In the 1920s it was common to believe that every culture corresponded to a race. For example, a widely read study of the "immigration problem" identified 56 distinct races employed in U.S. industry. Its authors, who were sympathetic to new arrivals from eastern and southern Europe, named as distinct races Poles, Slovaks, South Italians, North Italians, Hebrews, Spaniards, and "native born white Americans" among the 56. The authors discussed physical features; they were not referring solely to culture (Sipress, 1997).

Highly respected European American professors continued into the twentieth century to delineate racist ideas as if they were scientific facts. One example was Dr. Robert Bennet Bean, professor of anatomy at the University of Virginia. His popular book, *The Races of Man*, published in 1932, was used in universities and secondary schools, and he wrote magazine and scholarly articles about race for more than 20 years. Bean simplified the basic racial types to three—the White Race, the Yellow-Brown Race, and the Black Race. Here is how he described, in *The Races of Man*, the mental characteristics of the three "races":

> In general, the brain of the White Race is large, the convolutions are rich, with deep fissures. The mental characteristics are activity, nervous and physical vivacity, strong ambitions and passions, and highly developed idealism. . . .
>
> The brain of the Yellow-Brown Race is about medium size, with medium to good convolutions, which are sometimes varied and deep. The mental characteristics of the Yellow-Browns need further study, but they seem to be less vivacious, with emotions and passions less evident than in the other two races. They possess moderate idealism and some love of sport, but have less spirit for exploration and adventure than the White Race.
>
> The size of the brain in the Black Race is below the medium both of the Whites and the Yellow-Browns, frequently with relatively more simple convolutions. . . . The psychic activities of the Black Race are a careless, jolly vivacity, emotions and passions of short duration, and a strong and somewhat irrational egoism. Idealism, ambition, and the co-operative faculties are weak. They love amusement and sport, but have little initiative and adventurous spirit. . . . They have poetry of a low order, are rather free from lasting worries, are cursed with superstitious fears, and have much emotionalism in religion. (Bean, 1935, pp. 94–95)

Bean exemplifies the academic respectability of extremely racist concepts, but by the early twentieth century scientific evidence was beginning to accumulate against the theory of race. In the first decade, investigations showed that the four basic blood groups are distributed over all the so-called races, not lining up with supposed racial categories (Diamond, 1980; Salmon, Cartron, & Rouger, 1984).

During the 1930s, courageous biologists in England, and sociologists and anthropologists in the United States, especially W. E. B. Du Bois, Franz Boas, and Ashley Montagu, took the lead in repudiating the concept of race. The balance of opinion among scientists may have tipped toward rejecting racist theory during the 1930s, but the general public did not begin to absorb this information until after World War II (Barkan, 1992; Williams, 1989, 1996).

Dominant public opinion in the United States and Europe continued to hold that humanity could be scientifically categorized by physical attributes into separate racial categories and that the white race is superior to others. White people's belief in racial superiority was demonstrated during World War II, when blood transfusions for wounded soldiers first became possible—in part as a result of the work of an African American physician, Charles Drew. At first the Red Cross announced in November 1941 a policy of excluding black donors, but after the outcry that ensued, it compromised by agreeing to accept blood from black people on the condition that it be kept segregated from the blood of whites. Scientists knew conclusively that this was not necessary, but the surgeons general of the army and navy and officials of the Red Cross believed that the program would not work otherwise. Too many white soldiers believed that skin color and "racial traits" could be transmitted through the blood; they feared having black children if they received "black" blood. Segregation of blood continued until December 1, 1950 (Egerton, 1994; Love, 1996).

Even while most European American U.S. soldiers believed in race as a physical reality, they experienced in World War II the extreme way in which Hitler used the idea of race to attack Jews and other "non-Aryans." The Nazi use of race to engage in "racial cleansing" revealed to many the lethal consequences of racist thinking. World War II diminished Europe's hegemony in the world; that continent's loss of strength resulted in its African and Asian colonies making successful bids for their independence in the decades following the war. Until then, white people could imagine themselves superior, but afterward it became more difficult.

As Western imperialism began to recede, the idea that had provided the rationale for Anglo-European dominance gradually lost its force; the concept that scientific racism was a falsehood began to gain a foothold in the minds of European Americans. By the 1960s and 1970s, a small majority of anthropologists acknowledged that the idea of race had no scientific validity or usefulnesss. Their arguments were summarized in the United States by James C. King in *The Biology of Race* (1971). Racial classification began to be seen as a hangover from an outdated phase of science, and by 1970 it was frequently being omitted from anthropology textbooks altogether (Shanklin, 1994; Smedley, 1993).

Yet at the same time, in the 1960s, a physical anthropologist from Harvard, Carleton S. Coon, was writing popular trade books about racial classifications, *The Origin of Races* (1962) and *The Living Races of Man* (1965). Coon considered Negro people to have started on the same evolutionary path as other human groups, and then to have "stood still for a half million years," presumably more like apes than other humans. Alfred Knopf Company published these books at the height of the civil rights movement, showing that the idea of biologically based racial categories is difficult to relinquish for many European Americans, in this case elite professors and publishers (Banton & Harwood, 1975).

Today most social and biological scientists agree that there is no scientific basis for dividing people into races. Race is not a valid biological category. Skin color has its own distribution independent of any other characteristics. Geneticists have found that there is more genetic variability between individuals than between any groups. As one team of biologists concludes: "The remarkable feature of human evolution and history has been the very small degree of divergence between geographical populations as compared with the genetic variation among individuals" (Lewontin, Rose, & Kamin, 1984, pp. 126–27).

The preliminary information coming in from the mapping of the human genome is reinforcing the amazing degree of similarity among all humans. At present the prevailing hypothesis is that Homo sapiens evolved in the savannas of eastern Africa, with each successive advance in human evolution occurring in Africa and spreading out from there to the rest of the world, meaning specifically that white-skinned people have evolved from black-skinned people. Everyone is African—the evidence is overwhelming that there is one mother continent. From the earliest times of Homo sapiens, people have intermixed so much on a worldwide basis that there has never been a "pure" population. People, or at the very least men, have traveled widely for millenia and have kept the mix brewing (Angier, 2000; Relethford, 1994; Shanklin, 1994).

So where is U.S. society now on the historical trajectory of white racism? After slavery, the worst European American violence and discrimination peaked in the period from the 1890s through the 1930s. Organized social and political resistance to racism began in the 1910s, as will be described below, while scientific undermining of the biological concept of race began in the 1930s and has come almost to its full conclusion with the preliminary reports from the Genome Project.

But the consequences of racial discrimination persist, and the idea of race remains in the minds of many nonscientists. It also remains embedded in the customs and the social, political, and economic institutions of the United States, making race a reality even though it has no biological reality. This amazing paradox must be widely understood in order to keep U.S. society moving in the direction of transformation from a race-based society into one that is multicultural with equal rights for everyone.

THE COURAGE TO RESIST WHITE SUPREMACY

Toward the end of the period in which segregation was being put in place in the South, two national, interracial organizations were formed in New York City to fight it—the National Association for the Advancement of Colored People (NAACP) in 1909 and the National Urban League in 1910. White allies Jane Addams and John Dewey were among the founders of the NAACP. W. E. B. Du Bois, Ida B. Wells, and Mary Church Terrell were among the African Americans who provided leadership. During the 1920s and 1930s, the NAACP published a journal, *The Crisis*, to challenge racist thinking, mainly through legal action and education. The National Urban League pursued the same goal of racial equality, although its approach was somewhat less confrontational than that of the NAACP (Egerton, 1994; Kellogg, 1967).

In the South, interracial groups formed later. The Commission on Interracial Cooperation, founded in 1919 by Will Alexander, a white Methodist minister, did not challenge segregation. Another interracial group, the Association of Southern Women for the Prevention of Lynching (1930), was led by Jesse Daniel Ames. The missionary societies of the Protestant churches and the Young Women's Christian Association (YWCA) provided the institutional foundation for southern women's involvement in the reform of race relations (Hall, 1979).

Another national organization that tackled racial discrimination in the 1920s was the Communist Party. In the late 1920s it supported the development of a separate "Black Republic" within the United States, but this idea won few adherents. During the early 1930s the Communist Party outmanuevered the NAACP and took to the Supreme Court cases defending young African American men falsely accused in Atlanta and Alabama. The two groups were hostile to each other, having different goals. The NAACP wanted for Negroes the full rights of other U.S. citizens, not the reform of economic structure that the Communists wanted. During the 1920s the Communist Party aimed at destroying the NAACP; during the early 1930s it tried to discredit the group. After 1935, during the years of the popular-front policy with the non-Communist Left, the Communist Party tried to penetrate the NAACP (Egerton, 1994; Klibaner, 1989, p. 94; Record, 1964, p. 20).

Alabama had the most active Communist Party. Birmingham became the Deep South headquarters of the American Communist Party after 1928, when the Communist International decreed that Negro peasants would be the advance guard of a Marxist revolution in the United States. But opposition and repression reduced Communist membership so that in 1935 there were only 24 dues-paying members in Birmingham, and by 1951 the tiny group of remaining members disbanded the Communist Party in Alabama (Egerton, 1994; Kelly, 1990; McWhorter, 2001, pp. 41, 46).

In the 1930s, the South, the 11 former Confederate states, was a culture separate from the rest of the country. It was an underdeveloped, agrarian society with 25% of the nation's people but only 10% of its wealth. Politically, the South can best be described as a feudal oligarchy of wealthy white men. Poll taxes, literacy requirements, and the other devices used to nullify civil rights for black people also disenfranchised women and poor whites. The power of the southern oligarchs reached beyond southern borders; they were able to return to Congress over many terms, building a longevity that gave them undue influence on national legislation. Resistance in this climate proved especially difficult (Egerton, 1994).

Opposition to segregation was not notable in Washington, D.C., until the 1930s. Segregation had started there in 1913, when the first southern president in 50 years, Woodrow Wilson, permitted some of the larger federal bureacracies to segregate federal employees of color. Eventually the city became as thoroughly segregated as any in the Deep South. After 1932, several courageous men who came to work for President Franklin D. Roosevelt began to reverse segregation in the federal bureaucracies. They included Harold Ickes, who ran the Department of the Interior and the Public Works Administration; and under him, Audrey Williams, the head of the National Youth Administration, which sponsored work relief for young adults and part-time jobs for students. Both men hired African Americans to work in previously all–European American offices (Egerton, 1994; Green, 1967).

Another white ally, Eleanor Roosevelt, took the leadership in fighting racial discrimination at the national level. Her grandmother's family had enslaved African Americans in Georgia, and at first Mrs. Roosevelt referred to the black staff in the White House as darkies and pickaninnies. But gradually, through her friendships and travels, she awoke to the discrimination against Negroes, even in New Deal Programs. Largely because of her, President Roosevelt signed an executive order in 1935 barring discrimination in the administration of Work Projects Administration (WPA) projects. This proved to be good politics as well as good principle; in 1936 Negro voters swung decisively into the Roosevelt coalition (Cook, 1999; Goodwin, 1994).

President Roosevelt wanted to help African Americans, but for his New Deal legislation he had to work with the southern senators who controlled key committees. In the mid-1930s, Roosevelt decided not to sign a federal antilynching order, in deference to the southern senators (Goodwin, 1994).

Meanwhile, Mrs. Roosevelt met repeatedly with A. Philip Randolph, who, as the organizer and head of the all-black union the Brotherhood of Sleeping Car Porters, was the most powerful Negro leader in the United States. A socialist, he also served as president of the National Negro Congress until 1940. In that year Randolph and Walter White of the NAACP demanded that Negroes be admitted into all facets of the armed services and that segregation in the armed services be abolished. (There were only 4,700 Negroes in an army of half a million and not one in the Marine Corps, the Tank Corps, the Signal Corps, or the Army Air Corps.) But the leaders of the armed services—General George Marshall, Secretary of Navy Frank Knox, and Secretary of War Henry Stimson—refused to yield their opposition to racial integration. They felt that they could not carry on a social experiment while carrying on a war, and President Roosevelt did not contradict them, despite his wife's entreaties (Egerton, 1994; Goodwin, 1994).

During the late 1930s and early 1940s, a union-based civil rights movement began to take shape. Half a million black workers joined unions affiliated with the Congress of Industrial Organizations (CIO), formed in 1935, whose leaders adoped a policy of racial equality. These workers constituted the vanguard in efforts to transform race relations (Korstad & Lichtenstein, 1988).

In the mushrooming defense industries, racial discrimination continued as usual. In the spring of 1941, A. Philip Randolph began organizing the March on Washington Movement, supported by the NAACP and almost all the black newpapers in the country. In June, when President Roosevelt met with Randolph, Randolph assured FDR that on July 1, 100,000 Negroes would be in the streets of Washington to demand an end to discrimination in the workplace, and he could not stop them without appropriate action from the president. On June 26, FDR signed Executive Order 8802, which called for employers and labor unions "to provide for full and equitable participation of all workers in defense industries, without discrimination because of race, creed, color, or national origin." In addition, this executive order established the Fair Employment Practice

Commission (FEPC). The first big step in breaking segregation had been taken; Randolph called off the march (Goodwin, 1994, pp. 246–253).

Across the South, primary elections, held to choose a party's candidate, were closed to black voters on the grounds that they constituted a private club of party members. Since Democrats almost always won elections in the South, the primary election usually proved the more important one. In 1944 the Supreme Court ruled the Texas "white man's" primary unconstitutional, and after the war federal judges across the South upheld the law, taking the second big step to break segregation (Yarbrough, 1987).

Between 1940 and 1948 northern black voters doubled their numbers as a result of Black migrations out of the South. President Truman had enough support to appoint, in 1946, a Committee on Civil Rights. In 1948, he took the third big step toward ending segregation by issuing executive orders against segregation in federal employment and in the armed services. Because the press and Congress kept quiet about the end of segregation in the military, the full impact of the new policy did not become generally known until 1953, at the end of the Korean War. But Truman also introduced the loyalty oath in 1948, and the intensified Red-baiting, or accusations of Communist Party membership, of union workers finished off the strength of the labor-based civil rights movement (Korstad & Lichtenstein, 1988; Woodward, 1996).

In the late 1940s, the NAACP seized the leadership of the fight for civil rights. It had won its first major Supreme Court victory in 1938 when the court had ordered Missouri's all-white law school to admit Lloyd Gaines. The membership of the NAACP rose from 50,000 in 1940 to almost 450,000 in 1946. Its lawyers moved to use the courts to end segregation, bringing the cases against school segregation that eventually reached the Supreme Court as *Brown v. Topeka School Board*. The hopes of egalitarians rested on the Supreme Court's ruling in April 1954 that segregation in schools was unconstitutional. In the South there was only fragmentary white dissent from the segregationist consensus before 1954, but with the *Brown* decision, a modest number of white southerners joined the struggle for racial justice.

However, the great majority of southern whites responded by refusing to implement the Supreme Court's decision. In response, black people created a popular movement, starting with the Montgomery bus boycott in January 1956, an event so momentous that it has been called the "third founding of our nation" (Burns, 1997, p. xii). After the Supreme Court ruled segregation on buses unconstitutional, African Americans still had to fight it in other areas of life. Through marches and protests in the streets, they revealed the violence of white supremacists such as Eugene "Bull" Connor in Birmingham and elicited the support of nonracists nationwide. Finally, in 1964 and 1965, only 37 years ago, Congress passed federal legislation that ended legal racial segregation everywhere and granted full voting rights to African Americans (Burns, 1997).

In the South, the passage of the Civil Rights Act of 1964 and the Voting Rights Act of 1965 made a difference. This legislation broke down the oligarchic system that had produced such disgraceful white leaders as Theodore G. Bilbo and James Eastland of Mississippi, Eugene Talmadge of Georgia, and L. Mendel Rivers of South Carolina. It opened the way for a just multicultural society to begin to develop. More white allies stepped up to work with African Americans to begin the creation of a New South, to which African Americans began returning from other parts of the nation after 1970 (Thernstrom & Thernstrom, 1997, p. 209). Racism has not vanished in the South, but it has become as subtle and hidden as in the rest of the nation.

In the North, the passage of the Civil Rights and Voting Rights acts made little significant difference. There Negroes had secured by 1948 nearly complete civic equality in public laws. But in practice, most white people discriminated fiercely to keep themselves as separate from black people as possible, particularly in employment, housing and, as a consequence, schooling.

In housing, these practices included the refusal of realtors and white owners to sell to black people. In 1924 the National Association of Real Estate Brokers wrote into its code of ethics that "a realtor should never be instrumental in introducing into a neighborhood . . . members of any race or nationality . . . whose presence will clearly be detrimental to property values in that neighborhood." This statement remained in the code until 1950 (Massey & Denton, 1993, p. 37). White property owners signed contractual agreements called restrictive covenants, which stated that they would not permit a black person to own, occupy, or lease their property. Following World War II, black veterans challenged the practice of restrictive covenants, and in 1948 the Supreme Court ruled that they were not enforceable in court. Nevertheless, the practice continued (Massey & Denton, 1993).

By the late 1960s residential segregation had grown from its levels in the 1940s. Black in-migration from the South had increased the size of northern ghettos, while white people fled to the suburbs, their flight fueled by federal highway construction and by loans from the Federal Housing Administration and the Veterans Administration. The federally sponsored public housing projects constructed from 1950 to 1970 created a second level of ghetto. In the summer of 1967, black ghettos in 60 U.S. cities exploded in rage and frustration, directed not at white individuals, but at the conditions of racial oppression and economic depression that had festered for 60 years. In March 1968, the Kerner Commission appointed by President

Johnson informed Americans that if then-current policies continued, the result would be the permanent division of the country into two separate societies. Congress responded by passing the 1968 Fair Housing Act, which banned discrimination in the sale or rental of housing, but the act was not implemented and its flaws had to be remedied by the 1989 Fair Housing Amendments Act (Massey & Denton, 1993, pp. 55–59; 208–212).

In the area of education, many schools in the North had been integrated until the migration of African Americans from the South in the 1920s became too threatening to white people. For example, in Chicago, 91.3% of all black students attended integrated public schools in 1916, but 14 years later, 82.4% of black students were in segregated schools, with black teachers clustered in predominantly black schools. By the end of the 1940s, the pattern of de facto segregation was firmly entrenched in Chicago, Philadelphia, New York, and other cities with large populations of black students (Foster, 1997, pp. xxvi, xxvii; Massey & Denton, 1993, p. 46).

During the 1960s and 1970s, school segregation in northern cities continued to grow, as residential segregation increased. For example, in Boston between 1965 and 1971, the number of schools with more than 50% black enrollment rose from 46 to 67 (Foster, 1997, p. xxviii). In 1974, when Boston attempted to implement desegregation in the schools by means of massive busing, white children made up about half the public school enrollment. Twenty-five years later, when the Boston School Committee abandoned its desegregation plan, white children constituted only 15% of the enrollment. During this time, suburban communities continued to build much less "affordable" housing than mandated by state law (Formisano, 1991, pp. 138–139; Staples, 1999, p. 13).

In the process of school desegregation in Boston and in many other cities, those of low income did the desegregating, the middle classes did the fleeing, and the affluent were exempt from the start. To succeed, desegregation would need to involve every social class, which would challenge many accepted procedures of U.S. life: the right of parents to send children to private schools, teachers' seniority rights, sanctity of city/suburb district lines, and local control of schools (Formisano, 1991, pp. 232–233).

By the 1980s and the 1990 census, residential segregation had not decreased, on the average, in northern metropolitan areas. Five or six cities had patterns of lessening segregation, but equal numbers of cities had more segregation. By 1991, two thirds of all black students and nearly three fourths of all Latinos attended schools that were predominantly black and Latino, while one third went to schools more than 90% black and Latino. These proportions are about the same that existed prior to court-ordered busing in the early 1970s (Bell, 1980, p. viii; Dyson, 2000, p. 117; Hacker,

1995, pp. 167–168; Harris & Curtis, 1999, pp. 130–131; Massey & Denton, 1993, pp. 221–223).

After centuries of resistance to racism, there continue to be inequality and injustice in U.S. political, educational, legal, housing, medical, and employment systems. There is still an unfair and uneven distribution of power, assets, land, and privileges favoring European Americans. The racist structure of American life has not yet been demolished. Many more strong, committed white allies are needed who are willing to dismantle the racist system that works in their favor.

The preceding capsule history is meant to create an overview of European American racism and resistance up to the present. It can form a context for the profiles of the four white allies that follow. History has many layers of reality, which I have simplified and condensed. But the "big story" needs to be told, to help us understand our current reality; repeated attempts to tell this story will bring a more nuanced refinement.

2

An Imperfect Lady:
Virginia Foster Durr

I~N~ N~OVEMBER~ 1938, a historic 4-day conference was held in Birmingham, Alabama, the hometown of Virginia Foster Durr. Never before had such a gathering—interracial and including all strata of society—been held in the South. Sponsored by a new organization called the Southern Conference for Human Welfare, it included all the groups working for the democratic and economic development of the South—the New Dealers, the Southern Policy Committee, labor unions, ministers, and professors. It had the blessing of President Franklin D. Roosevelt because he wanted to defeat the southerners in Congress, who were killing his New Deal Reforms. Virginia Durr and her husband, Clifford, had helped organize the meeting from suburban Washington, D.C., where they had been living since Clifford had become a lawyer for the New Deal administration.

On the opening Sunday night, several thousand people crowded into the Municipal Auditorium, a quarter of them of African descent. Many of those attending defied, or forgot, the rules of segregation and sat intermingled together, singing and preaching. "Oh, it was just a love feast," Virginia Durr remembered. "We all went away from there that night just full of love and gratitude. The whole South was coming together to make a new day" (1985, p. 120).

The next day, police chief Eugene "Bull" Connor arrived to enforce the city ordinance that banned racially mixed meetings. Black people would have to sit on one side of the central aisle and white people on the other. The following afternoon, when Eleanor Roosevelt arrived late to make a speech, she sat down in the front row on the colored side, as she put it later, without noticing the segregated seating. When someone pointed out the required seating, Mrs. Roosevelt refused to acquiese. "Rather than give in," she explained, "I asked that chairs be placed for us with the speakers facing the whole group." For the duration of the 4-day conference, Mrs. Roosevelt sat on a folding chair set up between segregated groups (Roosevelt, 1949, p. 180; Cook, 1999).

By the time of this conference, Virginia Durr was 35 years old and had come to believe that segregation was a terrible wrong. She had been raised in a Presbyterian minister's family to be an aristocratic southern belle, but gradually over time she rejected her former beliefs in the superiority of upper-class white people. This occurred as she spent 2 years at Wellesley College and as she witnessed the effect of the Depression in Birmingham on poor people, black and white. After moving to suburban Washington, D.C., in 1933, and extending her friendships, she began to grasp the effects of racism on both its victims and its perpetrators.

Durr chose, as her special cause, to fight the poll tax so that white women and black men and women in the South could vote. From 1941 to 1948, she served as vice chairman of the National Committee to Abolish the Poll Tax. In 1948, she ran for U.S. senator from Virginia on the Progressive Party ticket to support the candidacy of Henry Wallace for president. When Harry Truman won, the Durrs gave up their privileged position in Washington to maintain their principle of opposing loyalty oaths. After 1951, when they moved to Montgomery, Alabama, Virginia formed friendships with the Kings, the Abernathys, and Rosa Parks and stood firmly by them in the decisive decade from 1955 to 1965.

GROWING UP IN BIRMINGHAM, 1903–1921

Virginia Foster was born in August 1903 in the parsonage of the South Highland Presbyterian Church in Birmingham, Alabama, where her father, Sterling Johnston Foster, was pastor. She arrived as a hungry, red-faced, squalling newborn, demanding from the beginning. Her mother, Ann Patterson Foster, nursed her for months, and if her mother was 15 minutes late, Virginia would cry so loudly the whole neighborhood would be upset, according to family stories.

Virginia took her place in the family as the youngest of three children. Her brother, Sterling, proceeded her by 5 or 6 years, and her sister, Josephine, by 4 years. Virginia always felt that her parents, especially her father, were disappointed by her arrival; they had wanted another son. She spent hours as a child trying to kiss her elbow, because she was told that if she accomplished that she would turn into a boy.

Virginia's father was fond of all his children, but Virginia believed that he favored Josephine, the angel of the family, an unusually sweet, beautiful child. Everyone adored her, even Virginia, who felt that she herself was the bad child of the family—obstinate, demanding, curious, and self-willed. But Virginia knew she was loved by her mother, who told her that she, too, was a sweet, beautiful child, that is, if she wanted to be and didn't lose her temper.

Virginia remembered her childhood until age 7 as a time of idyllic bliss. Her immediate household consisted of eight people: her parents and their three children; two black servants—Alice Spraggs, whom they called Nursie, and Sally, the cook. Nursie had a daughter, Sarah, who was the same age as Virginia. Nursie was a second mother to Virginia, as much a symbol of safety as her own mother. Nursie took care of her, bathed and dressed her, and put her to bed at night, often with Sarah in the same bed. Virginia grew up in a little cocoon of love, care, and devotion.

In Birmingham, the life of the Fosters, as befitted their station as the preacher's family, was absorbed by church activities. They had prayer every morning before breakfast. On Sundays they attended Sunday school and church, then the young people's group in the afternoon, and church again in the evening. On Wednesdays they went to prayer meeting, and her mother also attended the ladies' meetings.

This routine was broken every Christmas and every summer by trips down to Union Springs, Alabama, where Virginia's paternal grandmother lived in a large plantation home built in 1852–1856, just before the Civil War. Birmingham is located in north-central Alabama; Union Springs lies in the southeastern part of the state, below Montgomery, an area known as the "black belt" because of the black fertile soil. Nursie and Sarah went along, too; they all stayed a week at Christmas and several weeks in the summer. Virginia remembered the plantation as the Garden of Eden.

Virginia's paternal grandfather died before she was born. He had gone to medical school in Philadelphia, then married Virginia Heard and headed west to settle in Union Springs. By the time of the Civil War he had prospered, using slaves to grow cotton. But he opposed the Civil War, believing that the United States should settle the issue of slavery the way England had, with the government recompensing the owners for their slaves. He refused to fight and bought a substitute to go for him, a disgrace among his friends. He also refused to invest in Confederate bonds and kept his money in England, in Liverpool with the banks that handled his cotton transactions. When the war ended, Grandfather Foster was one of the few men in Alabama who remained wealthy.

With the saved money, the Foster family was able to extend the plantation to include about 35,000 acres of land. When Virginia was a child, the backyard of the plantation still had slave cabins that housed old men and women who had been slaves. They had earned a little money but not enough to leave, and they were still being fed on the plantation. Virginia was raised on the overly romantic tradition of a benevolent slave system. Her people still spoke the language of supposed chivalry and honor and denied the cruelty and violence that had been needed to keep slavery in place.

In Virginia's childhood, the plantation was run by two strong women—Grandmother Virginia Foster, her paternal grandmother, a white woman who had married at 15 and had 15 children, and Easter, a black woman who had been a slave.

Virginia remembered her grandmother as a woman with very red hair who was full of laughter. She had two carriages, one lined with red satin; two or three buggies; and a coachman who wore a high silk hat. When she went shopping, storekeepers brought out to her carriage the goods for her to choose from. She made a procession into church, whose upkeep she provided. She was the queen bee, whom everybody loved and was obligated to. As a child, Virginia wanted to be just like her.

Meanwhile, Easter kept the plantation running. Virginia remembered her as one of the smartest women she ever knew. She wore the keys to the plantation, planned the meals, and was in charge of the white children, who obeyed her to the letter.

Virginia's father had a sister, May, who brought about the end of Virginia's idyllic innocence by introducing a racial divide. Aunt May lived a life of high fashion in New York City, supported by money from the plantation. When she visited the summer that Virginia was 6, Aunt May heard the little black children calling Virginia's sister "Sis." Aunt May sent Easter out to tell them that they must not call her Sis but "Miss Josephine." The children, black and white, who had been playing together all their lives, were hurt and astonished. Josephine solved the problem by telling them: "Now, you don't have to call me 'Miss Josephine.' You just call me 'Miss Sis,'" which afterward all the children, black and white, did.

On Virginia's 7th birthday her family tried to impose the racial segregation expected of older children. Virginia always celebrated her summer birthday at her grandmother's plantation. They would have a barbecue in the backyard with the black children, digging a pit in the sand and grilling chicken over it. The children would be allowed to baste and turn the chickens, which, by the time they were cooked, were filled with sand. But to Virginia this was a great event, because she was presiding over the cooking.

On the day of the party Virginia was told that none of the black children could come, only white children, perfect strangers they would pick up downtown. Virginia had a fit of temper; she stood by her black friends and would not betray them. Finally, it was agreed that they would have a barbecue in the backyard with the black children in the morning, and a party in the front yard with the white children in the afternoon.

Everything went fine at the barbecue until Aunt May's daughter, Elizabeth, said to Nursie's daughter, Sarah: "Don't give me any chicken out of that black hand of yours. I'm not going to eat any chicken that your black hand has touched, you little nigger" (Durr, 1985, p. 17).

Furious, Virginia told Elizabeth to go to hell. The grownups put Virginia to bed, saying *she* would go to hell, for being so bad. At the afternoon party, with the strange white children, Virginia had another fit, bashed in the cake, and was put to bed again. That night at dinner, in the presence of Virginia, Aunt May told Virginia's mother that Virginia was the worst child she had ever known and that she should do something about her. Virginia threw a knife at Aunt May and was sent to the back porch, where she curled up in Nursie's lap and heard, through the window, Aunt May saying: "Annie, the trouble with Virginia is that nurse. She spoils her to death. And besides, I think it's terrible that you let her sit in her lap and sleep with her and kiss and hug her. You know all those black women are diseased" (Durr, 1985, p. 17).

Virginia could feel Nursie's muscles tighten beneath her. Nursie put her to bed that night, and in the morning she was gone. She took a different job in the neighborhood and refused to come back. It was a great trauma for Virginia. After that summer she attended school where there were only white children. The family had a succession of cooks and servants, and gradually Virginia was taught that they were not like the Fosters (Durr, 1985; V. Durr, interview with author, February 8, 1981).

Soon after Nursie left the Fosters, Virginia's family suffered another trauma. Her father was thrown out of his pulpit at South Highland Presbyterian Church, whose members were wealthy, leading citizens with deeply fundamentalist beliefs. Dr. Foster had received a theological education at Princeton Theological Seminary and at Edinburgh, Heidelberg, and the University of Berlin. In Heidelberg and Berlin he had learned the new theology—that the Bible was history and myth, rather than the literal truth in every word.

Dr. Foster's parishioners asked him to declare under oath that he believed as literal truth that Jonah stayed in the whale for 3 days and was spewed up alive. When Dr. Foster told them he did not believe in a literal interpretation of this story, he was dismissed from his church, brought before the presbytery as a heretic, and never assigned another church. He had a nervous breakdown, and the family temporarily moved to Memphis. They were able to return to Birmingham when Grandmother Foster bought the parsonage for them; Dr. Foster sold insurance to black people until his mother died and he inherited his share of her estate—9,000 to 10,000 acres with tenants, which the bank managed for him.

After the inheritance, the Fosters bought a bigger house and lived even more fashionably. Sometimes they had plenty, and sometimes they did not, depending on the price of cotton. Often they lived in genteel poverty, trying to keep up appearances on very little money.

The Fosters lived in a city with extremes of wealth and poverty. Birmingham had become a commercial center after two railway lines converged there and coal and iron ore were discovered in the valley. The large northern iron and steel companies established plants in Birmingham—U.S. Steel, Tennessee Coal, Republic Steel. It was a company town, colonized after the Civil War, bought up on the cheap by northern corporations. The air was so full of pollution that people's noses stopped up and white gloves always got dirty, but it meant prosperity for the upper classes. The city was tightly controlled by absentee capitalists, speculators, entrepreneurs, and calculating politicians. The worst fear of the manufacturers was that their labor force might organize into a union. Klan activity was strong during the 1920s; after 1925, agents of the Invisible Empire controlled the city's government. Only one fifth of the voting-age population were registered to vote, and fewer than half of them usually voted (Egerton, 1994; McWhorter, 2001; Salmond, 1990).

The coal and iron mines were located on the other side of the mountains. On Saturday mornings the mining families would come walking down Virginia's street on their way into Birmingham, since there was no public transportation. These large families looked pale and stunted. Pellegra (caused by a lack of niacin in the diet), worms, and malaria were common. These poor whites had replaced convict labor, mostly black, in the mines. Late in the afternoon the families would return, the children hollering and the adults falling down from drunkenness. Virginia's parents taught her that they were born to be white trash, that it was "'in their blood.' It was a very comforting thought, you see, because when you saw people starving and poor and miserable, you thought, 'Well, it isn't my fault. I didn't do anything to cause it. God just ordained it this way'" (Durr, 1985, p. 32).

At first Virginia went to public school, where her best friends were Jewish boys. But when she began to date, they were put off limits by both sets of parents. Virginia's sister, Josephine, had grown into an extremely beautiful and popular young woman. For 2 years, Virginia's father sent Josephine to New York City, to be polished at a school run by Aunt Mamie, who finally persuaded him to send Virginia, too. Aunt Mamie told Virginia's mother: "Virginia is absolutely impossible. She talks too much, and too loud. Her voice is too high, she asks too many questions, and she is very rawboned and nearsighted. Annie, Virginia will never marry well unless you do something to get her polished up" (Durr, 1985, p. 30).

Virginia spent about a year in New York City, then a year in public school in Birmingham. For her senior year she attended National Cathedral School in Washington, D.C. There Virginia met girls from all over the South, most of whom wanted to return home, make their debut, and marry well. Only a few went on to college, the bluestocking intellectuals. Virginia wanted to be popular and marry well, but she also loved her studies and hoped to attend college.

In February of her senior year, Virginia was called home to be the maid of honor in the wedding of her sister, Josephine, who had decided to marry Hugo Black, a young lawyer who eventually would become a justice of the U.S. Supreme Court. Black was a Baptist, which the Fosters held against him, and he represented unions in their struggle to be legal, which they also disapproved. But overall they liked him, and during his courtship he had been a wonderful influence on Virginia, bringing her books to read and talking with her as an equal.

Virginia's adolescent mind was filled with the contradictions offered her by southern white aristocratic culture. The most important issues were never discussed; it was assumed that one believed them. The white upper class was rendered mute by the moral tensions implicit in a society ostensibly Christian, democratic, and genteel, but in fact based on institutionalized racism and still proud of its heritage of slavery.

In Virginia's world the topic of money was never brought up; that would be "common" rather than "proper." Sexual facts and dilemmas were never mentioned; women were supposed to be "chased and chaste." If an unmarried girl had a baby, she just disappeared. Virginia knew that could happen to her, too, but she couldn't find out what a girl did to bring on a baby. Black people lived in the house with the Fosters, whose lives depended on them, yet they were considered outside the entire social order. Black men had never been anything other than kind and loving, yet she kept hearing about rape. She didn't know what it was and didn't want to ask, for fear she didn't want to know. When she watched the parades of the Ku Klux Klan, she wondered why all the marchers had such miserable, worn-out old shoes. She had been taught to think of the Klan as aristocrats riding off on white horses to save pure white southern womanhood. She felt that she was pure white southern womanhood; had the whole Civil War been fought to save her? From what? As a confused 18-year-old, Virginia was able to raise these questions; it was more than most white teenagers could do, surrounded by a white supremacist system.

COLLEGE AND MARRIAGE, 1922–1933

Wanting to find some answers, Virginia persuaded her father to send her to Wellesley College, an academically prestigious women's college outside Boston, Massachusetts. After one year at Wellesley, on the first evening of her sophomore year, Virginia Foster sat down at her assigned table and found a Negro girl sitting across from her. Virginia arose at once and asked the headmistress to reassign her to a different table, since her father would be furious if she ate with a Negro girl.

The headmistress explained to Virginia that she would have to follow Wellesley's rules of changing tables every month and that if she did not wish to, she could withdraw.

Virginia returned to her room amazed that anyone would take such an attitude. Greatly upset, Virginia described her dilemma to her room-mate, Emmie, who responded: "I don't know what's wrong with you. I just think you're crazy. Last summer when I was visiting you down in Alabama, you kissed and hugged that old black woman who was cooking for you. I wouldn't have kissed and hugged an old black woman, but you did. Why would you kiss and hug them and not eat with them?"

Virginia responded, "Why, I just love the cook, but I don't eat with her" (Durr, 1985, p. 57). But she was having a hard time making any sense of race relations or of her own logic. She stayed awake all night, imagining her father's fury if he ever heard of her eating with a Negro. She did not want to leave Wellesley, because she was having the time of her life. She felt completely free and did not want to give up her rich social and intellectual life.

About dawn Virginia found the way out—if she did not tell him, her father would never find out about the situation, and she would get to stay at Wellesley. Virginia ate with the Negro girl for a month and discovered that she was intelligent, well-mannered, and a southerner, too. Over time, Virginia came to understand that she did not fear the Negro girl, but rather her father's reaction. This was her first experience in discovering that some people considered her attitude toward Negroes foolish and intolerable.

Virginia only stayed at Wellesley until the end of her sophomore year; in the summer of 1923 she had to return to Birmingham. Her father could not afford to send her for another year because boll weevils had ruined his cotton crop. He was too proud to allow her to live in the Self Help House at Wellesley, where girls did the cooking and cleaning for themselves.

But in her 2 years at Wellesley Virginia had made many breakthroughs. She had learned to use her mind and get pleasure from it. She had realized that women could make a living and be happy, even if they did not have a husband. She had confirmed her view of the Bible as history instead of revelation, and she had grasped enough economics to know that people have a hard time making a living and do not get paid enough. She was no longer the thoroughly upper-crust, racist, southern lady she had been raised to be.

After 2 years of college in the North, Virginia returned to Birmingham to face the white woman's duty of marrying well. She spent her entire first year back making her debut. She went to parties both in Birmingham and in Memphis, visiting her aunt. Her mother gave a buffet supper for her, because they couldn't afford a fancy party. She had one or two proposals, but nothing that appealed to her.

The following year the Fosters were especially hard up. The furnace, the roof, and the plumbing needed to be renovated, so Virginia went downtown and got a half-time job at the county bar association's law library. This was an embarrassment to Dr. Foster, who said it ruined his credit at the bank, since they knew he had no money if his daughter had to take a job. But with the price of cotton down to almost nothing, Foster was beginning to sell off his land. When the law librarian became ill, Virginia took the job full-time.

In the spring of 1925 Virginia's family expressed anxiety that she would never get married. She was 21 years old, and they had almost given up on her. They thought she was too critical, that nobody suited her.

But soon, at church, she met Clifford Durr, son of a friend of Virginia's father from his preaching days and a fraternity brother of her brother. The next Sunday Clifford came to dinner; they courted for a year and married on Easter Sunday 1926. There were eight bridesmaids and more than 500 guests at the reception. Virginia's mother was triumphant; here was a daughter who had married well indeed.

Clifford Durr worked as a lawyer for a corporate law firm representing the local power company. He came from a wealthy Presbyterian family in Montgomery; his father owned Durr Drug Company, one of the most prominent wholesale drug houses in the South. Clifford had been a Rhodes scholar, Phi Beta Kappa, and the head of a fraternity at the University of Alabama. At first, he and Virginia lived with her parents, who were still clinging to her. Virginia returned from their honeymoon pregnant and delivered a healthy baby girl whom they named Ann, for Virginia's mother. Cliff and Virginia were deeply happy, and in 1931 they moved into their own apartment (Durr, 1985; Salmond, 1990).

Now that Durr had married well, she felt free to turn her attention to other matters; she no longer felt that she had to do what other people wanted her to in order to be accepted. Since she had a cook and a nurse for her child, Durr was able to become active in the Junior League, the church, and a bridge club. But she was also becoming aware of the dreadful state of the national and local economy. The corporations were shutting down everything because they could no longer make a profit. The smelting furnaces were closing down; people were losing their jobs. More beggars came to the door, and people lurked in the alleys. Durr's father and mother lost everything they had mortgaged. The plantation had to be sold for little more than back taxes. In the early 1930s, the Great Depression was in full force.

When Durr became aware that the dairies were pouring milk into the gutters because they couldn't sell it, she talked the Junior League into a project to give milk to the poor. She talked the firemen and the policemen into giving free concerts with their bands. Through the Junior League she began to work for the Red Cross, the only relief organization in town. She drove into the workers' areas and saw the absolute misery. There were no lights, water, or heat, and there was one water tap per block.

Most people around Durr blamed the poor for their problems. If only they had saved their money, they would have enough. No one said the problem was the economic or political system. What bothered Durr most was that the poor blamed themselves. They never said, "We are destitute because U.S. Steel treats its mules better than it treats us." Instead, they felt guilty that they had bought a radio. The preachers, especially the hellfire-and-damnation variety, told the poor they were suffering because they had sinned and would go to hell if they didn't come to God. Durr blamed the northern corporations for not paying their workers better. The Depression seemed a revelation to Durr:

> Up to this time I had been a conformist, a Southern snob. I actually thought the only people who amounted to anything were the very small group I belonged to. I valued the idea of being well-born. What I learned during the Depression changed all that. I saw a blinding light like Saul on the road to Damascus. It was the first time I had seen the other side of the tracks. The rickets, the pellegra—it shook me up. I saw the world as it really was. (Sullivan, 1996, p. 110)

The years 1931 to early 1933 were personally difficult for the Durrs. Virginia suffered a complicated miscarriage, the second since her first child had been born. Her parents, because of their financial circumstances, moved in with them, and Clifford lost his job at the law firm. The only hopeful events were the elections of Franklin D. Roosevelt as president on the Democratic ticket and of Hugo Black, Virginia's brother-in-law, as Democratic senator from Alabama. Early in 1933 Black called to say that the Reconstruction Finance Corporation was looking for corporate lawyers who could set up programs to save the banks. Clifford was offered a job, and the Durrs moved to Washington to become part of Roosevelt's New Deal.

WASHINGTON AND THE NEW DEAL, 1933–1938

Clifford and Virginia bought a big, sprawling white farmhouse on two acres in suburban Virginia, about seven miles from Washington. In September 1935 they celebrated the arrival of Clifford, Jr.; in January 1937 of Lucy; and in September 1939 of Virginia Foster (nicknamed Tilla). Since they could afford four servants, Durr continued her volunteer work. After meeting Eleanor Roosevelt at a garden party, Durr found her so attractive that she decided to work for the Women's Division of the Democratic National Committee.

The goal of the Women's Division was to repeal the poll tax so that southern white women could vote. There were no Negroes in the Women's Division and no mention of black votes. The poll tax had been instituted in southern states after 1900 as a means of disenfranchising black male voters. After the woman's-suffrage amendment in 1920, the poll tax had effectively disenfranchised black and white women, too, since very few women in the South ever had any money of their own. In Alabama the poll tax was retroactive to age 21 even if one started voting at age 45 (Durr, 1985, pp. 101–102).

In the presidential election of 1936 three out of four of the voting-age population cast a ballot, except in the eight poll tax states, where only one in four voted. The Democrats wanted to add women voters in these states. In the southern oligarchy of white men where no women served on Democratic committees, the goal of the Women's Division was to reach 50% women on party committees (Durr, 1985; Sullivan, 1996).

Durr threw herself into the fight for the white women of the South. She had personal experience with the poll tax in Birmingham. She had paid a dollar and a half in poll tax when she was 21, not realizing she had to pay it every year. After she married Clifford, he had to pay her tax for all the intervening years before she could vote again. Virginia gradually realized how much she resented the role that southern girls had to play—fooling the men to try to get a husband, being nice and putting up with anything to be popular. This resentment expressed itself in her early poll tax fight before she could articulate it.

Through her southern friends who were also working for the New Deal, Durr began to confront her own belief in white supremacy. Clark H. Foreman from Atlanta, whom she had met at Harvard when she was at Wellesley, worked as advisor on Negro affairs to Harold Ickes, secretary of the interior and head of the Public Works Administration. Foreman had worked with the Commission on Interracial Cooperation in Atlanta and the Rosenwald Fund. Now, working in the nation's capital, he hired a Negro secretary, with the support of Ickes, who was trying to integrate the bathrooms and cafeteria in the Department of the Interior.

This caused a storm. Durr, too, accused Foreman of betraying all the traditions of the South. He told that her that she was a bigoted, prejudiced, provincial girl. Their friendship continued nevertheless, and Durr began to realize that deep down she agreed with him. When Foreman arranged for Mattiwilda Dobbs, a black opera singer from Atlanta, to have a concert in Washington, the Durrs served tea at the reception to the whole Dobbs family, one of Virginia's first public acts in solidarity with Negroes.

By meeting professional black people at Clark Foreman's house and by talking with her southern friends who had lived outside the South, Durr became aware over a 5-year period of the diseased contradictions of segregation. For the first time she realized that light-skinned Negroes had white fathers or grandfathers and that these fathers were repudiating their own children. She understood the damage it did to her, and to all whites, to think that everyone not white was inferior.

Durr loved people of all persuasions. Immensely gregarious, she and Clifford entertained an unusually varied range of guests—judicial dignitaries, New Deal functionaries, young radicals, and conservative southern legislators, whom Virginia was forever trying to proselytise for the cause of the anti–poll tax. She was not interested in cooking and used the same basic menu: spaghetti, salad and, for dessert, three kinds of frozen fruit. She had a thick southern accent and a warm manner, especially toward men. Her approach to conversation was the direct-question method, no matter how delicate the subject: "Jack, I hear you-all had a falling out with John L. the other night. Whatever happened? I thought you-all were just about as thick as thieves" (M. Frantz, interview with author, December 7, 1980; Mitford, 1960, 1977, pp. 254–257).

In early spring 1938, President Roosevelt appointed Clifford Durr to a task force called the Committee on Economic Conditions in the South. This committee wrote a document that became a battle call against the conservative southern congressmen who were defeating the New Deal reforms. The committee often met at the Durrs' house, where Virginia served food and drinks, and in July it delivered to the president its *Report on Economic Conditions in the South.*

To publicize the report, the Southern Conference for Human Welfare was organized and held its first meeting in Birmingham in November 1938, as described earlier. By the time of this conference, Durr's thinking about race had changed, and she was opposed to segregation.

During the conference, Durr's childhood friends took her to lunch and told her how they hated the New Deal and Mrs. Roosevelt. They said she was encouraging the rabble to take over, and they spread the rumor that Negroes were forming Eleanor Clubs. Durr heard repeatedly, to her distress: "I'm sure my cook has joined the Eleanor Club" (Durr, 1985; pp. 114, 124; Goodwin, 1994).

After hearing stories about Eleanor Clubs all over the South, Mrs. Roosevelt asked the Federal Bureau of Investigation (FBI) to determine whether they existed. The FBI concluded that no such club actually existed. White women were having trouble retaining their Negro servants in the face of higher-paying wartime jobs, and they blamed Eleanor, considered by many southerners the most dangerous individual in the United States (Goodwin, 1994; O'Reilly, 1989).

Durr disagreed with her former friends' view on race. In her few years in Washington, D.C., she had begun to see the South as a small area of the United States where people's basic rights were being denied by a selfish ruling caste. In 1938 she decided to work with the Southern Conference for Human Welfare (SCHW) as vice-chairman of the SCHW's subcommittee on abolishing the poll tax, expanding her work to include voting rights for Negroes as well as white women. She considered this the broadest possible issue—securing the right to vote for poor whites, women, and blacks, a fundamental right in a democracy, she believed. Negro leaders told her that after the poll tax was abolished, they would still have to deal with unjust registration and literacy requirements, but they supported the work against the poll tax as the first step. By the mid-1940s, Durr would emerge as probably the most effective organizer on behalf of the national effort to defeat state poll taxes (Colby & Damon, 1992; Durr, 1985; Sullivan, 1996).

WORLD WAR II AND ITS AFTERMATH, 1939–1950

In 1939, when Hitler began invading Europe, both Clifford and Virginia Durr were interventionists. They had already opposed Franco as the dictator of Spain and had supported the Lincoln Brigade, who went to Spain to fight for the Republic. The Durrs believed that the United States would have to go to war; either it would be attacked or it would have to go to the defense of Britain. U.S. corporations did not want to go to war; they were afraid that if they built defense plants, they would have no orders and lose money. Working for the Reconstruction Finance Corporation (RFC), Clifford created a plan in which the federal government would pay for the plants and buy whatever they produced. Clifford expected this arrangement to resemble the Tennessee Valley Authority (TVA), which was owned and managed by the federal government. After the war was over, the corporations would give the defense plants back to the government to manage.

Instead, under President Truman, the corporations got to keep the defense plants; the government just gave them away, the Durrs felt.

In the early days of her work to abolish the poll tax, Durr enjoyed the support of both Eleanor Roosevelt and Franklin D. Roosevelt. But the majority of southern congressmen solidly opposed any national repeal of the poll tax. They saw it as the federal government trying to control the election machinery of the South. In early 1941, Virginia Durr and Lee Giver, Republican from Los Angeles, organized an umbrella organization for all the groups who were against the poll tax, the National Committee to Abolish the Poll Tax (NCAPT). In late 1941, FDR withdrew his support. He depended so much on southern senators' support for his war-preparedness policies that he could not afford to antagonize them on the poll tax. The NCAPT succeeded in 1942 in abolishing the poll tax for soldiers, and they got a bill introduced every single year until 1948, but they never were able to get a law through the Congress (Durr, 1985; Sullivan, 1996).

Durr said she had a one-track mind. She focused on the single issue of the abolition of the poll tax and refused to get pulled into other factionalizing controversies. She was rooted in her Virginia neighborhood, where people were polite, conservative, and genteel, were not engaged in any issues, and regarded the New Deal itself as radical. At the same time, she socialized with Communists and people of every other political persuasion and enjoyed maintaining friendships with those with whom she disagreed. She believed that that was a fundamental characteristic of the United States—a place where people can disagree, yet keep up their personal friendships.

Durr knew very well that the House of Representatives disagreed with her. In May 1938 the House had established the Committee on Un-American Activities (HUAC) to investigate extremist groups associated with Nazis, Fascists, Bolsheviks, and other foreign interests. The chair was Martin Dies, Jr., Democratic congressman from east Texas. Within months, the committee heard testimony that charged that Communists secretly controlled Hollywood, the Congress of Industrial Organizations and other labor unions, and a wide range of liberal and progressive social-action groups, including SCHW. The city commissioner of Birmingham, Jimmie Jones, requested that the Dies committee investigate SCHW shortly after its historic conference in Birmingham in November 1938, even though Jones himself had been a participant (Egerton, 1994; Kelley, 1990).

During World War II, HUAC continued its efforts to uncover Communists in the United States, and after the war this activity intensified. The two organizations that Virginia Durr worked for—the Southern Conference for Human Welfare and the National Committee to Abolish the Poll Tax (NCAPT) were frequently accused of having members who were Communists. This accusation was based on the fact that in the 1930s the Communist Party of America had a clear mandate to fight racism and southern segregation. Supporters of segregation used this history to claim, illogically but effectively, that anyone who supported racial equality must be a Communist (Record, 1964).

Durr took the position that the NCAPT had one rule. It accepted support from any organization or person who wanted to abolish the poll tax. Whatever else they believed in did not concern her. She knew that the NCAPT received some support from labor groups that included Communist members, but she was not willing to try to purge the NCAPT of Communists. Virginia was never tempted to join the Communist Party, since she felt its members were not free to think for themselves. She did not believe in complete government ownership of the means of production, but in some form of modified capitalism with government management of selected industries. In 1946 Virginia was able to visit the Soviet Union with Clifford, and in 1948 they visited Poland.

In the years after World War II, a coalition of interests in the United States feared the ideas of socialism and communism, attacked people with these ideas, and promulgated the view that these ideas were so dangerous as to be "un-American." In 1947 Truman issued an order requiring a loyalty oath from everyone who worked for the government; he also encouraged the FBI to investigate everyone suspected of being a Communist. During these investigations, people were accused on the basis of what one or another FBI agent said, but the accused were never able to learn the identity of the agent or the specific so-called data. Both Virginia and Clifford Durr believed this practice of letting a person lose a job on the word of some nameless FBI informer was unconstitutional. It violated everything they believed in (Durr, 1985; Egerton, 1994).

Durr felt personally confident in the midst of the Red-baiting that was encouraged by Truman's loyalty oath in 1947:

> I felt absolutely safe. I was an American. It was my country. I had my administration in the White House. The wife of the president was my friend. I went to the White House for receptions. My husband was in the government. My brother-in-law was on the Supreme Court of the U.S. I felt perfectly safe. Who in the world could accuse me of anything illegal or underhand? (Durr, 1985, p. 165)

But in 1948, both of the organizations Durr worked with dissolved under the Red-baiting of their members. The Southern Conference for Human Welfare evolved into the Southern Conference Education Fund. When the National Coalition Against the Poll Tax ended in 1948, four southern states had repealed their poll taxes—North Carolina, Louisiana, Florida, and Georgia. The 24th Amendment to the U.S. Constitution in 1964 finally abolished the poll tax for federal elections; Alabama was one of the five southern states that clung to it to the end (Egerton, 1994).

In the presidential election of 1948, two splinter parties broke off the Democratic Party—the Dixiecrats running Strom Thurmond and the Progressive Party running Henry Wallace. In this situation Durr supported Wallace, the only one in her family to do so. Wallace took an unambiguous stand against segregation. To help his campaign, Durr ran for U.S.

Virginia Durr, director, Progressive Party of Virginia, and 1948 candidate for U.S. Senate, Virginia. From Records of the Progressive Party, courtesy Special Collections Department, University of Iowa Libraries, Iowa City.

senator from Virginia on the Progressive ticket. She chaired the Progressive Party in Virginia when it was founded in June 1948. She made speeches, mostly to black audiences, and was amazed when black people nationwide voted for Truman rather than Wallace (Durr, 1985; Sullivan, 1996).

After President Truman narrowly won the election, he asked Clifford to accept reappointment to the Federal Communications Commission (FCC), to which Clifford had been appointed in 1941, ignoring the fact that Clifford's wife had supported Wallace. Clifford refused, because his conscience would not let him enforce an anti-Communist loyalty oath from the employees of the FCC; he did not believe that people should be accused by faceless informants.

This decision became a turning point in the Durrs' lives. By making it, they renounced their privileged position in the government to stand by their principles. At the time, Clifford was 49, Virginia 45; they had four daughters from 21 to 1 ½ years of age. (Their son had died of appendicitis in 1938 when he was 3, and Lulah was born in 1947.) The Durrs had no specific plans for what they would do next. Several corporations in New York wanted Clifford to work for them, to use what he had learned at the FCC to fight against that agency. But Clifford would not even consider doing that. Durr remembered later:

> We had no inkling at the time Cliff turned down reappointment to the FCC that the next years were going to be as hard as they turned out to be. Cliff had been offered a job at Yale earlier, but he refused it at the time because he wanted to finish out his term on the FCC. Cliff thought that when we got back from Poland he would be going to Yale, but the offer never was renewed.
>
> We were still not scared, even though we didn't know what we were going to do. We thought surely we'd land on our feet. It's curious that we weren't scared, but we really never were. We were naive, I suppose. (Durr, 1985, pp. 219–220)

Clifford wanted to return to Alabama, but, since Virginia did not want to face the pain of disagreeing with their families about the race issue, he opened a law practice in Washington, D.C., and defended people accused of "disloyalty." Virginia taught English to supplement their income. No corporate clients would come to Clifford after word got around of his first "disloyalty" client.

Two years later Clifford accepted an offer to work for the Farmers' Union in Denver. Within a year he lost this job, because Virginia publicly opposed bombing China (communist since 1948) as part of the Korean War. She was given a chance to save his job by retracting her opinion, but neither she nor Clifford would agree to it. Once again, they lost Clifford's job in order to maintain their principles. Clifford suffered serious back problems, necessitating an operation. Their savings from the sale of their house in Virginia ran out; they had little choice but to return to Alabama and move in with Clifford's mother in Montgomery.

MONTGOMERY AND THE MOVEMENT, 1951–1964

Clifford lay flat on his back for a year recovering from his back ailment, while Virginia worked in the insurance department of the state government, earning $125 a month. Once recovered, Cliff opened a law office with Virginia as his secretary; he said he could not find anyone else who could spell. Virginia felt that, since they were dependent on her mother-in-law, she would have to lead a quiet, traditional life; she resigned her membership in the Women's Division of the Democratic Party and in the American Civil Liberties Union (ACLU).

Those years were miserable for Virginia, who had little to do and could not speak out against injustice and unfairness. But she did find one way to work for racial equality. In Montgomery there were two separate groups of the United Church Women, one white and one black. Some members of each group, including Virginia, Coretta King, and Juanita Abernathy, broke away and formed an integrated group that started by praying in the mornings at Virginia's house and later met in black churches. They grew to be about 100 women from all over the state, until a local retired admiral took down all the license numbers of cars parked outside a meeting and then published the owners' names and phone numbers in the newspaper. The women received harassing phone calls at night and never met again. Several husbands took out notices in the paper disassociating themselves from their own wives; Virginia was fortunate to have Clifford behind her.

Clifford took legal cases brought by poor black people against whites who had cheated them. Wealthier blacks hired the top white lawyers, because juries were more likely to be persuaded by them. The president of the NAACP chapter in Montgomery, E. D. Nixon, brought its cases to Clifford.

By early 1954, word got out that the Supreme Court would soon hand down a decision about segregation in the schools. A senator from Mississippi, Jim Eastland, was campaigning with the argument that if the Supreme Court voted to desegregate the public schools, that would demonstrate that the court was an arm of a Communist conspiracy. The Senate Internal Security Subcommittee (ISS), analogous to the House Un-American Activities Committee, was holding hearings to investigate whether people were Communists. Jim Eastland served as the chair of the ISS and, deciding to use it to help him win reelection, scheduled a hearing in New Orleans.

One Monday morning in March, a marshal appeared at the Durr law office with a subpoena for Virginia to appear before the Eastland hearing.

Virginia knew the background of Jim Eastland. About her age, he had attended the University of Alabama. She knew that he was from the hill country, not a southern aristocrat at all by her family's definitions, and the thought of him trying to call her to account made Virginia furious. She had never been a Communist, but, since she had refused to purge Communists from organizations she led, she had had dealings with them. She was what Eastland called a "fellow traveler." She knew that Eastland was coming after her to discredit her brother-in-law, Hugo Black, and to make the Supreme Court appear Communist leaning.

The Durrs went to New Orleans, and after one day of watching the committee function, Virginia moved into a state of rage so fierce that she rose in the middle of the night and drafted a statement that opened: "I have the highest respect for the investigatory powers of the Congress. I think that is an important function. But from what I saw going on yesterday, this is not a proper exercise of Congressonal powers—this is nothing but a Kangaroo Court." She ended the statement by turning the tables on the committee: "I stand in utter and complete contempt of this committee" (Durr, 1985, p. 259).

Durr decided she would not invoke the First Amendment or the Fifth; she simply would not speak at all. When put on the stand, she identified herself, then tried to read her statement, and when Eastland would not permit her to, she handed it to the press. When the committee questioned her, she remained silent or said, "I stand mute," coolly pausing to powder her nose before leaving the stand.

The hearing continued for a week, investigating three other southerners who were officers of the Southern Conference Education Fund (SCEF): Jim Dombrowski, the executive director; Myles Horton of Highlander Folk School; and Aubrey Williams, editor of the *Southern Farmer,* the last two both members of the board of SCEF. Eastland hired two ex-Communists as witnesses to testify against the accused. On the last day of the hearing, one of the ex-Communists, Paul Crouch, testified that Mrs. Durr had full knowledge of a Communist espionage ring operating inside the White House. Clifford Durr lunged at him, reportedly shouting, "You dirty dog, I'll kill you for lying about my wife"; the strain on his heart put Clifford in the hospital for a week afterward (Egerton, 1994, pp. 579–571; Salmond, 1990, p. 165).

Eastland vowed he would cite all the defendants for contempt and have them jailed, but he never did. Instead of supporting Eastland, newspaper reporters described how unfair the procedures were, and Eastland called off his plans to hold a second hearing.

The Durrs' lives changed drastically as a result of the Eastland hearing. They moved out of Clifford's mother's house into an apartment of their own, because they thought they might be attacked or crosses might be burned. Bobby Shelton, who was head of the Ku Klux Klan, referred to Clifford Durr in all his speeches. That frightened Clifford, thinking it might stir up unstable people. Clifford received several job offers from other places, but he had no intention of leaving Alabama, where he now felt he belonged.

The Durrs experienced no burning crosses or violence, only harassing phone calls. But their children suffered enormously for being the nieces of Hugo Black, who was held responsible locally for the *Brown* ruling in May 1954 that segregation was unconstitutional. One of the Durrs' daughters, Tilla, was 12 or 13 at the time of the *Brown* decision; her teacher told her in front of the class: "You just tell your uncle I'm not going to teach any nigger children. I don't care how many laws they pass" (Durr, 1985, p. 269). Lulah, 6 years old, was disinvited to a birthday party after she was all dressed up and ready to go. Soon the girls' lives became impossible in Montgomery, and they were sent to boarding school in Massachusetts.

Virginia felt liberated by the Eastland hearing; the publicity meant that everyone in Montgomery knew where she stood. As soon as the Durrs moved into their own apartment, Virginia started going to meetings of the Council on Human Relations, the only interracial group in the city. While she was in New Orleans, she had received a supportive telegram from the Women's Political Council of Montgomery, signed by a lot of women she did not know. When she returned, she got to know them—educated black women working to improve their life. They had supported her because they thought if Eastland was after her, she must be all right. It was a tremendous relief for Virginia to be able to voice her opinions and be among people who were against segregation (Chappell, 1994, p. 54).

After the *Brown* decision, black people in Alabama rejoiced as if it were the second Emancipation Proclamation. But most white people resisted; only the power of the federal government forced them to accept integration. Governor George Wallace made preserving school segregation his great crusade; he sent troops in to close schools, and he personally stood in the door of the University of Alabama trying to prevent U.S. law from being carried out.

Over the years, the Durrs stayed in touch with their friend Myles Horton, the founder of Highlander Folk School in the mountains of Tennessee near Chattanooga, just north of Alabama. Highlander sponsored interracial residential workshops for grassroots leaders and union organizers. In the 1940s, the Durrs visited there several times, and Virginia "developed into one of our favorite visiting teachers," according to Horton, who liked to go fishing with Clifford. Virginia wished she had a million dollars to endow Highlander, with the one condition that she be able to visit whenever she wished. It was the only place in the South where people of any race could eat together and spend the night (Letters of Myles Horton and Zilphia Horton and Virginia Durr, in the Papers of the Highlander Research and Education Center, Wisconsin Historical Society).

During the summer of 1955, Myles Horton called Virginia from Highlander to say that he had a scholarship for 2 weeks to award to a local leader, preferably black, from Montgomery. Durr immediately thought of Rosa Parks, the secretary of the NAACP and a seamstress at the Montgomery Fair Department Store (Burns, 1997; Chappell, 1994).

Durr had got to know Mrs. Parks when the Durrs had first moved to town. Durr, too poor to buy clothes for her daughters, received hand-me-downs from her sister, Mrs. Hugo Black. But since the clothes needed to be altered, Durr took them to Parks, and they became friends. Durr offered Parks the scholarship to Highlander and helped her get ready to go. At Highlander, Parks found herself for the first time in an integrated situation where race was not discussed at all; she felt supported in her work by

Virginia Durr and Rosa Parks at the 50th anniversary of Highlander Research and Education Center, October 1982. Courtesy Birmingham Public Library, Department of Archives and Manuscripts.

like-minded people who would help her if she ever got in trouble (Branch, 1988; Durr, 1985; Parks, 1992; Terkel, 1973).

Four months after her trip to Highlander, on December 1, 1955, Parks refused to give her seat in the black section of the bus to a white man. When Clifford and Virginia arrived home that day, E. D. Nixon, president of the NAACP, was on the phone asking them to come down to the jail to help post bail. The Durrs did not have any money for bail, but Nixon did, money that the police would accept only if the Durrs would vouch for it.

The Durrs rushed down to the jail, where Virginia was upset to see the gentle Parks being brought through several locked doors. When Parks emerged from her cell, she saw Virginia looking at her with tears in her eyes. The police accepted Nixon's bail, and the Durrs joined Parks's family to discuss how to proceed. Parks agreed to test the constitutionality of the law upholding segregation, even though that would mean a long drawn-out process of appeal that might go to the Supreme Court and would require financial support from the NAACP.

The following Monday night, Virginia and Clifford went to a mass meeting in support of Parks. Virginia felt on such friendly terms with the black community that she had not the slightest fear of being the only white couple there. But they could not get inside; the crowds were too overwhelming. That night Dr. Martin Luther King, Jr., established himself as the spokesperson for the bus boycott and for the civil rights movement that was being born.

A month later, on January 30, 1956, Durr wrote to Myles Horton about Rosa Parks:

> When she came back [from Highlander] she was so happy and felt so liberated and then as time went on she said the discrimination got worse and worse to bear AFTER having, for the first time in her life, been free of it at Highlander. I am sure that had a lot to do with her daring to risk arrest as she is naturally a very quiet and retiring person, although she has a fierce sense of pride and is in my opinion a really noble woman. (Glen, 1988, p. 136)

A few days later, Durr wrote to another friend describing the behavior of white people in Montgomery:

> Things are really getting rough and it looks as though it might develop into a real sort of race war. Even the more or less decent white people say that all white people have to stand together whether the cause is right or wrong, but the solidarity of the white race must be preserved. I still think most Southern people are amenable to reason if it comes in the form of something concrete. Of course if the big Federal military installations would have the guts to declare all these seething Southern towns out of bounds for the military,

then they would calm down in a minute as the towns draw their life blood from these installations. To show you how silly this whole thing really is, Maxwell Field [Air Force Base] is now completely integrated, and thousands of white people from here work out there and accept Negroes in the Library, Cafeteria, work by them, and even in some areas, go swimming with them, BUT let them get back to Montgomery and they go nuts. It is not fear of the Negroes but a fear of each other, what people will think about them. They all have a sort of schizophrenia. (Burns, 1997, p. 153)

The boycott lasted the entire year, December 1955 to December 1956. Virginia picked up black people who needed a ride, even after the police began to give violation tickets to whites who did this. Many white women picked up the black women who cooked and cleaned for them. The mayor of Montgomery, Tacky Gayle, issued a plea for the white women to stop picking up their maids, but they responded with a roar of indignation. If Tacky Gayle wanted to do their washing and ironing and cleaning and cooking and looking after their children, they would stop; otherwise, they were going to drive their maids.

Parks's case went all the way to the U.S. Supreme Court, which declared segregation on buses anywhere in the United States illegal, and black people resumed riding buses, sitting where they pleased.

Virginia and Clifford Durr continued to work for Negro rights, defending people arrested for violating segregation. A black lawyer in town, Fred Gray, usually took the black defendants, while Clifford took the white ones. His biggest case involved a sociology professor and 15 students from a Methodist college in Jacksonville, Illinois, who were arrested for eating in a local black restaurant. Clifford had to take the professor's case to the Fifth Circuit Court of Appeals in New Orleans to get his conviction overturned.

In the summer of 1957, the Durrs celebrated the wedding, in Montgomery, of their second oldest daughter, Lucy. They invited Josephine Black, Lucy's cousin and the daughter of Virginia's sister, Josephine, and Supreme Court Justice Hugo Black. They also invited their friends, some of whom were Communists or had been, including the writer Jessica Mitford. Such was the impact of the Red-baiting at that time that Justice Black kept his daughter from attending the wedding, because he feared that her presence there might give segregationists an excuse to attack him and the Court (Schrecker, 1998).

For the Durrs, living in Montgomery in the early 1960s was living in the eye of a storm. They didn't know what would happen next. The best part was that many young people with Student Nonviolent Coordinating Committee (SNCC) and other northern supporters stopped to spend the night on their way to Mississippi. The worst time, for Virginia, was on May 20, 1961, when the Freedom Riders came to Montgomery by bus. They had been escorted by state troopers to the city limits, where the city police were supposed to take over. But the commissioner of public safety, Lester Sullivan, had promised local segregationists that he would give them half an hour to beat up "those God-damned sons of bitches [Freedom Riders]." Virginia and her friend Jessica Mitford watched it happen from Clifford's second-floor law office. The ordinary crowd of Saturday shoppers had turned into a raving mob, yelling, "Go get the niggers! Go get the niggers!" People held up their babies to "see the niggers run." Within half an hour, every Freedom Rider had managed to run and hide or had been beaten up. Ambulances waited half an hour to take them to the hospital. Virginia saw the attorney general of the state drive up with a local judge and both just stand there rubbing their hands in delight.

Virginia felt stark terror. During the past 10 years she had begun to build up confidence that white southerners were after all decent people, but here they revealed themselves as deep down full of bigotry and meanness. Virginia felt that she would live and die among people who could be absolute brutes; and how could she be sure they wouldn't turn on her? She had nightmares about it for long afterward (Durr, 1985, pp. 296–299).

The day following the attack on the Freedom Riders, President Kennedy ordered 500 U.S. marshals to Montgomery; they were reinforced by the Alabama National Guard, and together they held off another mob that evening at a rally at Ralph Abernathy's First Baptist Church. The federal government was forced to act in order to insure the safety of those who were against segregation in Montgomery (O'Reilly, 1989).

Four years later, in 1965, with the passage of the Voting Rights Act, Durr felt a great victory. Getting the vote had been her life's work. Finally, the poll tax and the literacy tests were abolished, and black people and women could vote. Yet whom did they elect? That old racist, George Wallace. Virginia saw the irony of her work; voting did not seem to be a solution to everything, and it certainly didn't bring black people the economic improvement that they wanted. After this, however, the South gave up its overt resistance to desegregation. Virginia was surprised at how southerners accepted change when they had to.

RETIREMENT, 1964–1999

Meanwhile, the Durrs' life gradually slowed down. Their children moved into adulthood, and no one was left in town from Clifford's family except his brother, James. Clifford had stopped teaching Sunday school at the First Presbyterian Church after the Eastland hearing; his students just never showed up again. Virginia and Clifford broke with their church completely when it barred its doors and would not let people in until they were seen to be white, even though Clifford had been a deacon and the fifth generation of Durrs to sit in the same pew. They began to spend most weekends on the Durr family farm, called Pea Level, near Wetumpka, about 15 miles from Montgomery. In 1964, when he was 64 and Virginia 61, Clifford retired from his law practice. In 1969 they moved permanently to the farm, where Clifford had built them a house, and where he gardened during his last years (Durr, 1985; Salmond, 1990).

In the early 1970s, Virginia and Clifford were invited to talk to students in a sociology class at Tuskegee Institute, the black college. The students were openly hostile, saying they did not want to listen to white people. None of them had registered to vote, and none of them trusted the courts. They wanted a good job, a house, and a car. It was a painful moment for Virginia, who felt they did not give a damn for that which she had worked so hard. But she understood that the whole struggle had entered a new stage, of which she was not really part. What could she tell them? She knew that people didn't seem to have any power at all, that government could not control the corporations, because the latter were more powerful. By the late 1970s, she believed it was going to be one hell of a struggle, waged on a different plane, and she would not live to see it resolved.

Virginia felt that this new fight would be for an alternative economic system, because she felt that capitalism did not work. She wanted a just, democratic economic system, which she knew might be asking too much. She was appalled at what the Soviets and the Chinese were doing; the idea of living in a society where she couldn't say what she wanted, or print what she wanted, or buy magazines and hear diverse opinions, was horrifying to her. But she believed that corporations had to be controlled somehow; she didn't know what the solution was going to be.

Nine years into his retirement, Clifford suddenly became a wealthy man, as a consequence of his father's business, the Durr Drug Company, selling its shares to the public. Four years later, in 1975, Clifford died. Virginia had been married to him for 49 years, and certainly no one had influenced her thinking as much as he had. Clifford was a highly principled person; he did what was right because he thought it was right. Virginia believed that this quality came out of the southern tradition of the principled, honorable gentleman, driven into him by his grandfather and his father. Clifford never cared much about money and the things it could buy—cars, clothes, and fine furniture. He was brought up without much money, and it held no temptation for him. Virginia saw her husband as a person of complete integrity, who never spoke or did a dishonorable thing. They fully supported each other at every step of their deepening commitment to civil rights and resistance to the anti-Communist movement; they shared a deep conviction that one must never compromise one's principles for expediency. Theirs had been a happy, loving marriage, indispensable to each in supporting their ability to take a principled stand in the world (Colby & Damon, 1992; Salmond, 1990).

After Clifford's death, Virginia experienced a period of depression and was hospitalized for a time. This had happened to her before, after the death of her son in 1938. Her parents had both gone through such periods, and she was not to escape them. Virginia continued to live at Pea Level Farm for about 4 years before she moved back to Montgomery. During these years she traveled to China, with one of the earliest groups to go after the country became open to visitors (Lucy Hackney, telephone interview with author, February 6, 1997).

During her years alone in Montgomery, Durr traveled several times to England, where she would rent a room from some friend of Jessica Mitford and stay for a month or so. She traveled widely within the United States, visiting Mitford in Berkeley, California, and visiting her daughters up and down the East Coast. She spent summers at Martha's Vineyard, where her daughter Lucy and Lucy's husband, Sheldon Hackney, had a house.

How was Virginia Durr able to stand up to the social and political pressure to conform? How could she sustain herself as the lonely nonconformist who, because of her beliefs, lived outside the magic circle in which she would have been a grande dame? When Durr was 87 years old, she was interviewed at length by Anne Colby and William Damon for their study of the development of lives of moral commitment. She revealed to them that she did not experience herself as a lonely nonconformist, or even as a radical. She knew that racial integration and the right to vote, the two things she especially worked on, were commonplace in almost every other developed country in the world. She just happened to live in a small area of the United States where these rights were denied by a selfish ruling caste, but she always felt that she belonged to the majority of people in the United States who were conforming to its laws (Colby & Damon, 1992).

Durr felt secure, the result of her loving upbringing in an aristocratic family. She expected to be loved, even when she wasn't. She liked to be around people and believed that by sticking together, people could accomplish great things.

Some had accused Virginia Durr of being too self-righteous, of thinking that she knew what was right. Well, she responded:

I did know what was right, and I felt that denying anybody the right to vote was wrong. I felt to segregate people was wrong. I never had any doubts about it. You see, you're terribly criticized when you do these things that are against the majority. If you don't know you're right, you have nothing to fall back on. I knew I was right. I was actually certain of it; I never had any doubts. (Colby & Damon, 1992, p. 124)

When things get rough, if you don't believe in what you are doing, then you might as well give up. That's the one thing that keeps you going. People would say, "How do you know you are right? Why do you think you have the wisdom of the ages?" Well, if you don't believe in what you are doing, why do you do it? You don't get anything out of it. You certainly don't get fame or glory or money or high position. You just do it because you believe it is right. (Durr, 1985, p. 337)

Durr was raised in a pastor's family and grew up in religion, but she felt that religion and faith in God played little or no role in her work and convictions:

I'm afraid my faith in the goodness of God is very weak. I cannot imagine a beneficient God, you know, letting the innocent suffer. . . . I've gone to church all my life, and I am religious in a way that I believe in a power in the universe beyond my comprehension, but I have never been able yet to feel, as some people do, the intimate power of God. I've had people tell me they felt that God was there. I've never been able to feel that. Well, I've felt always it's more people being with me, supporting me. (Colby & Damon, 1992, pp. 122, 129)

The southern tradition of honor played a major role in Durr's life. Her father lost his pastorship because he would not lie about his personal beliefs. Her paternal grandfather would not support the Confederacy. Her husband resigned from his federal job rather than investigate employees' political beliefs. It was a matter of course to her that one must act on one's beliefs and take the consequences.

But the costs of integrity had been great for Virginia and Clifford. Looking back on their life together, Virginia did not regret the lack of money or the turmoil of being in the fray or the loss of social status. But she did regret not having spent more time with her children, and she greatly regretted the suffering that the younger children endured during the hardest times in Montgomery: "My children certainly don't look back on Montgomery with happiness. Too hard, and too many threats, and too poor and didn't feel any sense of real pleasure. . . . And you feel kind of guilty that you got them in that position. . . . And I had to send them off to school. They were perfectly miserable. . . . That is the most painful part of the whole thing" (Colby & Damon, 1992, pp. 126–127).

But assessing it all, Durr was clear that, despite her regrets about the consequences for her children, if she had to do it over, she would do the same thing. For her, "Well, there were no choices to be made" (Colby & Damon, 1992, p. 127).

> My children, as they reached young adulthood, would sometimes say they wished I had stayed at home and baked brownies as other mothers did. But what good were brownies in a society that tolerated poverty and denied people the education to enable them to get out of poverty? What good were brownies in a society that denied people the right to vote? (Durr, 1985, pp. 336–337)

Durr's 90th birthday was celebrated in August 1993 at Martha's Vineyard, where she held court to receive the homage of her devoted friends and admirers. Eight years earlier her autobiography had been published; she was being recognized for her wit, her brilliance, her effectiveness, her integrity, and most of all, for being right. Within a few more years, her brilliant mind began to deteriorate. When she died on February 24, 1999, at the age of 95, the state of Alabama flew its flags at half-mast in tribute. President William Jefferson Clinton said: "Her courage and steely conviction in the earliest days of the Civil Rights Movement helped to change this nation forever." Rosa Parks wrote Virginia's family as if to Virginia: "We still have a long ways to go, but you, my friend, have made it easier for all of us" (Obituary, *New York Times*, February 26, 1999).

3

Reborn on the Bench:
J. Waties Waring

J. Waties Waring was born in 1880 in Charleston, South Carolina, a generation before Virginia Durr. As a young adult, Waring did not feel the contradictions of his society as strongly as she did, perhaps in part because he did not leave Charleston for his education. His antiracism did not emerge publicly until the 7th decade of his life.

Waring was born and educated and lived and practiced law within a few blocks in lower Charleston, south of Broad Street, where white blueblood society resided. He attended the Episcopal Church, belonged to all the exclusive societies (St. Cecilia Society, the Charleston Club, the South Carolina Society, and the Charleston Light Dragoons), and functioned as a popular member of Charlestonian aristocracy.

During the 1930s, when Waring was in his 50s, he served as city attorney and key advisor to the city's remarkable mayor, Burnett Maybank. Maybank and Waring strongly supported Franklin D. Roosevelt's policies, an unusual position for southern Democrats.

After 1942, when Waring was appointed a federal judge, he experienced a 6-year conversion that transformed him into an outspoken champion of racial justice. By requiring state politicians to open the 1948 primary election to black voters, he renounced his racism and gave up many of the privileges that it had bestowed on him. Like Virginia Durr, he rejected gradualism as a strategy and stood firm in the conviction that the time had come to abolish segregation completely. For this, Judge Waring became an outcast in white society in South Carolina and, in turn, "our judge" to black people.

WHO WAS WATIES WARING BEFORE 1942? 1880–1942

Waties Waring was an eighth-generation Charlestonian. His ancestors arrived at the township of Charleston, South Carolina, soon after its founding in 1670. His paternal forbears, the Warings, arrived from England in 1689 and secured 700 acres of land along the Ashley River, one of the two rivers that bordered the city. His maternal ancestors, the Waties, shipped from Wales and settled in 1694 on 250 acres along the coast (Yarbrough, 1987).

Waties Waring's father, Edward Perry Waring, came from a large Charleston family; he graduated from military school in time to fight for the Confederacy in the final year of the Civil War. After the war, with the cotton economy ruined, he married Anna Thomasina Waties and found a job as a clerk with the South Carolina Railroad Company. Eventually, he rose to a good position there, but after 22 years he lost his job when the firm was swallowed up by the Southern Railway Company. The family experienced difficult times until, in 1904, Edward Waring was elected superintendent of schools, a position he held until his death in 1916 (Yarbrough, 1987).

Waties remembered his father as an extrovert, "thoroughly saturated with the Confederate cause. . . . He didn't read much. He read newspapers, current events, and was friendly with people, did his work, but wasn't what you'd call a literary man" (Yarbrough, 1987, p. 4).

By contrast, Waties's mother read extensively; he remembered her as a "person of rather independent thought," with whom he enjoyed a different relationship from that he had with his father. "[Father] was very fond of children, [a] cheerful, bright fellow that played with kids. He liked to carry on that way. We were awfully fond of father. I think that mother was more intellectual. I talked problems with her more, but I had fun with him" (Waring, 1955–1957, pp. 5–6).

Waties was born on July 27, 1880, the fourth child, following Thomas, Edward, and Margaret. His father still held his position with South Carolina Railway Company and the city of Charleston was enjoying economic recovery after the war, with the use of phosphate fertilizer restoring the area's agricultural productivity. In that year, electrical lighting was introduced, although it remained a novelty for several more years. The city included more than 52,000 people, of whom slightly more than half, 54%, were African Americans. They lived a semislave existence, possessing less than 4% of the city's wealth (Yarbrough, 1987, p. 3).

About Charleston, Waring once observed: "It has a charm, a fashion, but it doesn't think much, and it doesn't think outside of its pattern. . . . It's not like the Bible Belt where hell and brimstone and eternal damnation is preached. There was none of that kind of thing" (Waring, 1955–1957, p. 8).

Reconstruction lasted in South Carolina until 1876, when an aristocratic former Confederate general, Wade Hampton, became governor. Under his tenure and with the withdrawal of Northern troops, the old master-slave relationships resumed, based on the economic, social, and psychological realities of white power.

As a child, Waties had a black nurse, an ex-slave named Hannah, whom he called "Dah"; the old families all had "Dahs" to raise the children. He never knew whether she had a last name.

> Most of the Negroes I knew were ex-slaves and you loved them, were good to them. We didn't give them any rights, but they never asked for any rights, and I didn't question it. . . . Now, as far as race relations were concerned, I practically never heard any discussion. For years I always thought that there was something wrong with the situation in race relations, but still it was what we had and we lived in it and we were pretty happy with it and why bring it up. It was that kind of attitude. (Waring, 1955–1957, pp. 9–12)

Of his siblings Waties recalled that Tom, 9 years older, was the most influential. As a boy, Tom read Greek mythology to Waties. Since their father was still earning well, Tom was able to attend an Episcopal college in New York City. When he returned, he assisted Waties with his homework and encouraged his interest in the classics. Tom "was pretty advanced and liberal in his thoughts," Waties recalled later: "he had a good deal to do with [my] intellectual development, if I ever had any" (Waring, 1955–1957, p. 4).

For high school Waties attended University School, a small private institution with a classical curriculum. The academic training he received proved unremarkable, but the ethical influence stayed with him for life. The headmaster, Walter McKenney, was a Virginia gentleman, highly educated and cultured. Later in life Waring gave great credit for his own ethical standards to McKenney, who maintained an honor system and imbued his students in this way:

> You couldn't lie to McKenney. You could do anything you wanted. You could talk, throw spit balls and that sort of thing, but if he said, "Did you do it?" you had to say, "Yes." If you said, "No," he accepted your word. [If] a new boy coming in would half lie, McKenney would look at him and say, "I thought I saw you talking, but if you tell me you didn't, of course I'll accept it." The fellow would shrivel up and never lie again. That was a pretty fine school. (Waring, 1955–1957, pp. 12–13)

Waties attended church all through adolescence; he felt he had no choice:

> My father wasn't a great questioner, and he followed along like most Epis-
> copalians who are good churchmen and don't worry too much about doc-
> trine. . . . [My mother] revolted a little bit from strict church doctrine, I think,
> though she continued to be a member. . . . In my early life, of course, I went
> to church. I went along. I had to go, but then the regime was relaxed . . . and
> I was left a good deal to my own devices so that by the time I got through
> high school and college I began to have a good many questions about the
> riddle of existence. (Waring, 1955–1957, pp. 5–6)

Throughout his life Waring continued to attend church, but he criticized it freely, and later, when he was being considered for a federal judgeship, a friend urged him not to talk about church. "Don't make fun of it.
It'll hurt you," the friend urged (Waring, 1955–1957, p. 7).

When Waring was ready for college, his father's financial situation had
gone from bad to worse, so he stayed in Charleston and attended the College of Charleston. There he read widely in the classics, including Horace,
Livy, Cicero, Catullus, and Virgil. He became an officer in the college literary society, taking part in debates, orations, and readings, and joined the
Alpha Tau Omega fraternity. In 1900 Waties graduated second in his class,
with honors (Yarbrough, 1987).

By his senior year, Waring had decided to become a lawyer. Several
of his mother's male ancestors had been lawyers, but there were no immediate family connections to law. Somehow his parents had expected him
to choose law; his mother spoke of it often and his father jokingly called
him "Judge" (Waring, 1955–1957, p. 26).

Since law school was out of the question, given the family's finances,
Waring stayed home and began to read law to prepare for the bar exam.
He did odd jobs, with no salary, at the firm of his father's friend, J. P.
Kennedy Bryan. Mostly he sat in a corner reading textbooks and asking
questions. After 2 years of this, he passed the bar examination.

For the next 11 years, Waring stayed at the Bryan law firm, taking
spillover cases and building up his own clients. During this time, he did
not marry, but socialized widely, gaining a reputation as one of Charleston's
foremost rakes, a lifestyle common for a man in his social class. He also
became active in Democratic Party politics. "Politics," he said, "gives you
a mixture with people and gets you known in the community. I went along
taking small parts in the political set up" (Waring, 1955–1957, pp. 51–53;
Yarbrough, 1987).

The few black voters in Charleston were staunch Republicans, loyal
to the party of Lincoln, until 1932, when FDR began bringing them into
the Democratic Party. Most black voters had been disenfranchised by the
new South Carolina state constitution of 1895, when Waring was 15. Legal

segregation came to Charleston by means of state laws adopted during the decade in which Waring began practicing law. Negroes increased their majority somewhat; by 1904 they constituted 57% of Charleston's population (Rosen, 1982, p. 128).

In 1913, Waring married Annie Gammell, a well-connected Charleston woman. She had studied drama in New York City and became a devotee of the great actress Sarah Bernhardt. Waties and Annie were married in Bronxville, New York. The next year they moved into Annie's house in Charleston, at an impeccable address south of Broad Street in the shadow of the historic Episcopal Church, which they attended. About 3 years later their only child was born and named for her mother, Anne. Sarah Bernhardt served as the child's godmother (Yarbrough, 1987).

In 1914 Waring's political connections paid off, and he was appointed assistant U.S. attorney for South Carolina's eastern district, a position he held for 6 years while he gained expertise in federal litigation. He was an admirer of Woodrow Wilson and thought it a tragedy that the United States failed to join the League of Nations. When a Republican, Warren Harding, was elected president in 1920, Waring chose to return to private practice, setting up his own firm with a partner (Yarbrough, 1987; Waring, 1955–1957).

Waring's firm thrived during the 1920s, with federal clients and real estate cases, and as counsel to the two largest newspapers in town. There were no Negro attorneys in Charleston, and Waring's firm had some Negro clients. Waring accepted white supremacy without examining it; he made certain that the city's property leased to the army as a recreation field would only be used by white soldiers. He called Negroes by their first names, as was customary, but individually he treated them with respect—perhaps a clue to his future behavior (Yarbrough, 1987, pp. 12–13).

In 1931 Burnett Rhett Maybank, Waring's close friend and mentor, became Charleston's mayor. The city council elected Waring to be the city's attorney, a position he held until his appointment as federal judge. Maybank, a firm supporter of Roosevelt, turned out to be an outstanding mayor during the difficult Depression era, and Waring served as his key advisor. Among other actions they took, they increased taxes and found new ways to collect them from the wealthy, who had not been paying (Yarbrough, 1987).

Ever since his first job as assistant U.S. attorney, Waring had wanted a permanent federal post. In 1930, he made a strong but unsuccessful bid for U.S. attorney in his district. In 1934, the seat of the judge of the the eastern district became open. (South Carolina had three federal judges—one for the eastern district, one for the western district, and one who roved, sharing the caseload of both districts.) Waring became a leading contender, but he was edged out by a close friend of South Carolina's junior senator.

In reviewing the contenders, the Justice Department had surveyed a number of Charlestonians about Waring; they frequently mentioned his "cold, aloof" personality. One claimed that he was "very smart, so much so that his smartness borders on insolence," and another that he was "lacking in humanity." But everyone praised his intellect, reputation, efficiency, and integrity, and several suggested that his "impersonal disposition" would be desirable in a judge (Yarbrough, 1987, p. 13).

Disappointed, Waring continued as city attorney. He and his wife were at the center of social life in Charleston. They entertained at home and at their summer cottage on Sullivan's Island, just off the coast. Their annual New Year's party was a social highlight of the year. Their daughter, Anne, attended college at Goucher in Baltimore, made her debut at the St. Cecilia Society in 1937, and soon afterward married and moved to Boston, then New York City. As city attorney, Waring often visited New York City during these years (Yarbrough, 1987).

In August 1940 the federal judge of the eastern district died, leaving the seat vacant. Again, Waring was a leading contender, but the political machinations took time, with the outcome uncertain. It did not help that Waring's law firm represented Charleston's *News and Courier,* one of the South's most vehemently anti-Roosevelt papers. Waring's law partner openly detested "Rooseveld," but Waring deeply supported Roosevelt and the many federal projects that came to Charleston through him.

Whether Waring would be appointed federal judge depended a great deal on his relationship with the senior senator from South Carolina, "Cotton Ed" Smith, who had the most longevity of any senator. If Smith objected to Waring, the Senate could be expected to invoke the custom of "senatorial courtesy" and deny confirmation.

Waring had got to know Smith back when Waring was assistant U.S. attorney to the man who served as Smith's campaign manager for many years. Waring had become Smith's campaign manager for Charleston. Smith had an odd combination of progressive and conservative views; he opposed the tariff, Wall Street, and big business, while also opposing labor legislation and woman's suffrage. Smith was an early supporter of FDR, but after 1935 he began to oppose crop controls and the National Recovery Administration. Early in his career Smith had avoided race-baiting, but as he aligned himself against Roosevelt, he became more demagogic, unleasing tirades against Negroes and antilynching legislation (Yarbrough, 1987).

Smith decided to support Waring, who thus secured the federal judgeship. Waring's relationship with Smith was an enduring one based on genuine affection. Even after Waring had served as federal judge, he still remembered Cotton Ed with fondness:

He was a good deal of a demagogue . . . his racial talks were to get the boys in the backwoods to vote for him, and they did. . . . I didn't have any admiration or particular respect for his opinions or the way he went on, but I had a kind of sneaking fondness for him. He was a nice old chap in a great many ways and very amusing and could make a wonderful speech to a half literate group of voters. (Waring, 1955–1957, pp. 130a–131a)

At noon on January 26, 1942, Waties Waring assumed the role of judge that his parents had predicted for him. At 61, Waring outwardly seemed to have everything a Charlestonian could aspire to—achievement, wealth, status, pleasure. He had performed just as had been expected of him and had reached the legal pinnacle of federal judgeship in the most cosmopolitan city of the South.

But inwardly, Waring continued to examine his society and come to his own conclusions. In the following 6 years, he would destroy the life he had carefully built and create a new one of far greater significance to himself and to his fellow citizens.

THE 6-YEAR CONVERSION, 1942–1948

When Judge Waring prepared his papers for preservation, he destroyed all but a few items from before 1945, seemingly to erase everything personal from before this time. Hence, there are few clues to the inner reality of his marriage to "Miss Annie," as she was known. Their friends considered them a model couple, thoroughly devoted to each other. Miss Annie testified at the divorce hearing that theirs had been an ideal marriage, that Waring had treated her with kindness always, that he had shown great affection in private, and that "we were considered the best and most completely happy couple in Charleston" (Yarbrough, 1987, p. 35).

The son of Waring's law partner later told Waring's biographer that "Miss Annie wasn't on the same intellectual level as Waties. She was a nice person and a completely devoted wife. . . . She worshipped the ground that Waties walked on, especially later when he became U.S. district judge. . . . But intellectually she didn't have the depth of Waties" (Yarbrough, 1987, p. 29).

In his oral history, given in 1957, Waring gave this brief explanation:

My first wife and I lived along pretty happily, and then her health wasn't very good, and there was a good deal of change, and things became pretty routine, not difficult but routine. Very little sympathy. Then I met my present wife and we fell in love. I discussed the matter very frankly with my first wife, and she agreed to a divorce and went to Florida and obtained it. Then

I married my present wife. We have been in thorough accord. (Waring, 1955–
1957, p. 402)

Whatever the issues between Judge Waring and his wife, Annie, sometime between 1942 and 1944, his first 2 years as federal judge, Waring met
and fell deeply in love with Elizabeth Avery Hoffman. She was the wife of
a wealthy Connecticut textile merchant, Henry Hoffman, who owned a
large home in Charleston, where wealthy Yankees liked to spend the winter. During the years of World War II, the Hoffmans lived in Charleston
and were among the many wealthy Yankees in the Warings' social circle.
The two couples became frequent bridge partners, and soon Elizabeth and
Waties also became lovers (Yarbrough, 1987).

Elizabeth Hoffman was a strikingly handsome woman 15 years
younger than Judge Waring, in her late 40s when they met. Henry Hoffman
was her second husband; her first marriage had lasted 20 years. In Charleston, as the wife of Henry Hoffman, she did volunteer work for the Red Cross
and the local Office of Price Administration (OPA) office (Yarbrough, 1987).

Divorce was not available in South Carolina in the 1940s. Except during Reconstruction, the state's legal code made no provision for it at all,
until a few years after Judge Waring's dilemma. Numerous houses of pros-
titution flourished in Charleston, and discreet affairs were acceptable. But
Judge Waring had fallen in love. One evening in late February 1945 he told
his wife of 32 years of his change in feelings and asked her to go to Florida,
where his sister-in-law lived, and obtain a divorce there.

Miss Annie was devastated by this news, but she carried out his wishes
and arrived in Jacksonville, Florida, on March 1. Elizabeth Hoffman went
to Reno to secure a Nevada divorce, and on June 15, one week after
Waring's divorce was final, Elizabeth and Waties were married in a municipal court in Greenwich, Connecticut. They returned to Charleston to
live in Waties and Annie's house, which apparently he had acquired in the
divorce settlement.

This news shocked and incensed upper-crust society in Charleston. It
could not approve of Judge Waring's forcing Annie out, or of divorced
women, or of Yankee ones, whom they found too aggressive and positive
in their views. Rumors circulated that Judge Waring had stolen Annie's
house and that he had moved Elizabeth into Annie's house—and bed—
before the divorce had even been granted (Yarbrough, 1987).

Shortly after their wedding, Waties and Elizabeth gave a large party
in Charleston. Few of those invited showed up. Invitations to the Warings
soon dwindled, and whenever they attended a party, the room they stood
in quickly emptied. Hurt and angered by this reception, Judge Waring

sometimes became brusque and curt. To make matters worse, after a year or so Miss Annie rented a small kitchen house less than 100 feet from her former home. There she lived a lonely, pathetic, often bedridden existence, eliciting the sympathy of Judge Waring's neighbors, until she died in 1954. After their marriage, Judge and Elizabeth Waring gradually became isolated from his traditional circle of friends and even from relatives; as his racial views began to change, this process accelerated to the point of completion (Yarbrough, 1987).

Judge Waring's former friends often blamed his change of heart about racial matters on his new Yankee wife, who they felt must have filled his ear with an outsider's rantings. Elizabeth Waring certainly assisted and supported her new husband's transformation, but the evidence suggests that he began to change his point of view soon after he became judge in January 1942. His changing views on race must have played a role in his falling in love with Elizabeth, as the two events occurred concurrently.

Judge Waring found that a lawyer's thinking changes in an impressive way when he puts on judicial robes. "It's kind of like being born again. It's an entirely different point of view. . . . When you're practicing law, you're representing a particular interest . . . when you're on the bench, you're not interested in who wins a case. You're interested in seeing the case handled justly and right" (Waring, 1955–1957, pp. 139a–140a).

In the interest of seeing cases handled justly and right, Judge Waring insisted that Negroes be addressed by their title, not by their first name. (He had done this previously in his correspondence as city attorney, when no one else did.) He had his bailiff move people around in the courtroom so that they wouldn't be racially segregated. There were few Negro jurors, but when there was one or two, they always came in last, after the white jurors. Waring stopped this by giving the jurors assigned seating. When he learned from a Negro juror that Negro jurors were being taken to the kitchen of restaurants to eat, he instructed his chief marshal to end this practice, ruling that it was clearly illegal to break up the jury and could invalidate his cases. This integrated at least one restaurant in Charleston. When complaints arose, he stood adamant. He knew these were little things, but he believed they meant a great deal. As Waring said, "I tried to introduce what I call the American creed into a court, even sitting in segregated South Carolina" (Waring, 1955–1957, p. 244).

Septima Clark, a black schoolteacher in Charleston, remembered that Judge Waring once said to her: "You know, a judge has to live with his conscience. I would sit in the courtroom, and I would see black men coming in that I knew were decent men, and they were considered bums and trash because they were black. And I would see white men that I knew were bums, and they were considered gentlemen. I just couldn't take it any longer" (Clark, 1986, p. 24).

The first cases brought to Waring that presented the issue of racial discrimination by public officials were two that challenged the inequality of pay for Negro teachers. In the first case, in 1943, the local NAACP chapter persuaded Viola Duvall to file a class action suit on behalf of Charleston's black teachers, who were paid substantially less than their white counterparts. Thurgood Marshall came from the New York office to argue the case. The school board was willing to right this wrong when it became clear that Judge Waring would insist on equality. The case was settled with the judge allowing until September 1946 for full equalization (Yarbrough, 1987, p. 43).

The second case was brought in Columbia, South Carolina, in 1944, by a black teacher asking for equal pay there. Waring ruled in May 1945 that the local school board had to develop standards for one pay scale, to be effective April 1946, retroactive for the academic year. Meanwhile, the legislature passed new qualifying regulations for all teachers, including a competence exam that helped determine the salary scale. Waring thought this was fine, since it was equal, and it helped eliminate both the ignorant teachers and the crooked ones, after several hundred got caught cheating on it (Yarbrough, 1987, pp. 44–46; Waring, 1955–1957). Looking back on these cases, Waring said:

> The general public [white] didn't particularly resent [the teachers' cases], and I didn't find any particular effects on me one way or the other, excepting internally. It made me begin to think an awful lot, because every time you looked into one of the things, the less reason you could see for resistance to what we commonly call the American creed of equality of all citizens of this country. Every time a case came up, or discussion came up politically or otherwise of these situations, you saw the old sophistry of trying to keep within the law, but declaring two classes of citizens, and that Negroes or people of partial Negro descent were not treated as ordinary American human beings, but were put in a separate classification—whether on pay or jobs or association or anything else. The whole thing worried me a great deal, and I knew the thing was coming to a showdown someday, and probably was coming in my state. The question arose as to whether I should dodge it or meet it. (Waring, 1955–1957, pp. 235–236)

The Negro general public, on the other hand, took great notice of these cases. Here was a federal judge who would rule in favor of black equality. Thurgood Marshall had been caught by surprise:

> When I took the teacher's salary case before him, I regarded him [Waring] as just another southern jurist who would give me the usual head-whipping

before I went along to the Circuit Court of Appeals. . . . [I]t turned out to be the only case I ever tried with my mouth hanging open half the time. Judge Waring was so fair that I found my apprehension totally unwarranted. He made his position clear and told them that the 14th Amendment was still in the Constitution and that it still prevailed for all citizens in his court. (Yarbrough, 1987, p. 43)

Soon after these cases, Judge Waring and Elizabeth Hoffman divorced their spouses, married each other, and were cut out of white society. With no other social outlet, Elizabeth began attending court, where she experienced the next race-discrimination case with the judge.

This particular case, which proved the most influential in changing the Warings' views, came to trial in Columbia in November 1946. It involved a Negro soldier, Isaac Woodward, who was on his way home to his wife in North Carolina after his discharge in Georgia from 3 years in the army, including 15 months fighting in the jungles of the South Pacific. During his ride homeward, Woodward was taken off the bus by local police in a small town and beaten severely on the head, which resulted in permanent blindness, since the constable had driven his nightstick into Woodward's eyes. The U.S. Department of Justice failed to prosecute aggressively; the defense appealed to the worst racist traditions; and the jury acquitted the police chief, to applause from the courtroom (Kluger, 1975).

This case had a tremendous impact on Judge Waring, who felt deeply hurt to have been made a party to it, simply by having it come before his court. Elizabeth returned from the courtroom to their hotel room in tears. The judge later said it was her baptism in the viciousness of race relations in the South, the part you could escape seeing, living there as a Yankee. When Elizabeth confessed her shock to a local white woman, her acquaintance responded: "Well, Mrs. Waring, that sort of thing happens all the time. It's dreadful, but what are we going to do about it?" (Waring, 1955–1957, pp. 223–224).

Elizabeth decided that she could, at the very least, educate herself about Negro reality in the South. To gain the Negro perspective, she borrowed materials from Samuel Fleming, a prosperous black shoemaker and the juror who had informed Judge Waring about black jurors not being allowed to eat with white jurors. Elizabeth also secured copies of studies now considered classics—W.J. Cash's *The Mind of the South* (1941) and Gunnar Myrdal's *An American Dilemma: The Negro Problem and Modern Democracy* (1944/1962). She read these materials to Judge Waring in the evenings as he rested his eyes, and he began to read as well. He found these books deeply disturbing: "I couldn't take it, at first. I used to say it wasn't true, it couldn't be. I'd put the books down, so troubled I couldn't look at them. We'd get in our car and drive through the night, miles and miles, just thinking and talking" (Yarbrough, 1987, p. 53).

Eventually Waties, like Elizabeth, embraced what they were reading. Both Cash and Myrdal, though in different ways, gave them a means with which to detach themselves from local southern culture and see it as a whole from the outside. Wilbur Cash was a southerner, a journalist from Gaffney, South Carolina, who had left the South to work for the Chicago *Post*. In *The Mind of the South* Cash examines the South as a civilization different from the rest of the United States, emphasizing the irrational hates and fears that dwell in the mind of white southerners. From Cash, the Warings concluded that white southerners were suffering from a serious disease that required drastic treatment (Clayton, 1987; Yarbrough, 1987).

Myrdal, however, looked at the whole of the United States from the perspective of a Swedish social economist. His project, a large work of investigative scholarship, was funded by the Carnegie Foundation. As an outsider with nothing to lose, Myrdal documented the depth and breadth of white racism. He pinpointed the moral dilemma of how to reconcile white people's discriminatory behavior with the ideal on which the nation was founded. He deftly analyzed the dilemma of white people:

> The popular beliefs rationalizing caste in America are no longer intellectually respectable. . . . Everybody who has acquired a higher education knows they are wrong. Most white people with a little education also have a hunch that they are wrong. There is today a queer feeling of *credo quia absurdum* hovering over the whole complex of popular beliefs sustaining racial discrimination. This makes the prejudiced white man nearly as pathetic as his Negro victim. (Myrdal, 1944/1962, vol. 2, p. 1003)

The hope for the future of America, Myrdal believed, was neither revolution nor status quo, but a middle road of responsible change to integration and equality (Egerton, 1994).

By 1947 Judge Waring had embraced these ideas and was ready to act on them; his next case completed his break with his society and his racist past. This case, which challenged South Carolina's white primaries, arose in Columbia, in the jurisdiction of the Western District of the federal court. The judge there, George Timmerman, had asked Waring to take a case that involved discrimination at the University of South Carolina, where Judge Timmerman was a trustee. Waring agreed, and asked as well to take the case challenging the primaries, since both suits involved claims of racial discrimination. Timmerman was all too happy to be rid of both cases (Yarbrough, 1987).

Before he took the case of the white primaries, Waring considered the possibilities in it:

I liked it because I felt it was an opportunity, and I felt that somebody in this country ought to take a stand. . . . I felt that my state was backward, that it had been blind to decency and right, and that somebody had at last to face the issue. I thought it was a fine opportunity. I confess that I had some feelings the other way, some worries. I discussed it with my wife. (Waring, 1955–1957, pp. 256–258)

Judge Waring told Elizabeth that if he struck down South Carolina's white primary, it might mean their total isolation from white society. They were still invited to white social events in Columbia and Florence, if not in Charleston, and had that yet to lose. She assured him she was with him from start to finish (Waring, 1955–1957).

South Carolina stood dead last in the nation in the percentage of its citizens who voted; in the 1940 general election not 1 in 20 citizens went to the polls. This feat was accomplished in part by means of a poll tax, which South Carolina kept until the early 1950s, but in larger part by white primaries, which had been used for years by southern states as the most ef-

A luncheon for visiting magazine writer Samuel Grafton, in early 1950. Pictured are Judge Waring at the head of the table and, counterclockwise from him, Lillian Wilson, John Fleming, Mildred Guenveur Cherry, Grafton (partially hidden), Elizabeth Waring, Susan Butler, Septima Clark, Ruby Cornwell, Dr. Roscoe Wilson, and Corinne Guenveur. Courtesy Moorland-Spingarn Research Center/Howard University.

fective way to block Negro participation in elections. After Reconstruction, the Democratic Party had become the only viable party in the South; excluding blacks from the primary election, when the Democratic candidates were chosen, effectively eliminated them from the election process. The Supreme Court upheld this arrangement in the early decades of the 20th century. In the 1930s it went back and forth over cases from Texas, but in a landmark case in 1944, in *Smith v. Allwright*, the Supreme Court unanimously declared the Texas white primary unconstitutional (Egerton, 1994).

After this decision, the political establishment in South Carolina moved quickly to preserve its version of the white primary. It erased all state legislation pertaining to primaries and put these regulations into the bylaws of the state Democratic Party. The conduct of the primaries was left entirely in the hands of party functionaries; the governor told the general assembly: "White supremacy will be maintained in our primaries. Let the chips fall where they may!" (Yarbrough, 1987, p. 62).

South Carolina Negroes moved to challenge these developments. A black merchant from Columbia, George Elmore, tried to vote and was refused in the primary held August 1946; NAACP lawyers, including Thurgood Marshall, prepared a class action suit. Judge Waring later commented that when he heard the case,

> it seemed to me that the law in the case was as plain as the nose on my face. . . . if you're going to judge people on the color of their skin and not on their ability or their capability, then you've abandoned the whole American system. . . . I don't know what the Caucasian race is and I don't think anyone else knows. It's entirely a false idea that was based on the fact that a fellow named [Blumenbach] discovered a skull in the Caucasus that he thought was the finest type of human race . . . Webster, I believe, describes the Anglo-Saxon race as a mixed race. I think all races are mixed races. (Waring, 1955–1957, pp. 269–270)

On July 12, 1947, Judge Waring upheld the right of Elmore to vote in the primary. He concluded his opinion with this advice: "It is time for South Carolina to rejoin the Union. It is time to fall in with the other states and to adopt the American way of conducting elections" (Yarbrough, 1987, p. 64). Five months later the case was upheld by the Court of Appeals for the Fourth Circuit, and the Supreme Court accepted the decision as self-evident, refusing to review it.

Waring's decision in the Elmore case won him the approval of the black community and the national press. No white politician in South Carolina agreed with Waring's decision, but opposition was restrained. Waring received a few letters of support from South Carolinians—people from his neighborhood and ministers around the state. This support encouraged

Waring to believe that there were decent people in the South who would gradually prevail on the traditional racists to give up the old way of white supremacy. Six months after the decree, Waring still believed that progress should be nurtured gradually; in December 1947 he wrote to George E. Zook, president of the American Council on Education:

> Too drastic measures may stifle it as it is not difficult for the agitators to stir up resistance against outside interference. In South Carolina, the spirit of secession is not dead and imitation halos of the Confederacy are still worn by our political candidates. . . . But there is a silent, thinking minority who are as yet little heard of. They must be encouraged gradually. (Yarbrough, 1987, p. 66)

But the litigation over white primaries was not finished, and the transformation of Judge Waring's racial views was not yet complete; in the following year he gave up on southern gradualism and become convinced that federal assistance would be necessary to compel the white southerners to grant basic democratic rights to African Americans.

Politicians in South Carolina refused to accept Judge Waring's decision that primary elections be open to Negroes. They played hardball and openly defied him by changing the rules of the Democratic Party to admit only whites to membership, while allowing blacks to vote, but only if they took an oath to support state rights and the social, religious, and educational segregation of the races, and to oppose the proposed federal Fair Employment Practices Commission law (Yarbrough, 1987).

Thurgood Marshall and his team filed a new suit in early July 1948 and sought an injunction to allow Negroes to vote in the coming August primary until the new case could be decided. Waring knew that the white politicians would challenge him to the hilt and that only the full and unambiguous exercise of his authority, with the power of the U.S. judicial system behind him, would be effective in overcoming them (Yarbrough, 1987).

On July 19 Judge Waring granted an injunction, ordering the white politicians of the Democratic Party to allow registered Negroes to vote in the August primary and to keep the registration books open through July. In his order, Waring said:

> It is the intent of this opinion that the full spirit hereof, as well as the letter be obeyed so that the Democratic organization of South Carolina, and the primaries which it holds, shall be freely open to all persons entitled to enter therein under the laws and Constitution of this country and state without discrimination of race, color or creed; and any violation of the terms of the order or of the laws set forth in this opinion by them or their successors in

office or those acting under them will be considered a contempt and will be proceeded against and punished. (Waring, 1955–1957, pp. 300–301)

In short, Waring told the party leaders that he would hold them personally responsible and send them to jail if the election did not proceed according to his order.

On election day, August 10, Judge Waring made his presence felt. He kept his chamber open for any complaints, and he and Elizabeth drove about Charleston, stopping at polling places with large black enrollments. Thirty thousand Negroes voted in that primary. Predictions had been made that the blood of racial warfare would flow in the streets and would be on Judge Waring's hands. But the white politicians backed down, and it proved to be the most orderly election in years. Two days later, after Judge Waring conferred with Marshall and other black lawyers, the Warings left Charleston by train for New York and California; they returned to Charleston only in mid-October, in time for a final decision on the case in late November (Yarbrough, 1987; Waring, 1955–1957).

As soon as Judge Waring issued his injunction, the harassment from the white community began. The Warings' phone rang incessantly, callers spewing out insults like "nigger-lover" or the receiver filled with heavy breathing. Judge Waring had a second line installed in order to be able to make outside calls, the harassment was so constant. When he drove through the streets, there were catcalls and whistles. People obstructed Elizabeth in shops and on the sidewalks; confronted with Judge Waring, they moved out of the way, pretending not to see him.

> You can go to a foreign country and there you expect to be different, because you don't know what the people think or what they do and what they talk about. But there, day after day, I met dozens of people whom I had known intimately and who talked my language and knew my way of thinking, excepting on one point. And that point completely separated me from the entire white community, the entire governing community. (Waring, 1955–1957, p. 331)

Meanwhile, South Carolina's politicians used Waring's decision in their efforts to win the November 1948 election. In South Carolina and three other Deep South states, the Dixiecrats took control of the Democratic Party organization and offered Strom Thurmond as candidate for president. The progressive wing of the Democratic Party broke off to support Henry Wallace on the Progressive ticket. With these two threats from within his own party, Harry Truman was facing close odds with Republican Thomas E. Dewey. One congressman from South Carolina introduced a resolution in the House to authorize an investigation of Waring's conduct; it never got scheduled. The most vicious assault came from Dixiecrat L. Mendel Rivers in the House of Representatives. His speech to that body gives some flavor of the vitriol that Waring's stand engendered among South Carolina's conservatives; the judge, he exclaimed, was

> as cold as a dead Eskimo in an abandoned igloo. Lemon juice flows in his frigid and calculating veins. By means of the FBI and the United States marshals, he has lampooned, lambasted, and vilified with unparalleled vituperation the comfort and ease of the outstanding members of the bar of South Carolina. At times he has literally banished some of them from his court by force. He should be removed by the force of a boot, if necessary, from office, because he is a disgrace to the Federal judiciary of South Carolina. Every lawyer in South Carolina lives in mortal fear of this monster and everyone who reads this speech will thank God that I made it because I am speaking for the vast majority of the bar of South Carolina. (Yarbrough, 1987, p. 90)

NO MORE GRADUALISM, 1948–1952

Judge and Elizabeth Waring returned to Charleston in early November to continued exclusion from their social world. People shunned them on the streets. Elizabeth was refused service in shops. Their car repeatedly broke down mysteriously; they believed that sugar was put in the gas tank (Yarbrough, 1987).

In the election of November 1948 Truman squeaked into the presidency, and in December Judge Waring went to Washington, D.C., to talk with President Truman and with Chief Justice Fred Vinson. In February 1949, Waring was in New York City, where the National Lawyers Guild honored him. There Clifford Durr, who had just months before given up his privileged position in Washington society by refusing to implement Truman's loyalty oath, said this of Judge Waring:

> Soldiers on a battle field draw courage from each other. . . . A courage of a greater and rarer kind is required to face the disapproval of society in defense of a basic democratic principle. It hurts to be shut off from one's own people. It hurts even more when they are good people—friendly, basically decent and kindly, and the only barrier is an idea. Loneliness can be more painful than the wounds of battle, and few are willing to risk it. It takes real courage for a judge, in opposition to the deep-seated folkways of those with whom he lives and will continue to live to say, "This is the law. It is my duty to enforce it and I will do my duty." It takes far more courage to say, "This law which you so strongly oppose is not only the law but it is morally right, it is elementary democracy." (Yarbrough, 1987, p. 104)

The support that Waring received outside Charleston had to sustain him there, in what increasingly felt to him like a foreign assignment in a country where the whole native population hated him. As a final outrage to his colleagues, in October 1948, Judge Waring appointed John Fleming, a Negro, as bailiff in his court. Waring arranged his judicial calendar to hold court in venues outside South Carolina as much as possible: 6 weeks in New York and 4 weeks in California each year (Yarbrough, 1987).

Back at home, Judge Waring resigned from the Charleston Club and the South Carolina Society—to applause from their members. Elizabeth Waring, an intensely social person, devised a way to be sociable in Charleston; if white people would not come to their house, maybe black people would. She persuaded her husband to buy a shiny green Cadillac, a symbol of success that Negroes would expect, she thought. Soon their table was filled with Negroes who had the courage to defy custom and accept the Warings' friendship. In the opinion of white people, she was taking revenge on the society that had dared to reject her (Yarbrough, 1987).

But African American society had its own caste system; people with lighter skin were considered of higher status than those who were darker. Someone like Septima Clark, of medium-dark skin tones and the daughter of an ex-slave, could not be invited to play bridge or have dinner in the homes of the lighter blacks, despite the fact that she had a middle-class income as a teacher and served as a civic leader in the local NAACP and YWCA, and in the Alpha Kappa Alpha Sorority. Clark decided to accept the Waring's invitation, despite the protestations of her family, neighbors, and school principal that it was a dangerous thing to do. At the Warings, Clark found herself welcomed by higher-class Negroes because she could talk so intelligently about history and current events. She reciprocated by inviting the Warings to tea at her house, which they accepted (Clark, 1986).

After Clark got to know Elizabeth Waring socially, she invited her to speak at the local black YWCA, in January 1950. Clark knew that Elizabeth Waring would say exactly what she thought and that black women would be encouraged by hearing a white person who could disagree with prevailing white behavior. Both blacks and whites tried to persuade Clark to retract her invitation, but she would not back down (Clark, 1986; Yarbrough, 1987).

Since Elizabeth Waring knew that the conservative newspapers in Charleston often twisted the news, she insisted that reporters print the full text of her speech. It rocked white society when they read it, for she had opened her address with these words:

> My very dear friends, it was brave of you to invite me to speak here and brave of all of you to come to hear me, for the white "powers that be" have done

everything in their power to keep me from speaking to you Negro people, even to defaming Judge Waring's and my character. But we only feel sorry for them, for their stupidity, as it will hurt them, and not us, for it is apparent to everyone what their real motive is in not wishing me to speak—fear of the judge and me. We to them are like the atom bomb which they are afraid we will use to destroy their selfish and savage white supremacy way of life, and they are quite correct. That is exactly what the judge and I are doing, and they know it and see the writing on the wall. But you know and we know and they *should* know that there is another use of atomic energy, and that is for building and healing and restoring a civilized way of life. That is what the judge is trying to do for the good of the white people down here as well as the Negro. (Yarbrough, 1987, p. 130)

Waring went on to say, "You Negro people have already picked up the torch of culture and achievement from the whites down here. . . . who are a sick, confused, and decadent people . . . full of pride and complacency, introverted, morally weak, and low" (Yarbrough, 1987, p. 130).

This speech catapulted Elizabeth Waring into the national press. The *New York Times* gave it ample space, and in February she made an effective appearance on NBC's *Meet the Press*. At home, Waring refused to be intimidated; the morning after their house had been stoned and a piece of concrete thrown through a window (October 9, 1950), she went shopping for a mousetrap and remarked defiantly to the clerk and the other customers: "You know, I'm about ten times as scared of a mouse as I am of the whole Ku Klux Klan." When a grateful Negro mother would say to her, "God bless you. I'm going to pray for you," she would respond: "They'll never stop me from showing my face. But for heaven's sake, don't pray for me. Get up off your knees and fight" (Rowan, 1952, pp. 90–93).

The Warings were sustained during these difficult years by their friendships in New York City. Among their staunchest friends there were Walter White, president of the NAACP, and his wife, Poppy Cannon. Walter was $1/_{64}$ black, with white skin, blue eyes, and blond hair—a man who could have passed as white. He had been in love with Poppy, a brunette white, for 20 years and finally had the courage to marry her in 1949. Their interracial marriage caused a storm of protest and confusion; Walter temporarily resigned from the NAACP, while in Europe people often thought Poppy was the person of color. The Warings offered them unwavering support and loved to visit them at their country place in Connecticut. There Waties helped Walter stop smoking by saying: "Walter, whenever you light a cigarette you ought to say, 'Here's to you, Jimmy Byrnes. Here's to you, Strom Thurmond. Here's to you, Senator Eastland.' For let me tell you, that when you die, they're going to declare a national holiday, they'll be so glad to get you off their necks" (Cannon, 1956, p. 220; Egerton, 1994).

As White liked to tell it, he began to feel a little green at once. He never lit another cigarette, and even the smell of smoke made him nauseous, in memory of Byrnes, Thurmond, Eastland, and their ilk.

The night that a piece of concrete was thrown through the front window in the Warings' house, Elizabeth called the Whites in New York City: "They've just thrown a rock through the window. I've turned out all the lights, and we're sitting here in the dark. I had to call you, just to re-assure myself that there is a civilized world . . . outside this jungle" (Cannon, 1956, p. 166).

In April 1950 the Warings were favorably profiled in *Collier's* magazine under the title "The Lonesomest Man in Town." A large photo showed them at dinner with their Negro friends. The author, Samuel Grafton, discussed the claims of white Charlestonians that the Warings were out to destroy white supremacy in revenge for being ostracized for their divorces and subsequent marriage to each other. But the author was not persuaded:

> To shrink this down into a story of a cold man and a divorce is, in an odd way, to make it more socially acceptable. For if Charlestonians were to concede that the judge suffered a sincere revulsion of feeling, they would imply that portents of impending social change have popped up in the heart of their society. By comparison, when they try to reduce it all to a mere social scandal, it is more acceptable. (Grafton, 1950, p. 20)

The article concluded that "the lonesomest man in town might very probably also be the happiest," after quoting Judge Waring as saying:

> It is an unpleasant situation to be in, to stand alone in a community. But after experiencing it . . . I feel that it is the happiest position I could be in. . . . My opponents are the most unhappy people you can find. They're all torn apart inside. They try to make you believe that things that are not all right are fine, and they sweat as they search for the words to do it with. I don't have to engage in those mental acrobatics. I'm almost seventy, and I've got a cause to live for and a job to do. That's pretty good. What can they do to me at seventy that would matter? (Grafton, 1950, p. 21)

By this time Judge Waring's views had developed into a position beyond that of many black leaders. Waring believed that the time had come to ensure full equality for African Americans; that white southerners would never do this voluntarily; and that the full force of federal authority must be exerted to defeat white supremacy, slavocracy, and segregation. He wanted a case that would go to the Supreme Court to enable it to overturn *Plessy v. Ferguson* and declare that segregation, per se, is unequal and unconstitutional. Local black leaders did not seem eager to create this case;

Waties and Elizabeth Waring, n.d. Courtesy Moorland-
Springarn Research Center/Howard University.

they agreed to accept scholarships to the black State College in Orangeburg
instead of attacking segregation at the College of Charleston. They also
settled for a segregated law school instead of insisting on black admission
to the University of South Carolina's law school (Yarbrough, 1987).

But the case Judge Waring hoped for did emerge from nearby rural
Clarendon County, 50 miles northwest of Charleston. There the public
schools served 2,375 white and 6,531 black students. In 1949–1950 the
county had spent $179 per white student and $43 per black student; class
size was sometimes 60–79 for blacks yet not more than 31 for whites
(Kluger, 1975, p. 8).

The case first filed asked only for equal facilities, not for desegregation. Waring was not satisfied; he advised the Negro lawyers, Thurgood
Marshall and Robert Carter, to ask for a dismissal of the case and then to
bring a new suit, charging directly that the schools of Clarendon County,
under the South Carolina constitution and statutes, are segregated, and that
those statutes "are unconstitutional, and that'll raise the issue for all time

as to whether a state can segregate by race its schools" (Kluger, 1975, p. 304). Astonished by this turn of events, Marshall and Carter agreed.

Under federal law, any case challenging the constitutionality of state laws had to be heard by a three-judge panel convened by the chief judge of the district. Marshall and Judge Waring both knew that Waring would surely be outvoted by any panel that he convened. But win or lose, Waring wanted segregation attacked, then and in his court. He was done with gradualism and pragmatism. He had nothing left to lose and called the question (Kluger, 1975).

In the months before the three-judge hearing, the Warings attempted to keep a low profile. But they granted a 7-hour interview to Carl Rowan, an African American reporter for the Minneapolis *Tribune*. Often with tears streaming down his face, Waties Waring told Rowan: "I admit I miss the shop talk. I miss chatting about this Supreme Court ruling or such and such a case. [But] socially, I miss no one. I lost small brains and found larger ones. I have met southern Negroes and northerners of both races whom I would not have known except for this" (Rowan, 1952, p. 94).

Waring told Rowan that he could understand his townspeople's commitment to the past, "to rice and recollections," as he often called it. "White supremacy is a way of life. You grow up in it and the moss gets in your eyes. You learn to rationalize away the evil and filth and you see magnolias instead." But once he had escaped that "web of prejudice and hatred," he had no regrets. When he and his wife drove through Charleston, black children would wave and smile, whispering to one another. "Then I realize the gain that I have made. I am not living a phony life. I can look myself in the face, confident that I am meting out justice." "Perhaps," he added,

> there could be nothing better than that the white supremacists should kill me. No, I am not foolish. I don't want to die. But it is time some white people die to wake up America. They kill Negroes like flies and, as a white Georgian put it after a lynching, "It's just another nigger. It didn't stop a checker game." It's time they killed a white federal judge. Let the people of the world see how insane this thing is, then perhaps it will wake up Americans. (Rowan, 1952, pp. 94)

The hearing for the new case, *Briggs v. Elliot*, Briggs an elementary school student and Elliot a school board member, lasted only 2 days, May 28 and 29, 1951, with Marshall bringing few witnesses and filing, in Waring's opinion, a lackluster brief that skirted the central issues. The Warings felt let down after the trial, especially about the lack of aggressiveness on the part of the NAACP and Negroes in general. Elizabeth Waring wrote in her diary on June 12 that the enemies of integration, both black and white, were rising up again, crawling out of their holes and spewing their venom. . . . The Negro variety [are] usually politicians, doctors, and dentists, preachers and worst and most vociferous of all, school teachers. . . . My beloved Waties has been even more disgusted and hopeless than John [Hammond, a black reporter for the New York *Compass*] and last week became so angry and upset that I had to talk and reason and soothe him . . . until after midnight . . . to get him back to his . . . normal self which is really more hopeful than I am. (Yarbrough, 1987, pp. 191–192)

On June 23, 1951, the opinions and decree of the court were issued. The other two judges ruled with the defendants, the Clarendon County Board of Education, while Judge Waring filed a strong dissent for Briggs, the plaintiff. Judge Waring gave Elizabeth an autographed copy of his dissent, inscribed: "To my precious Elizabeth. This could not have been done without her *love* and *encouragement* and *support*." The previous week they had celebrated their sixth wedding anniversary (Yarbrough, 1987, p. 193).

In his dissent Judge Waring used strong language, less temperate than many people expected from the bench:

If [Negroes] are entitled to any rights of American citizens, they are entitled to have these rights now and not in the future, and no excuse can be made to deny them these rights which are theirs under the Constitution and laws of America, by the use of the false doctrine and power called "separate but equal." It is the duty of the court to meet these issues simply and factually, and without fear, sophistry and evasion. . . . if the suggestion made by these defendants [to equalize the schools] is to be adopted as the type of justice to be meted out by this court, then I want no part of it. (Waring, 1955–1957, p. 360)

As Waring had hoped, the NAACP eventually developed four other cases similar to the one in Clarendon County (*Briggs v. Elliot*) and took all five to the Supreme Court, as *Brown v. Topeka Board of Education*. But with his dissent in *Briggs v. Elliot*, Judge Waring knew that he had done all he could do. His life as a judge was no longer useful or pleasant, especially in his own jurisdiction in Charleston. As soon as he had served 10 years and could retire with his full salary, he did so—on February 15, 1952, when he was 5 months short of 72 years old.

RETIREMENT IN NEW YORK CITY, 1952–1968

Judge Waring had once thought of retiring to San Francisco, but the Warings had too many ties to New York City to consider living anywhere else. His daughter, Anne, lived there with her husband, Stanley Warren, and the couple found a small apartment for the Warings at 952 Fifth Avenue. On February 18 the Warings boarded a train to leave the South, promising their black friends that they would not return so long as segregation remained the law of the land (Yarbrough, 1987).

The first spring in New York was a busy time for the Warings. In March Waties spoke at the annual banquet of the Harvard Law Review Association and at an NAACP meeting in Philadelphia. In April the New York chapter of the ACLU gave a luncheon in the Warings' honor; in June, Howard University awarded the judge a doctor of laws degree, and in Chicago the Warings were given a tumultuous reception at the general conference of the African Methodist Episcopal (AME) church. In all these appearances, Waring made clear his opposition to gradualism in racial change, condemning northern black "Uncle Toms" as well as southern liberals. He also refused to appear before any black organization that excluded whites from its membership (Yarbrough, 1987).

To be useful in his retirement, Judge Waring became a member of the board of the National Urban League in 1954, after a fight within the organization about his extremist views, and later a member of the board of the ACLU. Waring believed that the ACLU should develop chapters in the South to pick up the work of the NAACP, which southern legislators had managed to attack and destroy in many southern states. He also created an organization called the National Committee for Rural Schools to deliver food and supplies to rural schools in the South (Yarbrough, 1987).

Judge Waring experienced tension with the staff of the NAACP on several occasions. The New York chapter wanted to hold a testimonial dinner for the judge, but he felt they were asking people to be toastmaster who were too moderate, and they all declined. By the time Dr. Ralph Bunche accepted, Waring did not want to go ahead with it. In June 1952 Waring agreed to address the NAACP's annual convention, but he withdrew at the last minute because the NAACP's officials seemed too committed to the Democratic Party, holding fast no matter what compromises they had to accept. It was a remarkable situation, as James Hicks described in the *Afro-American*: "Thus we have the unusual situation of a prominent Southern-born white man, who has given up most of the things he holds dear in life, charging a group of colored men with not having the courage to go as far and fight as hard as he is willing to fight for the things which are most dear to them" (Yarbrough, 1987, p. 219).

Judge Waring was a staunch anti-Communist throughout the Cold War days. Yet he criticized the House Committee on Un-American Activities and signed petitions seeking its abolition. He recognized that Redbaiting was a favorite tactic of segregationists. He opposed one-man hearings and thought that Jim Eastland (Democrat of Mississippi), the white-supremacist senator investigating advocates of racial justice, made a mockery of due process. Yet he refused to join Eleanor Roosevelt, Mary McLeod Bethune, and others in protesting Eastland's activities, and he was disappointed that Virginia Durr chose silence rather than outspoken indignation as her defense. He thought she should not set up legal objections to the inquiry itself, but rather refute the charges head on. For Waring, the abolition of racial segregation was the paramount cause (Yarbrough, 1987).

Judge Waring's language had a harsh, uncompromising tone that alienated those who negotiated and compromised. His conversion to racial justice had been painful and gradual, but once he had seen the light he would not get bogged down in complexities and ambiguities. When Adlai Stevenson chose John Sparkman, senator from Alabama, as his running mate to try to hold southern Democrats in the party, Waring showed that he had no patience for Sparkman's remarks on civil rights and wrote Stevenson:

> Unless clearly repudiated by you, Governor, [Sparkman's remarks] will and should definitely drive away from supporting you those of us who believe that the time has come for America to cleanse itself of this evil disease of racial prejudice which is gnawing at the vitals of our body politic and is making a sham of our loud but hypocritical show of democracy. (Yarbrough, 1987, pp. 214–215)

On May 17, 1954, the Supreme Court announced its decision in *Brown v. Topeka Board of Education*, deciding unanimously in favor of the plaintiffs, the black schoolchildren damaged by segregation. Even though Judge Waring had steadfastly believed that he would be vindicated, he never expected a unanimous decision. Earl Warren, who had become chief justice the previous December, had worked tirelessly to achieve unanimity. Of the 15 federal judges whose opinions were being considered in the five cases, Judge Waring was the only one who had ruled that segregation was unconstitutional. Yet strangely, Judge Waring's dissent had not been mentioned during the court hearings, nor did Warren mention it in his opinion for the court. Waring regretted the omission, but expressed pleasure with the opinion itself. He felt that Warren had done better in 8 pages than he had done in 20 and was especially satisfied that Warren had not tried to make an academic case, going through endless precedents and points of law. Soon afterward Judge Waring said: "The great beauty of the Warren decision is that it's not a learned opinion. It's not an opinion that cites a great mass of cases. . . . I think you can summarize it by saying that segregation isn't fair, that's all" (Waring, 1955–1957, p. 367).

Elizabeth Waring began calling friends as soon as the decision was announced in the early afternoon. The judge put whiskey and ice on the kitchen counter, and many friends came to celebrate both the decision and their hosts: Alan Paton, author of *Cry the Beloved Country;* Walter and Poppy White; Henry Moon and Robert Carter of the NAACP legal staff. For the rest of the year, steady praise would come in, mostly from African Americans (Cannon, 1956).

Judge Waring had promised not to return to Charleston until segregation had been overturned, and he kept his word. In 1952, he declined an invitation to speak at an academic conference at a black college in Columbia. But after the *Brown* decision, the Warings felt free to return to Charleston. In November 1954, they were met at the train station by several hundred cheering African Americans, then taken by motorcade to the home of Ruby Cornwell, where they stayed. That evening an audience of 300 attended ceremonies at a black elementary school. In his acceptance of a plaque, Judge Waring reminded his audience of Victor Hugo's injunction that "a man should so live that he will be cursed by the past and blessed by the future." Waring joked about the length of his dissent in the Clarendon County case and added, "Maybe I should have said, 'It's all nonsense' and signed my name." The next day Septima Clark entertained in the afternoon, and Ruby Cornwell held a reception at night.

In the years after the *Brown* decision, the Warings preferred to stay at home. The judge found his work reduced by the rigors of old age—failing sight, hearing, and energy. He continued to follow national politics on radio and television, and Elizabeth devotedly read aloud to him. They were clearly in love to the end (Yarbrough, 1987).

Judge Waring's relations with his daughter, Anne, proved more stormy. He seemed to need, after his isolation, total approval and acceptance from her and felt that she did not always provide it. He could be coldly contemptuous of anyone who did not share his complete commitment and zeal; his daughter seemed to perceive this aspect of his personality more acutely than others (Yarbrough, 1987).

Judge Waring prepared for death by giving his papers to the Moorland-Spingarn Research Center at Howard University. By late 1967 he was suffering indigestion and intestinal blockage, almost certainly malignant. He decided to forgo surgery and remained in his apartment until the day before he died, on January 20, 1968, almost 88 years old. His body was returned to Charleston for burial, where 200 black people and 12 whites attended his funeral. He had one last laugh from his grave; in his will he left scholarships to the College of Charleston—to be used only by black students (Clark, 1986).

Elizabeth Waring entered a nursing home soon after Waties's death and died 9 months later, on October 30, 1968. Her body was returned to Charleston to lie beside his. Six blacks and three whites attended her funeral. She had said she wanted no hypocrites at her graveside, and there were none, according to her friend Septima Clark. The Warings were buried in a segregated cemetery. Vandals uprooted the magnolia tree planted by Waties Waring's daughter at his grave site, but by 1981 the city of Charleston had erected a bronze sculpture in his honor (Clark, 1986; Yarbrough, 1987).

At the end of his oral history, Judge Waring made this summary of his life's beliefs:

> More and more I began to understand the complexity of the thing [racism] and come to the conclusion that the solution was to get rid of the complexity, and adopt a simple doctrine that all people in this country are equal and should have equal opportunity, that they should have complete freedom of association. If I don't want to associate with a Chinese, I don't want anybody to tell me that I have to. If I do want to associate with a Chinese, I want complete liberty to be with a Chinese, have him in my home, visit his home, and mix with him on the street or socially or any other way that I choose. I think that's what Americanism means. It's what America means. It's what Judaism or Christianity or Hinduism or any other religion—you can put any name to it—means to me. That's about my religion, that human beings should have complete right of association and complete right of opportunity, and that any restrictions on that are bad and wrong. I realize that goal is far off, but I believe we're stumbling towards it, and I believe that's why Jefferson wrote the Declaration of Independence, and that's why America is, and that's why America, I believe, will be.
>
> That's about my doctrine of faith, my doctrine of policy, and my doctrine of religion, and you can make it just as broad as you want. (Waring, 1955–1957, p. 405)

4

The Other America:
Anne McCarty Braden

AT THE AGE OF 75, Anne Braden still works from 4 a.m. until midnight, driven by the never-ending crises of consulting with local leaders, holding press conferences, helping individuals in trouble with the police, appearing in court, and dealing with the flow of people in and out of the Carl Braden Memorial Center in Louisville, Kentucky.

The Braden Center, named for her deceased husband, is a modest house in an African American neighborhood of Louisville. Anne's desk on the second floor is piled high with manila folders; she has an outdated computer and no secretarial assistance. Nor does the center have janitorial services—the rugs are stained with coffee; books and papers are scattered everywhere.

The rooms are seldom empty. People wait until they can have some time with Anne, dressed in jeans and a turtleneck, energized by coffee and cigarettes, not taking time for meals. Every morning Anne makes a daily agenda, but she seldom advances through more than half of it, many nights working until she simply falls asleep.

No one would guess that Braden had been raised to be an upper-middle-class white southern lady. Between the ages of 23 and 29 Braden committed class suicide. She turned herself inside out to become a working-class woman, holding low-paying jobs while organizing her community for racial equality, the development of strong unions, and socialist ideals.

At the age of 30, in 1954, Braden, with her husband, Carl, purchased a home in suburban Louisville in order to deed it over to an African American couple. For this, the Bradens were charged with sedition against the state of Kentucky. Carl was convicted and sentenced to 15 years. Anne freed him through her efforts of traveling around the country, appealing to the national conscience, and raising money. This set her on her lifelong course of traveling the South to create a regional network of people fighting for the causes she believed in—racial equality, working peoples' rights, and freedom of speech and belief.

No one understood better than Anne Braden the interconnections between national anticommunism and the fight of white southerners to preserve segregation. If anticommunism had not occurred simultaneously with the black push for integration, she believed, enough liberal white southerners might have challenged segregationists to defeat racial segregation. But being branded a traitor to their country was too much for most liberals, and they retreated into silence. Anne Braden had the courage to fight both anticommunists and segregationists—and the insight to see that, in places of power, they were often one and the same.

SOUTHERN YOUTH, 1924–1947

In her 30s, after she had been charged with sedition as a communist and people were saying, "Go back to Russia," Braden liked to retort that she was descended from the first white child born in Kentucky. She would stand up in public forums and say that she had been in Kentucky longer than most folks, and they could go back to Russia if they wanted to (Braden, 1981, 1984).

Braden was always interested in her great-great-great-great-great-grandmother, Ann Pogue, who brought the first spinning wheel into Kentucky over the Cumberland Gap, the route through the mountains from Virginia and Tennessee, to settle at Fort Harrod. Anne knew she would have liked Ann Pogue; she was one of those strong pioneer women who knew how to run things. She had five husbands, four of whom were killed by Indians:

> What I always heard—and this must have been word-of-mouth come down in the family—was that she ran the fort. Not only did she bring in the first spinning wheel, she also set up the first school in the fort. She insisted they have a school so the children could get some learning. She was apparently considered something of a tyrant by the men, even though they kept marrying her, because she insisted they stick around the fort and till the land. Their inclination was to go out and fight the Indians, but she wanted the land tilled so they would have corn and vegetables. (Braden, 1984, p. 81)

Anne says she remembers wondering, when her family would take her to visit restored Fort Harrod as a child, why the men killed the Indians. She recalls that when she asked her mother, she replied: "They had to, because the Indians were trying to kill them." But Anne was not satisfied; she remembers thinking that they wouldn't have been killed if they had stayed home and planted corn, as Ann Pogue told them to. This was the earliest question regarding social justice that Ann Braden remembers articulating (A. Braden, personal communication, March 20, 1999).

Braden was born in Louisville, Kentucky, on July 28, 1924, the second child of Anita Crabbe and Gambrell McCarty. She was named for both of them, Anne Gambrell McCarty. Her older brother, Lindsay, 4½ years old at the time of her birth, did not play an important role in her life. Her father came from a pharmacist's family in Owensboro, Kentucky. He worked as a traveling salesman for Allied Mills, a feed company that, until Anne was 7, moved him around frequently. The family finally settled in Anniston, Alabama, where Anne grew up and graduated from high school in 1941 (Braden, 1981, 1984).

Anniston's wealth derived from cotton mills and the manufacturing of iron pipes. A city of about 25,000 people when Anne was growing up, Anniston was clearly demarcated into sections reflecting class and race. To the right of the main downtown street, Noble Street, lived those who were better off; to the left lived poor people, black and white in different areas, with black people in South Anniston living along dirt streets (Braden, 1979).

When the McCarty's moved to Anniston, Anne's mother joined the Episcopal Church and put her children in Sunday school there, while her father joined one of the big Baptist churches. Anne wished she could go to a Presbyterian or Baptist church, because they had more children and sounded like more fun, but her mother wanted her children in the Episcopal Church, because it was the church she had grown up in and the church of some of Anniston's "first families" (Braden, 1984; A. Braden, personal communication, March 20, 1999).

Anne's father threw himself into his job and later his farm; he "worked like a dog all his life," Anne said. Her mother later joked about the "McCarty drive," which she believed her husband and her children all had. Had she known about it 50 years earlier, she thought "she would have run screaming in the other direction," for she was a widow to her husband's work for years (Braden, 1984, pp. 81–82).

When Anne Gambrell started kindergarten, she was advanced to first grade and stayed a year ahead until graduation. School offered few, if any, challenges; instead, Anne became deeply religious as a child; she read the Bible and worried that her family was not religious enough.

The passage from the Bible that impressed Anne most was from Matthew: "For I was hungry, and ye gave me no meat; I was thirsty, and ye gave me no drink; I was a stranger, and ye took me not in; naked, and ye clothed me not. . . . Verily I say unto you, inasmuch as ye did it not to one of the least of these, ye did it not to me" (Braden, 1999, p. 23).

Anne lived amid the hunger of the Great Depression. Her family tried to do what Christ taught; they fed most of the beggars who came to their door, sometimes 20 in an evening. Occasionally, when her mother grew tired of it and refused to help, Anne stayed awake worrying whether her mother would go to hell. Her parents made sure that the Negro family who worked for them from time to time had shelter, food, and clothes. Her father sometimes paid their rent, and her mother gave them the McCarty family's cast-off clothes. (A. Braden, personal communication, March 20, 1999). "But," said Braden,

> something happened to me each time I looked at the Negro girl who always inherited my clothes. Sometimes she would come to our house with her mother, wearing one of the dresses I had discarded. The dresses never fitted her because she was fatter than I was. She would sit in a straight chair in our kitchen waiting for her mother, because of course she could not sit in one of our comfortable chairs in the living room. She would sit there looking uncomfortable, my old faded dress binding her at the waist and throat. And some way I knew that this was not what Jesus meant when he said to clothe the naked. I recalled that Jesus had also said, "Therefore all things whatsoever ye would that men should do to you, do ye even so to them." And I knew that if I were in her place, if I had no clothes, I would not want the old abandoned dresses of a person who would not even invite me to come into her living room to sit down. And I could not talk to her because I felt ashamed. And as I watched her, I would feel a binding sensation around my own throat. And I would feel to see if my own dress was too tight. But of course it was not. My clothes were always well cut and perfectly fitted. Instead there was a small straitjacket around my soul. (Braden, 1999, pp. 23–24)

The minister at Anne's Episcopal Church, the Reverend Jim Stoney, tried to overcome his parishioners' denial of poverty. He set up missions on the other side of town and invited poor children from the missions to Anne's Sunday school. He wanted the wealthier people in Anniston to become aware of what poverty was like and take some action. He had a decisive influence on Anne, who adored him:

> I had never been around poor people, just like I had never been around black people. But at the church, I would be with the children from the cotton mill villages, and would hear Jim Stoney talk, and I developed a feeling about religion as something that was supposed to *do* something about these things. (Braden, 1984, p. 82)

In her teens Anne attended young peoples' meetings at the church. Once she asked a question that displayed some doubt about segregation: "I'm not even sure I knew the term segregation; I just knew that people lived apart. The assistant minister came up to me afterwards and said I shouldn't say things like that or people would think I was a communist. And I didn't even know what a communist was" (Braden, 1984, p. 82).

In Anne's world, people thought they were in their privileged position because they actually were better than others, and that God had willed it so. When Anne heard about strikes in Anniston and about the Scottsboro case—in which in 1931 nine young black men were falsely convicted of raping two white teenagers hoboing on a train—it was with the explanation that outside agitators were causing trouble. Anne also heard that Eleanor Roosevelt was stirring up people, but she had no way of finding out what was happening (Braden, 1984).

For college, Anne headed north as far as Virginia. She considered going to the University of Alabama, the usual choice of women in her situation, as a place to find eligible men. But Anne's college years coincided precisely with U.S. participation in World War II, and she realized there were practially no men left at the University of Alabama—they were off to war. So she chose women's colleges, beginning at Stratford Junior College in Danville, Virginia, and finishing at Randolph-Macon Woman's College in Lynchburg, Virginia.

Stratford consisted of a few hundred people and one large building with dormitories upstairs, classrooms downstairs, and a dining room in the basement. Within this small scope, Anne was able to excel at everything, becoming president of her class and editor of the paper and playing all the roles in *Joan of Arc* (Braden, 1984).

At Stratford, Anne's McCarty drive began to emerge. In her freshman year, she decided, at the last minute, not to go home with her roommate for Thanksgiving, but to stay and work on the school paper. She considered that a turning point, the first time she chose to work instead of taking time to enjoy life. She discovered that she enjoyed working more than anything else, and that is how she continued to live her life.

The person who most influenced Anne at Stratford was Harriet Fitzgerald, the older sister of the dean of women, Ida Fitzgerald. Anne met Harriet at a cookout held by the dean for students. Harriet, about 40 then, lived in Greenwich Village, in New York City, as an artist. After her artwork was shown in New York, it was displayed at Randolph-Macon, where Anne was able to see it. Harriet became a role model for Anne and urged her to attend Randoph-Macon, where Harriet was an alumna and a trustee.

Harriet Fitzgerald belonged to the generation of white women in the 1920s who decided to seek careers instead of marriage. Influenced by

Fitzgerald, during her college years Anne rejected the traditional role of the southern white woman:

> And in that period I made up my mind that I would never get married, because marriage seemed like a living death, that this meant going back home and living in the kind of society that I'd grown up in, where women were supposed to take care of—well, I didn't worry too much then about taking care of the house and that sort of thing, but it was mostly the thing of being an ornament and not a human being. That just seemed to me that that would be the worst thing that could happen to me, would be to go back home and get married and end up living this life of going to the country club on Saturday night and bridge parties in the afternoon, which is what women usually did. (Braden, 1979, pp. 8–9)

Harriet Fitzgerald opened up a world of ideas to Anne. She introduced her to the work of Karl Marx and Sigmund Freud; she explained what the labor movement was about, and that the CIO, the Congress of Industrial Organizations, was against segregation. Fitzgerald's father was the owner of the Dan River Mills, scene of a bitter textile strike in the early 1930s. Fitzgerald changed sides in the class struggle, even while she maintained loving personal relationships with her family. She became a good friend of Lucy Randolph Mason, the roving ambassador of the CIO in the South. Fitzgerald was prolabor, pro-Roosevelt, and the first person Anne ever met who was actively working against segregation:

> She was just a profound influence in my life, and I think was the first person I was ever in love with. It was not any overt homosexual relationship; that would have scared me to death because that just wasn't accepted in those days as it is now. I'm talking about love in that she was what made life exciting and interesting. Exploring a world of ideas with someone else just made the world more exciting. Compared to this excitement, the relationships I'd had with men were so barren. I had learned the lesson well that one must appear to have no brains in order to be attractive to men. Until I met Harriet, I had never experienced the excitement of real intellectual companionship; I didn't know such relationships existed. And, of course, that's the kind of relationship I found with Carl later. (Braden, 1984, p. 83)

Segregation had never been mentioned when Anne was growing up. Only when she was in college, while the United States was engaged in a war against the racist ideology of Nazism, did people around her begin to discuss segregation.

> Now that the subject was open for discussion, I began to understand the things that had been bothering me so long. I don't think anyone gave me any

new ideas; I discovered them buried in my own mind when the channels were opened through which they could flow. And I discovered too that many of my friends in Anniston were also beginning to discuss these things and that many of them had felt the same conflicts I had—they, too, unable to articulate them, unable to understand them because they had been bottled up in the netherland of the undiscussable. (Braden, 1999, p. 26)

In 1944, during her junior year at college, Anne got her first chance to really know a Negro. Harriet Fitzgerald invited McCarty to visit her in New York and arranged a dinner with a friend of hers, a young Negro woman playing a part in a Broadway play. As McCarty recalled in 1958:

I went to the meeting with some misgivings. Never in my life had I eaten with a Negro. I was intellectually pleased at the opportunity to break this lifelong pattern, but I was somewhat ill at ease in the face of a new experience. She of course was much more mature. She too was from the South, and I think looking back on it that she must have realized my feelings. She undoubtedly went out of her way to put me at ease. Soon we were talking—talking, talking—discussing all the things in which we were mutually interested. To me she was a wonder, for she was a success in a field that I at the moment aspired to. Suddenly, in the midst of the conversation, the realization swept over me that I had completely forgotten that there was a difference in our color. We were no longer white and Negro—we were just two young women talking about things we liked to talk about. Somewhere inside of me a voice seemed to say: "Why, there is no race problem at all! There are only the people who have not realized it yet." . . . Here, for a moment, I glimpsed a vision of the world as it should be: where people are people, and spirits have room to grow. I never got over it. (Braden, 1999, pp. 27–28)

Anne used her college summers to explore career options. Between her freshman and sophomore years, she participated in summer theater near Plymouth, Massachusetts, on the Cape. One of her teachers told her that she shouldn't go into theater unless she loved it so much that she would rather sweep floors in a theater than do a top job anywhere else. Anne realized that's how she felt, not about the theater, however, but about newspaper work.

The following summer Anne McCarty tried her first newspaper job—reading proofs at the *Anniston Star,* in her hometown. She worked there another summer, and after she graduated in June 1945, she took a full-time position on the *Anniston Star.* Since most of the men were still away at war, the paper was short-staffed, and McCarty got experience that otherwise a woman could never have had. She wrote editorials and headlines, and even handled sports off the wire; they simply didn't have anyone else.

The owner of the *Anniston Star,* Colonel Harry Ayers, was a New Dealer, a Roosevelt liberal, who did not oppose segregation but rather talked about justice and more opportunity. Ayers accepted McCarty's editorials against the poll tax, but her father snorted, "That's ridiculous!" (Braden, 1984, p. 84).

After working in Anniston a year, McCarty decided she needed a broader experience and moved to Birmingham, the South's industrial city. She was assigned to cover the courthouse for two newspapers, the *Birmingham News,* an afternoon daily, and the *Age-Herald,* a morning paper under the same ownership. She worked in a little press room at the courthouse from early morning until late at night, phoning in stories. She had almost no social life, nor did she want any. She had many college friends in Birmingham, including daughters of the judges whose courts she was covering, but she never contacted them.

Instead, McCarty threw herself into reporting state politics from her point of view. Jim Folsom, a populist, was running for governor in November 1946. McCarty had covered his campaign in the Democratic primary for the *Anniston Star,* when he carried around a wash bucket and a mop, saying he was going down to Montgomery to clean out the rich folks so poor people would have a chance. Also on the ballot was the Boswell Amendment to the state constitution, designed to keep Negroes from voting. McCarty was able to interview Folsom and elicit his comment that he was opposed to the Boswell Amendment. That was worth a large headline in the *Birmingham News.* It was the courthouse itself, however, that had the greatest impact on McCarty:

> It exposed me to a whole new world, different from the sheltered world I'd grown up in, and one where I could see close up the crushed lives. I remember one case where a black man got twenty years in prison because they said he had looked at a white woman across the road in an insulting way; the charge was assault with intent to ravish. I began to feel that everything was wrong in the society I lived in, began to realize what it does to people, how it destroys people—both black and white. (Braden, 1984, p. 25)

McCarty made friends with people around the courthouse in an effort to obtain stories. Once a deputy sheriff was telling her about a murder in Birmingham that had never been solved. When McCarty expressed interest, he brought out a skull and said:

> "It never will be solved, because that man was a nigger and the man that killed him was white." He was kind of twinkling; he thought this was a nice little secret that he'd let me in on and that I would think that way, too. I was

just horrified! I looked at it, and the skull just got bigger and bigger. I just turned around and ran almost to get out of there. (Braden, 1984, p. 25)

With one final event, McCarty decided to leave the South. One morning she sat down with a friend to have breakfast, knowing she would have to get up and go to her office if any important stories had happened overnight. She asked her friend to order breakfast for her while she called the sheriff's office. When she returned to the table, her friend asked, "Anything doing?" and McCarty replied:

"No, just a colored murder," which meant that I had time to eat breakfast; I didn't have to go to the courthouse . . . it just wasn't news when a black person killed another black person. They might put a paragraph about it in the newspaper, but it wasn't anything to get excited about. Just as I said that— it was like a piece of electricity—a black waitress was putting our things on the table, and it suddenly dawned on me what I'd said.

I didn't want to look at her, but I looked up and her expression didn't change. I can see her face now. Her hand sort of shook as she was putting down my coffee, but her face was like a mask. And it just came over me how awful this was, and I wanted to say, "I didn't mean that. *I'm* not the one who says it's not news, the paper says that. I didn't mean that it didn't matter that one of your people was killed; I'm not the one who says what news is."

But I didn't say anything, because as I sat there, it suddenly dawned on me that I did mean it! It was like an octopus, it was getting me, too. I knew that if I stayed that I was going to become a part of that world, that you can't be neutral. You are either part of it or you are against it. And I didn't know how to be against it. It was that morning that I decided to leave! It was just this devastating sort of thing, and I had to get away. It seemed like my whole world was just death and destruction. It was that skull. (Braden, 1984, p. 85)

In March 1947, when McCarty had been in Birmingham for only 6 months, an editor from the *Louisville Times,* the afternoon paper of the *Courier Journal,* wrote that they had an opening in the news department, and she accepted.

A NEW IDENTITY, 1947–1953

In April 1947, McCarty arrived in Louisville, which she saw as a temporary transition to leaving the South altogether. To her surprise, she learned that segregation in Louisville was little different from what it was in Birmingham, except that buses and streetcars were integrated.

But in Louisville the postwar tensions appeared more out in the open. Black veterans who returned from fighting for democracy in Europe wanted to have some of it at home, while workers, who had forgone striking during the war, organized militantly and refused to work, in an effort to increase their suppressed wages. The National Association for the Advancement of Colored People (NAACP) was highly active, filing suits against segregation in public institutions, or threatening suits to precipitate action. Bus drivers organized and held a successful strike in 1946. International Harvester built a large plant in Louisville, and its workers were organized by the Farm Equipment Workers, a militant union in the CIO. McCarty joined the NAACP and became acquainted with people in the militant unions (Braden, 1979).

Meanwhile, back at the desk, McCarty had developed a special relationship with one of her colleagues, the labor editor, Carl Braden. Braden had married young and had grown, taking a different direction from that of his wife. He was 10 years older than McCarty, had grown up in Louisville, and had been in the newspaper business since he was 17. He was born to a Catholic mother and a Socialist father, who named him for Karl Marx, although adjusting the spelling, because the priest would not allow the parents to spell Carl with a *K*. Carl's father worked all his life in industrial shops, first for the Louisville and Nashville Railroad, then for the Ford Motor Company. For Carl Braden, as for his father, the most compelling ideas were provided by Eugene Debs, the great socialist leader and five-time presidential candidate in the early 20th century (Braden, 1979, 1981, 1999).

Recognizing McCarty's talents, Braden sent her to cover labor stories on his days off. To fill in her ignorance about the labor movement, he provided books about Debs and labor history and opened up a world of ideas she had never known. The period between April 1947 and a year later, when Carl had got a divorce and Anne and Carl began living together, proved to be a crucial time of Anne's life in personal terms. Carl's influence pervaded this period, for he opened to Anne the working-class world:

> I had to really cope with the conclusion that everything about the society I'd grown up in had been wrong, and I went through I guess a lot of guilt things, like you do if you're white and if you come from a privileged sort of background. I'm glad I didn't get hung up in that for too long, because I don't think guilt is very useful, but I felt I had to get away from everything in my background and start life over. . . . the hard part of it is deciding, or coming to grips with the fact that your own society and the things you've benefited from and the people you love and the people you've known are really totally wrong, and that's hard for people to do, and that's one reason people believe lies instead of doing that. . . . You know, white Southerners believ-

ing it when people told them, and telling themselves, that "black people were happy until the Communists came" or the outside agitators came, or the Yankees came—this sort of thing. People believe that, because it's very hard to face this truth that their society is totally wrong. (Braden, 1979, pp. 19–22)

Anne McCarty and Carl Braden lived together for a few months before they were married, in June 1948. Since their families were of different class backgrounds, planning a wedding proved difficult; one morning they decided to go to a Unitarian minister and marry that very day (Braden, 1981).

After their wedding, both Bradens began to feel impatient with newspaper work. They wanted their lives to be useful, to make a difference by being directly involved, and reporting seemed a form of noninvolvement. Carl resigned his job first, and then Anne did. He drove a cab for a time while she worked as a waitress, then in a tobacco factory, in a cigar plant, and on a large bakery line. Eventually they handled public relations and a small newspaper for a group of militant labor unions (Braden, 1979). In Braden's words,

> It was all as if the world had been turned upside down, and my memory of these first years in Louisville is of some rapid floodwaters rushing over my soul, tugging at my entrails, pulling me up by the roots. I was falling in love with Carl and seeing the world from an entirely new vantage point, his vantage point, the vantage point of a different place in society. The roots aren't really washed away, of course. They never are. No one ever completely breaks away from the earth that nourished him, and if he did or could his spirit would probably die. But when the floodwaters subsided, I knew that some of the old soil had been carried downstream: the old concept of *noblesse oblige*, the old belief in superiority conferred by social class; and with it had gone some of the filth of race prejudice. Not all perhaps, and who can say that one of my environment will ever lose it all. But some of it, at least, I knew was gone. (Braden, 1999, pp. 32–33)

In 1950 Carl returned to newspaper work as a copyeditor on the *Courier Journal*, while Anne quit work to have a baby, something they had not originally planned for when they married, but on which she had changed her mind. James Braden was born in September 1951, and Anita arrived 17 months later, in February 1953 (Braden, 1981).

After Anne Braden's first child was born, she redoubled her efforts to end segregation so that this child would not have to endure its poison. She worked with the Negro Labor Council in Louisville to fight job discrimination against Negroes; she served as a team captain of the NAACP's membership drives, with the task of recruiting more white members. She also worked on a statewide committee trying to repeal Kentucky's school segregation law. Always she favored the more radical course of action on the question of segregation. She simply could not see the argument of being prudent and going slowly. Writing in 1958, she said:

> I have been told that the intensity of my feeling about segregation is neurotic. I have never denied that this may be so. I grew up in a sick society, and a sick society makes neurotics—of one kind or another, on one side or another. It makes people like those who could take pleasure in killing and mutilating Emmett Till, and it makes people like me. The United States Supreme Court in its historic decision against segregation in the schools outlines what segregation does to the Negro child. The justices might have added some discussion of what it does to the white child. There are many white "neurotics" like myself in my generation in the South—if that is what we are. The people who describe themselves as "sane" and more "practical" and more "moderate" tell us to wait, not to go too fast. But that is no answer. They may persuade some of us to take a slower course, but they can never convince us all. As long as segregation remains a fact in communities all over the South, there will be people like us who are compelled to act. (Braden, 1999, p. 35)

Several months before the birth of her first child, Anne took the train to Jackson, Mississippi, to protest the pending execution of Willie McGee, a black man accused of raping a white woman. She reported back to several African American churches, who had raised money for her to go. After this trip, William L. Patterson, a black leader of the Civil Rights Congress and a Communist, took time to write Anne that she need not be talking to Negroes; she ought to be talking to white people. Patterson told her that she didn't have to be part of the world of the lynchers; she could join the "other America," the one that has been here since the first slave ship, the one of Negroes and whites who fought against slavery, lynchings, and injustice of any kind. On this point, Anne said:

> That's what I feel like I joined, I joined the "other America." It's a real reality to me. . . . that's what keeps me going. I've got this sense that I'm part of this long movement that's like a chain back into the past and will go on after I'm gone. I'm a part of it. That gives me my identity. . . . I had to reject the whole background I came from, and you've got to have roots somewhere; people get real confused if they don't. I found my roots in "the other America." (A. Braden, interview with author, December 1997)

As Anne got to know Louisville in these intense years of transformation, she discovered that the city, although segregated, differed significantly from Birmingham or Anniston. Not only could African Americans ride buses that were integrated, they could vote and had been doing so for a long time. Although they were only 15% of the population, they sometimes provided the swing vote. News about the NAACP and the Urban League appeared in the newspaper. Some white people openly opposed segregation; a considerable portion of white leadership was liberal as applied to segregation, meaning they opposed it in varying degrees. Both the *Courier Journal* and the *Louisville Times* had always worked against segregation, sometimes quietly and other times more openly. The publisher of the two papers, Mark Ethridge, had fought the Ku Klux Klan in Georgia in his youth and had worked during World War II for the Fair Employment Practices Committee. The University of Louisville decided, just as the NAACP was preparing a suit, to admit African Americans, and by 1954 they were enrolled in modest numbers. The main public library opened to African Americans in the later 1940s, and in the early 1950s it opened its branch libraries. Hospitals began to admit African Americans. A suit by the NAACP ended segregation on the city golf courses, although the parks remained segregated, except for one ampitheater. On the surface the city appeared to be moving toward full integration.

For most white people in Louisville in 1954, however, segregation was still very much a way of life that one did not question. Most lived behind walls in their white world. African Americans lived either in slums in the central section of the city or in the West End, where white people were leaving for the suburbs to the south and east. In 1947 almost all residential property was covered by restrictive covenants, and that did not change even after the Supreme Court ruled in 1948 that these covenants could not be enforced in court. Bankers, real estate agents, and builders had unwritten agreements not to sell or lend money on property in white sections to African Americans, except when realtors decided in advance to "break a block" by selling one house to a black family in order to turn that section into an all-black one, selling houses at prices inflated by the pent-up demand (Braden, 1999).

In addition to fighting against segregation, Carl and Anne continued working in the labor movement, which in the early 1950s was being broken up by the anticommunist forces personified by Senator Joe McCarthy. They also organized against the Korean War. They saw their efforts as part of the resistance movement against the push toward a police state taking place at that time (Braden, 1979).

INDICTED FOR SEDITION, 1954–1956

In March 1954 Anne's life was flowing along smoothly in her new identity. She had been married for 6 years in a marriage of equality, highly unconventional at that time. Since Carl worked, as a copyeditor, at night, he could care for their children during the day while Anne continued her community activism, focused on fighting segregation in all its manifestations. They lived in a small four-room cottage in an old section of town on the west side, into which African Americans had been moving for a number of years. They both led a highly political life, working as a team on many of the same committees and at home (Braden, 1979, 1999).

One day, a casual acquaintance, Andrew Wade IV, asked them to buy a house and transfer it to him; he, of course, would put up the money for the down payment. Wade was an African American veteran of World War II; he and his wife, Charlotte, who was pregnant with their second child, wanted a new house out of town where their children could play. They had tried repeatedly to buy a house, but whenever the realtors discovered that the buyers were African American, the deal fell through. The Wades had asked several white people to buy for them, to no avail.

The Bradens had known Wade, an electrician, for 4 or 5 years before he asked them to buy a house for him. They had never refused to act when someone requested help in breaking down segregation. To Wade, they said, "Of course," and went on with their daily business, not realizing that they had just made one of the major decisions of their lives (Braden, 1999).

The house the Wades chose was located near the tiny hamlet of Shively. The seller worked part-time on construction, building one house at a time on his own property. On May 15, 1954, the first night the Wades moved into their new home, a cross was burned in the next field at about 10:00 p.m.; and at 2 a.m., 10 rifle shots rang through the kitchen. The next day, reporters from the *Courier Journal* asked the Bradens why they had bought the house solely to transfer it to the Wades. The *Courier Journal* printed their statement the following morning; the story became front-page news: "We feel that every man has a right to live where he wants to, regardless of the color of his skin. This is the test of democracy. Either you practice what you preach, or you shut up believing in democracy" (in Braden, 1999, p. 69).

The liberals in Louisville—the *Courier Journal* and *Louisville Times;* the clergy—blamed the Bradens more than they did the Wades. According to the *Louisville Times:* "The family of Andrew Wade IV made, we believe, an understandable error when it moved into a white neighborhood in Shively. . . . Mr. and Mrs. Carl Braden, in our opinion, made an inexcusable blunder when they made that mistake possible by buying the home and then transferring it to the Wades" (quoted in Braden, 1999, p. 82).

No decisive action to prevent further violence came from any liberals, nor did it come from the Bradens or Wades, who declined to press charges against the Wades' neighbors, in the hope that they might yet accept the Wades.

Two days after the Wades moved in, the Supreme Court declared segregation in schools illegal in its *Brown* decision. That compounded the shock of the Wades' suburban neighbors. When the weekly suburban newspaper came out on Thursday, questions were raised about whether the Bradens had acted alone or whether it could be "the cause of the Communists in this country to encourage panic, chaos and riot to lower the morale of the American people?" (quoted in Braden, 1999, p. 89). The editorial writer pointed out that Henry Wallace's Progressive Party, to which the Bradens had formerly belonged, contained a few Communist sympathizers, but failed to mention that the Progressive Party had long since disintegrated in Louisville.

Within a few weeks, the bank demanded full payment of the Wades' mortgage, on the grounds that transferring the property without the bank's written consent violated the terms of the contract. The bank went to court to foreclose against the Wades and the Bradens, but the Wades refused to move, since the banks had never before enforced this clause. The Wades and the Bradens then found an attorney willing to defend them (Braden, 1999).

Six weeks after the Wades moved in, on the night of Saturday, June 26, shortly after midnight, sticks of dynamite placed under the house blew up, destroying half the building. The Wades and a friend were sitting on the front porch on the opposite side from the bomb and escaped harm; their daughter had stayed overnight with her grandparents.

The county police failed to arrest those who planted the dynamite, although there is evidence that they knew who did it and that the lawbreakers included the developer who built and sold the house. Following the explosion at the Wades', the Bradens received repeated threats to their house. After staying up many nights defending their house, Anne suffered a miscarriage of their third child at 2 months' gestation.

A month later, invoking a statute passed during the Red Scares after World War I, a grand jury charged Carl and Anne Braden, together with five other white people who had supported the Wades, with sedition, claiming that the sale of the house and the bombing had been a Communist plot to stir up trouble between the races and bring about the overthrow of the government of Kentucky and the United States. Such charges could bring a penalty of 21 years in prison and a $10,000 fine. The defendants were arrested on October 1; Anne was in jail for a week and Carl for 3 weeks before they could post their pretrial bond of $10,000 each. Meanwhile, Anne's parents came to take the two children to Anniston while Anne and Carl were in the local county jail (Braden, 1999).

Anne's parents completely disagreed with her on the subject of segregation and thoroughly disapproved of her activities to abolish it. They had not even heard about the Wade incident—and she had not told them—until a week before the indictments. She asked them not to come, but since they cared deeply for their grandchildren, they came anyway. Within a week, her father was able to make bond for her, with no strings attached, borrowing the money from a wealthy friend.

While Anne and Carl were in jail, the prosecution raided their personal library at home, where they had collected hundreds of books representing every conceivable point of view, including many by Marx, Lenin, and Stalin, as well as books on socialism by noncommunists. The Bradens had foreseen the possibility of a raid, but had refused to be cowed into removing any of their books. They later heard stories from friends who were Negro domestic servants about wealthy whites who removed books that they felt might be questionable, wrapped them in old sheets, and dropped them into the Ohio River, weighed down with rocks (Braden, 1999).

After their release from jail, Anne and Carl asked to be tried separately. Carl's trial was set first, to start November 29, 1954, eight weeks after his indictment. Lawyers, both black and white, came forward to help the Bradens. The white ones hesitated briefly, knowing they were risking their careers, but once they decided to help, they proved loyal to the end.

The prosecution designed its case to prove two points: that Carl was a Communist and that racial incidents are deliberately planned by Communists to arouse class conflict. The prosecution found willing assistance from two members of the House Un-American Activities Committee (HUAC), who came down from Washington, D.C., to help. They provided several witnesses who made a living testifying as ex-Communists against people charged with being Communist. None of these witnesses claimed to know Carl personally, just Communists in general. A white woman from Louisville also testified that, as an undercover agent for the FBI, she had attended Communist meetings at the Bradens' house (Braden, 1999; O'Reilly, 1989).

The trial proved to be an early example of segregationists' labeling every move toward desegregation in the South as "Communistic." This idea, put forward by the editor of the county newspaper, who had reported the bombing of the Wades' house, found ready adherents in the federal Congress, as well as in the general populace, who badly wanted a simple way to place the blame for the complex wrongs of racism on someone other than themselves.

Carl's trial lasted 13 days; during it he stated that he had never been a member of the Communist Party, in order to rebut the charges of the undercover FBI agent. But the courthouse was filled with people eager to see him convicted, and the jury found him guilty of sedition. They held out only to decide whether to extract the maximum sentence of 21 years. They settled for 15 years, plus a fine of $5,000 (Braden, 1999).

At the defense table. Left to right, Carl Braden, Anne Braden, attorney
Louis Lusky. Louisville, December 11, 1954. © *The Courier Journal.*

Carl Braden later regretted that he had stated directly that he was not
a Communist. He was under pressure from his lawyers, who passionately
wanted to win his case. He never again answered the question "Are you a
member of the Communist Party?" and a few years later went to prison
specifically for refusing to answer it before HUAC. Anne never answered
it and still refuses to do so. She says:

> In those days, if you had any principles at all, you just did not
> answer. This question was a political test that cut off all discussion
> of real issues. If you answered, no matter whether your answer was
> "yes" or "no," you were giving in to that syndrome, feeding the
> atmosphere that said the opinions of people in a group that had
> been designated "villains" were not to be considered. This meant
> some ideas were just not to be considered, which stifles real creative
> discussion of social issues. (A. Braden, personal communication,
> March 20, 1999)

Carl served 42 days in solitary confinement, and Anne was not able
to visit him for 3 months, since she had recently been in jail herself. After
that, she could visit once a week. Jimmy and Anita Braden stayed with their
grandparents all winter, since Anne's trial was expected to come up soon.

It was set for February 28, then postponed twice. Anne has no memory of these winter months; she believes that she did not behave very heroically; she had doubted whether a continued fight would be worth the pain and difficulty. Carl wrote her from prison that she should decide whether to appeal his sentence; he would abide by her decision (Braden, 1999, pp. 273, 284).

When Anne went to her lawyer with her decision to quit, he was able to bring her back to her responsibilities. If she quit now, he argued, they would all be living in a police state; how could she let that happen to everyone (Braden, 1999)?

Anne went back to the reflex centers built in her childhood, to draw on words from her mother: "You can never live a worthwhile life, Anne Gambrell, if you think only of yourself. It's the things you do for other people that make life worthwhile"; and from the New Testament: "Whoever shall seek to gain his life shall lose it, but whoever shall lose his life shall preserve it." How could she teach her children to live by any standards worth having if they knew their parents had run away from theirs? Anne realized she had to fight (Braden, 1999, p. 275).

By postponing Anne's trial, the prosecution gave her a chance to recover her courage and to organize. Within a week of Carl's imprisonment, Anne was in New York City raising money for his defense at a party of friends. By spring 1955, she decided to appeal his conviction and had lined up the national ACLU to prepare his appeal. His bail on appeal was set at $40,000, and with the help of the Emergency Civil Liberties Committee the bail was raised; Carl walked out of prison on July 12, 1955, after serving 7 months. An enormous outpouring of support came from people and organizations in all parts of the country, north and south: churches, especially the Episcopal League for Social Action; labor organizations, especially the United Packinghouse Workers and the United Automobile Workers; civil liberties organizations such as the Bill of Rights Fund and the National Lawyers Guild; and southern liberal groups, such as the Southern Conference Educational Fund; plus virtually every left-wing political organization in the United States, including the Socialist Party (Braden, 1979, 1999).

Fourteen months after Carl's release, the prosecution dropped its charges against him, on the basis of a Supreme Court ruling in a Pennsylvania case against state sedition laws. The Wades were finally able to take possession of their house, when a white couple in Chicago loaned them the money to pay off the mortgage, claim the insurance money, and rebuild. But Charlotte Wade decided that she could never feel safe there, and they bought an old house in Louisville's West End, then still a checkerboard pattern of one block black, the next white (Braden, 1999, p. 308).

In many senses the Wades and the Bradens had lost—the Wades were not able to live where they wanted; the house bombers were never caught; the city had panicked in hysteria; liberals were frightened into silence; the personal lives of the Wade and Braden families were severely disrupted. But in a larger sense they had won. Louisville desegregated its full school system in September 1956, with open support from white liberals who did not want their city further disgraced. Carl had lost his job at the *Courier Journal*, but the case had won support throughout the nation. After Carl's release, the Bradens brought their children back and provided a family life for them, taking turns with their political activity. Between them, the Bradens crisscrossed the country, building support for the struggle they were engaged in. Twenty years later, Anne felt that the ordeal between 1954 and 1957 had been one of the richest experiences of her life, allowing her to discover the resistance movement of this country. It was not, however, a positive experience for the Wade family—another example of how deep racism runs in this society, she felt (Braden, 1999).

After it was over, the Bradens felt minimal animosity in response to the torrent of hatred that had been turned on them. Anne wanted to tell their story, as an illustration of the vast problems of black-white relations that society must summon up the capacity to resolve or else face disaster. She told the story in a book called *The Wall Between*, published in 1958 by the Monthly Review Press after being rejected by mainstream publishers. In the book, she cast no heroes or villains, simply people doing what they had to do, impelled by forces that had their roots far back in previous generations. This book was a runner-up for the National Book Award in 1958 and was republished in 1999 by the University of Tennessee Press, with a new epilogue by Anne analyzing developments of the past 40 years.

FIGHTING SEGREGATION HEAD ON, 1957–1974

With the charges of sedition behind them, Carl and Anne Braden began reconstructing their life. They had no employment: their children were 6 and 3. Because of male supremacist attitudes, wherein a man is viewed as more dangerous than a woman, Anne was able to get a job first—as a typist in the office of a small company. Since Carl could not be hired in Louisville, he took care of the children while the parents considered what their next move would be (Braden, 1979, 1999).

At this time, the Bradens were working with a few people nationwide to begin organizing a national committee to abolish the House Un-American Activities Committee. A group in Chicago wanted the Bradens to move there to help organize this work, but Anne felt that they should not leave Louisville, not let people drive them out, even if they could not be effective there for the moment.

By this time, the Bradens had become acquainted with Jim Dombrowski, the guiding spirit of the Southern Conference Educational Fund (SCEF) in New Orleans. SCEF, usually called "skeff," was a continuation of the Southern Conference for Human Welfare, the organization Virginia Durr had worked with, which had disbanded in 1948. Both SCHW and SCEF were interracial, reform organizations working within the U.S. system for peaceful social change. Neither organization was Marxist or revolutionary in its aims or methods, although segregationists portrayed them as such. SCEF pursued a single program: ending segregation in the South immediately through Negro and white people working together. Dombrowski himself was a Christian socialist (Klibaner, 1989).

By 1957, SCEF, along with Myles Horton and the Highlander Folk School, was setting goals against segregation that were far ahead of other organizations. As a result of the Eastland hearings of March 1954, when SCEF's leaders were subpoenaed to New Orleans, many of its allies abandoned it as a "Communist front" or "pink" organization. Benjamin Mays, president of Morehouse College, resigned as vice-president; the national Leadership Council on Civil Rights refused to admit SCEF as a member; many New Deal leaders refused to support it after the Eastland hearing. Eleanor Roosevelt continued to support it until 1960, when she, too, publicly separated herself from it, fearing it might be a Communist front (Klibaner, 1989).

But SCEF's leaders refused to be cowed. They wanted someone to travel around the South to reach white people, to help them realize that they should support the historic dismantling of segregation. After months of discussion, the Bradens accepted the job of field secretaries for SCEF, beginning in September 1957, at a joint salary of about $4,000. For the following 10 years they scoured the South, usually taking turns so that one parent could be at home with the children. Anne felt that she had a lucky life—from 1957 to 1966, the period of historic upsurge in the South, it was her job to get to know the people who made it happen (Adams, 1992; Braden, 1979; Egerton, 1994).

One of the first trips that Anne made for SCEF took place on Labor Day weekend in 1957, to attend the 25th-anniversary celebration at Highlander Folk School at Monteagle, near Chattanooga, Tennessee. Anne thought it would be a good place to meet helpful people from around the South. Anne drove down by herself to Monteagle and met about 180 friends of Highlander, including Martin Luther King, Jr., who spoke at the final session. Since the National Baptist Convention was meeting in Louisville soon afterward, Reverend King and Reverend Ralph Abernathy needed to get there, and Anne offered them a ride, which they accepted. They were amazed that a southern white woman would drive alone through the countryside with two black men; she didn't give it a thought, but afterward realized that they were the ones in danger.

Anne and Carl developed a modus operandi of visiting people in places where action against segregation was occurring, then reporting it in a positive way in the newsheet of SCEF, the *Southern Patriot,* which Anne edited. For example, immediately after Highlander's celebration, on September 4, the governor of Arkansas, Orval Faubus, ordered the National Guard to prevent nine Negro students from enrolling in all-white Central High School. Three weeks of white resistance ensued, until President Dwight D. Eisenhower sent in 1,000 soldiers from the 101st Airborne Division to restore order and enforce integration at Central High. Later, the Bradens drove to Little Rock to meet Rev. Dunbar Ogden, the white Presbyterian minister who had walked with the students. They gave him the support of SCEF, then spread the news about him through the *Southern Patriot* and through their information network of black, labor, religious, and national newspapers (Braden, 1981).

In July 1958, less than a year after the Bradens took their jobs with SCEF, they were subpoenaed to appear before hearings to be held by HUAC in Atlanta. These hearings were called just 6 months after SCEF had led a conference in Washington, D.C., about violations of voting rights in the South. Every person who received a subpoena from HUAC was white and actively involved in opposing segregation, except one black person. This outrage provoked the first mass opposition to HUAC; 200 leading Negroes signed a letter asking why HUAC wasn't investigating such un-American activities as the deaths of Negroes who tried to vote, or the bombings of Negro churches and Jewish synagogues. "It is increasingly difficult to find white people who are willing to support our efforts for full citizenship," the letter continued. "It is unthinkable that they should instead be harassed by committees of the United States Congress." SCEF sent the letter to every congressperson, and it appeared as a full-page ad in the *Washington Post,* but the *Atlanta Constitution* refused to print it, saying it libeled the congressional investigators (Adams, 1992; Klibaner, 1989).

Anne Braden never appeared before HUAC, because she refused to leave Rhode Island, where the Bradens were vacationing with their children, unless the committee paid to fly her children to Atlanta with her; and federal marshals excused her. Carl appeared and declined to answer questions, saying that, since the First Amendment guaranteed freedom of opinion, the committee had no right to ask his opinion. At this session, HUAC also interrogated Frank Wilkinson, who refused to answer on the same grounds. (Wilkinson had been targeted by the FBI in the 1950s for managing the first integrated housing project in Los Angeles.) After the hearing, the U.S. House of Representatives, except for one African American congressman, Robert C. Nix of Philadelphia, cited Braden and Wilkinson for contempt of Congress. In January 1959, after a short trial, they were both sentenced to one year in jail.

Carl Braden and Wilkinson appealed their conviction to the Supreme Court, which in February 1961 ruled five to four that they were guilty. On May 1 they entered federal prison in Greenville, South Carolina, which they would leave on parole 10 months later. In his dissent, Justice Hugo Black noted: "This is a decision which may well strip the Negro of the aid of many of the white people who have been willing to speak up in his behalf" (Schrecker, 1998, p. 392; see also Adams, 1992; O'Reilly, 1983; F. Wilkinson, telephone interview with author, February 2, 1998).

Key African American organizations debated whether or not to support SCEF and fight HUAC. The NAACP decided not to fight HUAC, but SCLC, although divided, did support SCEF and the campaign for clemency for Wilkinson and Braden. Its leader, Dr. King, defied enormous pressure to give his personal support. The young leaders of the Student Nonviolent Coordinating Committee stood resolutely with SCEF against HUAC; the Bradens became close allies of theirs. Another key African American in the fight against HUAC was Rev. Fred Shuttlesworth, who would lead the mass movement that broke segregation in Birmingham in 1963. Shuttlesworth, a leader in the SCLC, also became president of SCEF and refused to be intimidated as a result of Red-baiting. When Shuttlesworth began as president of SCEF, he argued: "Blacks are concerned about civil rights, having a job, and persecution. But here [resisting HUAC] we are talking about what democracy means in its fullest sense, and how to persevere in the struggle to make democracy real. Civil liberties is an extra burden, but it is an extra burden we must take up" (Adams, 1992, p. 248).

Early in 1964, Anne Braden realized with deep clarity that HUAC was the old southern oligarchy fighting to keep segregation and stay in power, and the rest of Congress was allowing them to proceed. Knowing that many people did not see the connection between HUAC and the southern oligarchs, Anne wrote a 45-page pamphlet called *House Un-American Activities Committee: Bulwark of Segregation*. It was published in 1964 by the National Committee to Abolish HUAC (NCAHUAC), formed in 1960, from its national office in Los Angeles. In this pamphlet, Braden raised the question of why there were so few white people, especially in the South, willing to support the freedom struggle. Her answer: Advocates of civil rights are persistently labeled Communists. This practice intensified in the 1950s and continued to increase in the 1960s, producing "a direct cause-and-effect relationship between this labeling process and the shortage of people ready to act for integration" (Braden, 1964). Very few other Americans saw this relationship, and no one stated it as clearly as Anne Braden did.

In her pamphlet, Braden showed that if one traces each charge of subversion, one finds the same common source: either HUAC; its counterpart in the U.S. Senate, the Senate Internal Security Subcommittee, headed by James O. Eastland of Mississippi; or one of several state committees modeled after these. What Braden could not know at the time was that the FBI was working hand in hand with HUAC; the FBI had a copy of Braden's pamphlet 3 weeks before its publication (Braden, 1964; O'Reilly, 1983).

Braden granted that the label of Communist doesn't always originate with these committees, but "they give weight to these reckless charges by placing upon them the stamp of approval of a government committee. . . . They have enabled the segregationist to tie his kite to the national issue of communism and thus pose, not as the defender of a corrupt Southern status quo, but as a guardian of the national security" (Braden, 1964, pp. 13–14).

Braden documented that many of the leading members of HUAC were southern racists—Rep. John Rankin of Mississippi, who made HUAC a permanent committee in 1945; Rep. John Wood of Georgia, a chair of HUAC in the late 1940s and early 1950s; Rep. Edwin Willis of Louisiana, who assumed the chair of HUAC in 1963 and led southern opposition to the civil rights bill in 1964. A few chairs of HUAC were not southerners, but the northerner who held the chair longest, from 1955 to 1963, Rep. Francis Walter of Pennsylvania, proved to be connected with organized racism (Braden, 1964).

Labeling the civil rights movement subversive had a greater chilling effect on white people than on black people, Braden believed:

> Perhaps this is because their families and friends are likely to believe the communist charges, whereas it is pretty hard to convince Negroes that the freedom movement is a communist plot. So the net result has been to keep whites out of action, leave Negroes alone on the front lines, and sometimes to encourage them to suspect the motives of the few whites who are active. Thus the gap has been widened between black and white. (Braden, 1964, p. 32)

The same year that Braden published her pamphlet, 1964, HUAC faced a large protest in San Francisco. After the death of FBI director J. Edgar Hoover in 1972 and the resignation of President Richard Nixon in 1973, the work of NCAHUAC paid off. The House of Representatives finally abolished HUAC, its name having been previously changed to House Internal Security Committee, in January 1975 (O'Reilly, 1983).

Through all this tumult, traveling, and separation, both chosen and forced, Anne and Carl managed to have a loving marriage and some semblance of family life. They had a third child, Elizabeth, born on February 7, 1960, a year before Carl entered prison for contempt of Congress. In June 1963, they learned that Anita was ill with a rare genetic disorder; it caused her death in June 1964, at the age of 11 (Braden, 1981).

During the 1960s, the Bradens' house was full of young people traveling back and forth between North and South. Often there were 15 to 20 for supper: "I tried to divide up chores and put them to work. I had never planned to stay at home and cook for my own family, much less the whole younger generation" (A. Braden, interview with author, March 21, 2000).

The Bradens' home life was hectic and filled with tension; often when they sat down to dinner the phone would ring with news of a fresh crisis. Their children saw their parents painted as villains on TV and had to compete with all the guests for their attention. Luckily, the schools they attended were friendly to them, because they served mostly black children—out in the suburbs the Braden children would have had a more difficult time.

Braden regrets that she was not a better mother, but accepts that she did the best she could under the circumstances:

> At the time our children were little—in the early 50s—we thought we were putting our finger in the dike to stop Fascism and World War III. All our friends did, and I think we might have been. I think our analysis of history was right. We just didn't have the luxury of sitting around thinking how we were going to create the best environment for our kids. I'm not sure if people do now—they think they do. (A. Braden, interview with author, March 21, 2000)

In the months following Carl Braden's release from jail in February 1962, SCEF's leaders tried to organize a broad-based conference of southern civil rights groups in Atlanta. At first, SCLC planned to cosponsor it, but when they decided not to, SCEF organized a workshop with SNCC. Anne was able to implement her plan of paying a white student to work on SNCC's staff to organize white student support for the freedom movement on college campuses. Anne hoped that it would be a woman, but instead Robert Zellner, a college student from Mobile, Alabama, held this job, with distinction (Fosl, 1999; Klibaner, 1989).

In October 1963 the Louisiana Joint Legislative Committee on Un-American Activities (LUAC) raided SCEF's office in New Orleans, removing all files, mailing lists, and books. SCEF's executive secretary, Jim Dombrowski, was arrested and his house searched and his papers removed. This resulted in complex suits and countersuits, which were finally resolved in April 1965 when the Supreme Court reached a decision, five to two, that Louisiana's statutes, illegal and overbroad, were being used to harass constitutionally guaranteed activities. SCEF's files were ordered returned, and Dombrowski had his victory in court. But within several months, he was forced into retirement by arthritis, and Carl and Anne Braden became the codirectors of SCEF (Adams, 1992; Braden, 1979; Klibaner, 1989).

By the end of 1965, Congress had passed civil rights legislation, and the attorney general's office was beginning to enforce it in the South. The mass civil rights movement had climaxed, but it inspired other democratic movements and groups—the women's movement, the peace movement, the civil liberties movement to stop HUAC, Students for a Democratic Society, the gay and lesbian movement, the environmental movement, the disabilities movement. Anne felt certain that all these protests grew out of the efforts of black people:

> If you're going to understand the dynamics of this country, then it's essential to understand that the thing that has always moved history forward is the black people's movement. And that's just because that's the way our country is structured. It's not because black people are virtuous or have some great corner on brains or anything else. Our society happened to have been built on slavery of black people, so blacks are at the base of society; so it's just always when they've moved, it's moved everything else. (Braden, 1979, pp. 89–90)

The Bradens moved the office of SCEF from New Orleans to Louisville in 1966. The organization bought a house for its office not far from where the Bradens lived, in a mixed neighborhood that would soon become all black. In 3 years, SCEF was able to buy the house next door as an educational center and meeting place. From Louisville the Bradens continued to run SCEF and publish the *Southern Patriot*. Eventually SCEF became an almost all-white organization, as it attracted young whites who left SNCC after that organization told them their job was to organize white people against racism. By the early 1970s, when SCEF was trying to conduct staff meetings of 50 to 60 volunteers, it became vulnerable to government infiltration. Internal debates over political ideology between various factions of socialists and communists caused its demise in 1973. This breakup of SCEF, which Anne had spent 16 years building, was one of the great traumas of her life, worse for her than the ordeal over the Wade house (Braden, 1997, 1981, 1999; A. Braden, personal communication, March 20, 1999).

Anne Braden believes that the dissension that destroyed SCEF was encouraged by the Counterintelligence Program (COINTELPRO), which the FBI used to disrupt organizations it considered dangerous. It especially targeted civil rights groups and African American organizations. Between 1960 and 1976 the FBI employed some 1,300 informers, at an estimated cost of $26 million, to infiltrate or monitor the Socialist Workers Party alone (O'Reilly, 1983). Braden sees these agents as part of the generalized repression against black movements that occurred in the late 1960s and early 1970s:

> During the civil-rights movement in the early 60s, racism was on the defensive. But in the late 1960s a massive counter-attack began. This took many forms: the framing and jailing of black organizers, and sometimes their murder; covert efforts to destroy civil-rights organizations; co-optation of movement energies with temporary federal programs; a new ideological onslaught of theories of racial superiority; and a re-emergence of the Ku Klux Klan. (Braden, 1977, p. 51)

Braden believes that the repression of the late 1960s was worse than that of the 1950s, in that more people died, and that it is yet little understood by white historians, perhaps because most of the victims were black. She was still traveling throughout the South during those years and wrote in 1983:

> I remember well that one could hardly visit any community without finding that its key black organizers were either in jail, on their way, or just out after much struggle. . . . Most of the charges were criminal, that later proved to be frame-ups. On August 25, 1967, F.B.I. director J. Edgar Hoover issued a directive ordering "experienced and imaginative" special agents to "expose, disrupt, misdirect, discredit, or otherwise neutralize" what he called "Black nationalist hate-type organizations." Among those targeted were: SNCC, SCLC, CORE, Nation of Islam, Stokely Carmichael, Rap Brown, and Elijah Muhammed. Six months later another memo expanded the scope of the first one and added Dr. King as a target, exactly one month before he was murdered. (Braden, 1983, pp. 21–22)

In 1971 Carl Braden resigned as codirector of SCEF and set up a related consulting organization, the Training Institute for Propaganda and Organizing, which conducted training programs for community organizers throughout the nation. Anne continued as director of SCEF, until it folded in 1973. Meanwhile, in 1972, Carl Braden and Angela Davis became two founders of the National Alliance against Racist and Political Repression.

In February 1975, after Carl, at the age of 60, returned from a monthlong series of training sessions in the Midwest and West, his 15-year-old daughter, Beth, found him on a couch, dead of a heart attack. Anne wrote in her press release: "Carl was tired. If he had slowed down, he might have lived longer—but I don't think he would have been happy, and he couldn't do it. He felt there was so much to do" (Braden & Braden, 1928–1972).

Even in 1975 the *Louisville Courier Journal*, in its editorial tribute to Carl, still criticized the Bradens. After admitting that sometimes protest had to be active, the editor wrote:

But sometimes, as in the Louisville of 1954, when Mr. Braden and his equally activist wife used subterfuge to buy a home for a Negro family, in a white neighborhood, the result was a setback for their cause. The whirlwind of bigotry, fear and witchhunting precipitated by this action actually delayed the community's advance toward better race relations. That the Bradens seemed to derive satisfaction from the storm they had created, and even from the ensuing trial for sedition, only compounded the error of their idealism turned to zealotry. (February 21, 1975)

This editorial revealed the depth of the *Courier Journal*'s commitment to the status quo and its need to distance itself from the Bradens, even 10 years after the huge victories of the civil rights movement and more than 20 years after the Wade house controversy.

CONFRONTING INJUSTICE, 1975–PRESENT

After Carl's death, Anne tried to do alone everything that the couple had done together as a team. Instead of deliberating what to do with the rest of her life, she went to whatever project called most for her attention. She is constitutionally unable to be selective; she wants to do everything. She never learned what can be accomplished in a given time. She thinks she might have been more effective if she could have been more focused (A. Braden, interview with author, March 21, 2000).

Braden's overarching political commitment has been to building a regional network that can change the racism and elitism of the South. She admits that the South has changed somewhat. "It's probably less segregated than the rest of the country and no more racist, which isn't saying much" (A. Braden, interview with author, December 1997).

With the demise of SCEF, Braden had to build a new organization capable of being a regional network. Determined never again to create a mostly white organization, as SCEF had become in its last years, she organized, with Rev. Ben Chavis, the Southern Organizing Committee for Economic and Social Justice (SOC). Its headquarters were in Birmingham, in the home of the paid staff person there. SOC was a multiracial, multiissue network with no membership, except its "board," which grew to more than 65 people.

Braden was responsible for much of the details of keeping SOC going, including raising money. She had no time to start another newspaper like the *Southern Patriot*, which is one of her chief regrets, but she has succeeded in building SOC as a multiracial organization that now has a paid staff of four and a rented office in Atlanta. It has a strong African American director and growing Latino and Native American participation (A. Braden, interview with author, December 1997; personal communication, March 20, 1999).

The most urgent issue that has arisen through the SOC network has been the issue of environmental justice. Toxics are being dumped in poor, black communities all over the South, and people are fighting back, with SOC's support. A task force of the United Church for Christ documented the facts in 1987 in a report called *Waste and Race*, and in September 1991, people of color organized the People of Color Environmental Leadership Conference in Washington, D.C. Braden served on an advisory committee and attended as a participant, given a voice but no vote; only people of color could be delegates with a vote. Braden says:

> I have never been as proud of my white brothers and sisters as I was there because not anybody peeped. No white person said one word, because there was nothing to say. . . . They adopted the seventeen principles of environmental justice, which is still the guiding document of the environmental justice movement, and a very eloquently written call to action against world-wide genocide. . . . It had a real impact on white environmental groups, who all began to add blacks to their staffs. . . . It changed the environmental movement forever, although we still have struggles with these white environmentalists who don't seem to see the importance . . . you know, they're not going to win by themselves. (A. Braden, interview with author, December 1997)

SOC followed up by organizing a multiethnic environmental conference in New Orleans in December 1992, with 300 or 400 participants expected; more than 2,500 showed up. Braden believes that since then, a real grassroots environmental movement has developed in the South based in communities of color and that nationally people are not aware of it (A. Braden, interview with author, December 1997).

After's Carl's death, Anne maintained her pattern of being at home about 50% of the time and out of town the other 50%. While in Louisville, she works mostly through the National Alliance against Racism and Political Repression and its state affiliate, the Kentucky Alliance. She believes that every community needs one multiethnic organization whose sole purpose is to fight racism and build an antiracist majority. That is how she sees the work of the Kentucky Alliance; the central issue has not changed:

> The Alliance has started saying white supremacy instead of racism because then you don't get into endless arguments about whether blacks can be racist. It says what we mean—the fact that this country was founded on racism, which I define as the assumption that everything should be run by white people for the benefit of white people. That's the reason why we haven't solved all these other problems—health insurance, part-time work, school systems falling apart. White su-

premacy has kept people divided. Otherwise, we would have had a movement
that would have changed who is running things. I'm pretty single-minded about
it. I'm going to be talking about racism as long as it's here. That just hasn't changed
in my life. I'm afraid it won't. (A. Braden, interview with author, December 1997)

Braden believes that the concept of reverse discrimination, that blacks
are taking something from whites, is the most dangerous idea ever let loose
in this country. It comes from the Klan and from academic circles, but
Braden says:

> The idea that blacks were taking something from whites is a plain, bald lie. The
> black movement never took a thing from white people—it helped them. Not just
> in spiritual or psychological terms, but in very practical things. Everything that
> blacks gained, white people, working-class white people especially, got the
> benefit of—PELL grants for college studies, CETA [Comprehensive Employment
> and Training Act], Medicare and Medicaid. Those all came out of the War on
> Poverty, when black Americans demanded opportunity. (A. Braden, interview
> with author, December 1997)

Braden worked enthusiastically on Jesse Jackson's campaign for president. She served as an alternative delegate to the Democratic convention
in San Francisco in 1984 and as a delegate to the one in Atlanta in 1988.
She points out that Jackson beat Gore and Clinton to win the South, forcing the Democrats to unite behind Dukakis in order to defeat Jackson. She
believes that the lack of growth of the Rainbow Coalition after 1988 has
been a political tragedy. She hopes it will revive, or some movement like
it will be formed, in order to bring fundamental change to the country
(A. Braden, interview with author, December 1997; personal communication, March 20, 1999).

Braden always belonged to an Episcopalian church in Louisville, but
she usually felt she had more important things to do on Sunday mornings
than attend. However, in recent years she has become active in a small
mission church, St. George's. She derives strength from it, in part because
her roots are there. Braden has also been active nationally in the Racial
Justice Working Group of the National Council of Churches; she finds that
most denominations in this country have both a reactionary and a progressive wing, the latter of which she calls the Christians (A. Braden, interview
with author, December 1997).

Braden's son, Jim, won a Rhodes scholarship and practices law in San
Francisco. Her daughter, Elizabeth, is a mother of two children, living in
Hawaii. Braden lives by herself in a house with two bedrooms so filled with
boxes of papers that there is no room even for visitors. Anne has given most

of the Braden papers to the Wisconsin Historical Society; when she has time she will donate the rest (A. Braden, interview with author, December 1997).

In recent years, Anne Braden has been transformed from an outcast into a role model. It's been a long time coming:

> I don't know what happened, but I think it's partly longevity. Most people now don't know what I did. They may have heard I was a little controversial, but they don't know why. Awards get to be contagious because people are looking for somebody to build a fundraiser around. All of a sudden people began giving me awards. It's a strange feeling that I really don't know how to handle. We learned to handle attacks.... When you are under attack, you use every attack as a platform from which to reach more people with what you were trying to say anyway. It works like a charm—they can't win and you can't lose. We did it all through the South on different battles in the 60s. So I know how to handle attacks. I just really haven't figured out how to handle the awards. (A. Braden, interview with author, December 1997)

One of Braden's deep regrets is that she has not had time to keep in touch with people she really loved. One of those was Virginia Durr who, after she retired, wanted Braden to come to Montgomery to visit her. Braden explained to her on the phone, "Virginia, *I* haven't retired," but Durr was hurt. Once Braden attended a reunion dinner of the codefendants in the Wade trial, and she was on the phone during half the dinner, which angered the hostess. Braden is pained by this, but it is a part of her that she accepts (A. Braden, interview with author, March 21, 2000).

Braden is not financially able to retire; she has no reserve of money to live on, even at her modest level. For income, she teaches one course at Northern Kentucky University in suburban Cincinnati and travels to small colleges giving speeches about racism and civil rights. She expects that one day she will just drop dead and hopes that it will not be soon, since she wants to see what happens next (A. Braden, interview with author, March 21, 2000).

Braden is amazingly healthy, given her poor diet, high stress, and constant smoking. She feels it is too late to stop smoking now. She started when she was 14, before people knew the dangers, considering it an aspect of growing up. She has quit twice, but resumed each time, and now it is part of her chemistry (A. Braden, interview with author, March 21, 2000).

Braden does not believe that she has paid a price for the choices she has made in her life. That is an important point for her, because many people say to her, "Oh, you gave up so much."

> I don't think I paid a price. Maybe I wasn't as good a mother as I could have been because of the strain of trying to do both. But I'm not sure I would have

Anne Braden about 2000. Photo by C. E. Branham. Courtesy *Louisville Eccentric Observer.*

been a good mother anyway, and I did the best I could. . . . I gained so much more than I ever gave up. I don't think I lived a life of self-sacrifice. I found a new world, the world I wanted to live in and that I was happy in. Sometimes I wish it had been more relaxed, because we were in a constant strain. But being part of that battle was what I wanted to do in my life. I feel very privileged and don't think I gave up anything. (A. Braden, interview with author, March 21, 2000)

When her book, *The Wall Between*, was reissued in 1999 because it was still timely and well-written, Braden wrote in her new epilogue:

Southern whites of my generation perhaps have something to say that the rest of this country needs to hear and heed. . . . We who came to maturity when the South was totally segregated and ruled by terror had to turn ourselves inside out to deal with this question. . . . what I and other white southerners went through in earlier times is a microcosm of what this entire nation must do. It must turn itself inside out, and turn its values, assumptions—*and* policies—

upside down. So far the country has only picked around the edge of the problem. (Braden, 1999, p. 339)

Braden changed her class allegiance to resist the white supremacy of her region and her nation. She had the single-minded determination it took to fight legal segregation, white racist violence, state prosecution, the FBI, and denunciation by committees of Congress. She has hope today because she sees in many local communities new movements of people of color demanding justice:

> Mass movements always come as the product of long years of mundane work by unsung heroes, but no one can predict when the upsurge will crystallize. No one could have predicted that it would happen in 1955 in Montgomery. We cannot predict today when it will happen again, and I am not at all sure I will live to see it. But as surely as I know that dawn will come tomorrow morning, I am convinced that it will happen. And when it does, a huge question will be how many white people will understand that this upsurge holds hope for their lives, too, and will therefore go through the personal metamorphosis that will be needed to join this new movement. (Braden, 1999, pp. 346–347)

5

Teaching for Hope:
Herbert R. Kohl

IN THE SPRING OF 2000 Herb Kohl was living in the Bernal Heights neighborhood of San Francisco with his wife, Judy, in a small house, which they shared with their golden retriever, Mazel Tov. Kohl had been a visiting professor of education for several years at the University of San Francisco and was starting a new program there in teacher education, one that would focus on teaching for social justice as well as on excellence of teaching. He was busy interviewing students, arranging student loans, and wondering how to help students find housing.

At this stage of his life, at age 62, Kohl was still deeply engaged in his lifetime goal—transforming the public schools of the United States to promote equity and social justice. For decades he has advocated for children—for their creativity, their personal and social imaginations—and for creating learning communities at school and with parents. As a consequence of these concerns, he has opposed racism as an impediment to the growth and learning of children. Over the years he has worked on these concerns from a number of vantage points—teaching at almost every grade level, setting up a non-profit organization to link professional writers with classroom instruction, administering an alternative public high school and an alternative teacher education program, and writing more than 40 books, many of them about how teaching could be improved in almost every field: in reading, math, theater, writing, literature, and the natural sciences.

Kohl's passion for children's learning began in New York City, where he grew up, in the Bronx, with his immigrant grandparents and native-born parents. When he began teaching in 1962, he encountered the shocking racism that the children of color in New York City were experiencing. Based on his work in Harlem, he wrote *Thirty-six Children* (1967), documenting the success of his students when they were supported in telling the truth about their lives.

Kohl came into adulthood at a time of racial turmoil. Legal segregation was being challenged; the civil rights movement was midway in its course. Kohl perceived early and clearly how the struggle played out in the schools, where racism was perpetuated by the refusal of many white families to educate their children with children of color and by the institutionalized failure of many white teachers to educate children of color. Kohl has been able to nurture hope, both in students and adults, and to support people's capacity for imagining ways in which the world could be better. But perhaps his greatest gift has been his performance as a tough, compassionate teacher of young people.

GROWING UP, 1937–1961

Herbert Ralph Cohen arrived in the world on August 22, 1937, the first-born of Marion and Samuel Cohen, the eldest son of the eldest son. He was named Herbert for his mother's father, Heschel, the most recently deceased in his family. The family name of Cohen had been assigned by an officer at Ellis Island; when Herb was 5 years old, his father changed it to Kohl, since he could not find work as a civil engineer with a name perceived as Jewish. Nor could he after he changed his name; he continued to work independently as a building contractor, along with his father (Kohl, 1978; interview with author, August 18, 1998).

In the Bronx, the Kohls resided in a working-class neighborhood in a two-flat house. Downstairs lived Herb, his mother, his father, and his younger brother and sister; upstairs were his father's father and mother, two uncles and a wife of one uncle. Under the first floor, the garage housed his father's and his grandfather's construction business, Herbert Construction Company. Across the street lived Herb's father's sister and her family, and around the corner, another sister. A few blocks away lived his mother's family, more bohemian, containing artists and printers, some of whom had mixed Italian and Jewish backgrounds (Kohl, 1978).

> The whole notion of simple family relationships in a rather post-1950s American way was not part of my growing up. I didn't experience that, thank God. I probably would have gone crazy because then you have to deal with the psychology of just your mother and just your father and their relationships, where I had uncles and aunts . . . so I had all kinds of adults to look at. Not one kind of adult,

not one kind of family, and not one set of values. (H. Kohl, interviews with author, April 4, June 5, 1997)

Many family members were influential in young Herb's life. Among them were two of his mother's sisters, Addie and Evy. Aunt Addie, married to an Italian American cab driver, taught Herb to read and to love books. His mother's side of the family celebrated Christmas, with a tree and Nativity scenes.

But the most influential person in Herb's young life was his grandfather, Morris (Moishe) Cohen, whom he called Pop. Grandfather Cohen loved anybody and everybody, as long as they weren't trying to boss other people around or use their money to exploit other people and keep them poor. He hated bosses.

Morris Cohen had come to the United States around 1905 from Bialystok, in the area of central Europe known as the Pale (Lithuania, Poland, Belarus, Ukraine), to which Russia restricted its Jews. An orphan, Morris Cohen managed to escape from service in the czar's army and travel to Hamburg and then to London, where he earned his fare to New York City. His commitment to democratic socialism remained unambiguous until he died in 1967. He worked as a framing carpenter and took an active part in the Arbeiter Ring, or Workmen's Circle, a socialist, prounion, profeminist, but non-Zionist organization and social club. Also a founding member of the Carpenter and Joiners Union, Morris Cohen was a secular Jew who had escaped the pogroms of imperial Russia.

> So I grew up basically in a family in which the notion that working people have rights and that nobody has a right to have more when someone is hungry was just part of chicken soup. . . . There is a social ambience, there is a political and social context in which you are born, there are moral values which you have to determine for yourself and have to either live or, if you don't live them, then you don't have them. (H. Kohl, interviews with author, April 4, June 6, 1997)

The Arbeiter Ring, as his grandparents called it in Yiddish, deeply influenced the young Herb. Its members were committed to democratic socialism but not to communism. They believed in workers' control of work, not in being told what to do. They considered it a weakness for a person to need to give orders or to want to give orders; they believed in using their own judgment in conversation with one's peers. Herb grew up unable to join any authoritarian organization that precluded the option of saying no (H. Kohl, interviews with author, April 4, June 6, 1997).

Herb's grandfather worked long hours as a rough carpenter, framing in walls with two-by-four's, wearing a truss to protect a hernia that could burst at any time. In his union activities he was a physically violent man who attacked scabs when they attempted to break the strikes of other unions. He went to jail numerous times for this, but the authorities could only arrest him; they couldn't issue an injunction against his own union, because it was not conducting the strike.

> This was a strategy used in the early union struggles when they were building the unions. They needed some people who were strong men willing to deal with violent confrontation, who could really go in and confront [the scabs]—because the people they hired to cross the picket line were thugs. . . . You have to decide which side you're on, but it never would occur to some people I grew up with that you wouldn't have to fight, and that you wouldn't suffer. So, for example, I am totally incapable of understanding New Age philosophy and people who want their own personal happiness and believe that because they're going to be happy, the world is going to be saved, and that they have a right to indulge themselves without suffering. I don't believe that. As a matter of deep conviction, I believe that as long as there is injustice in the world you have to keep other people's suffering in your mind, and you have to redeem their suffering through your actions. Redemption is through action, and there is some absolute necessity not to rest in comfort. (H. Kohl, interviews with author, April 4, June 6, 1997)

When Herb was 8 or 9, his grandfather's union went on strike. His union colleagues sat around the family table and talked about their difficulties buying food and paying their rent. People cried, and everyone had a story to tell. Herb's grandfather passed around Canadian Club whiskey, encouraged people to figure out how to help one another in a difficult situation, and told stories about what the world could be like for workers. Herb couldn't understand the content of the stories because they were told in a mixture of Yiddish and English, but he could understand that they warmed everyone more than the whiskey did, that they built comradeship and dedication to social struggle (Kohl, 1995).

Herb's grandmother worked at times as a pieceworker for the garment industry. Her family and its network attempted to translate their social ideals into action in their everyday lives; they shared money and food, making sure that nobody went hungry. Later Herb reflected that the next generation—his parents and their siblings—began to lose that communal sense of "we" as they began to succeed as capitalists.

Morris Cohen's best friend was an African American laborer, Rogers Williams, who worked with him as a team for 30 years. Williams came to the Cohens' apartment every day after work for a drink. Herb felt the deep bond between the two men when he worked with them.

Other members of Herb's family would talk about the "Schwartzer," the blacks. As they were becoming Americans, the Kohls talked about the people they were climbing over. Yet they were more prejudiced against the Irish, who were closer down the block. Herb was the first person on his father's side to marry a non-Jewish woman—of his paternal relatives only his grandfather had a positive response to this. On his mother's side, by contrast, where intermarriage had already taken place, relatives celebrated (H. Kohl, interviews with author, April 4, June 6, 1997).

The Kohls' immediate community consisted primarily of working-class people, mostly first generation with a mixture of immigrants. Since New York City was a port of entry, an international city, immigrant culture dominated. An Irish community existed several houses away, while around the corner three different Italian communities flourished—the Neapolitans, the Sicilians, and the Calabrese. Within the larger Jewish community there was a Reform, an Orthodox, and a Conservative community. There were Ashkenazi Jews from eastern Europe, Sephardic Jews from Spain, and German Jews, who didn't speak to eastern European Jews. Divisions characterized Herb's community; there was no majority point of view, no sense of being part of the majority. It was clear to him that "boundaries define who you are and where you are. Where you stand and whether you walk across boundaries or stay in your own community is everybody's problem from the day they are born" (H. Kohl, interviews with author, April 4, June 6, 1997).

When Herb began to attend public school, the diversity became simpler rather than more complex. In his school there were about eight classes per grade; most of the Jewish children were put in the top two or three classes. The rest of the classes were mostly Italian, with a smattering of African American, Puerto Rican, and Jewish. The Irish children were in Catholic schools. Previously many of the teachers had been Irish, but by the time Herb started school many were Jewish. The class assignments were made on the basis of so-called objective criteria of academic performance.

> But academic performance had to do with the fact that by the time I hit school many of the teachers were Jewish and therefore most of the teachers really responded to Jewish kids as their kids and other kids as foreigners—foreigners who had been in the country as long as they had, by the way. . . . Jewish teachers knew the parents of the Jewish kids and used the public schools basically as a way to promote the economic and social advancement of the Jewish community. . . . The whole nature of success changed in the system, which is one of my theses, which is why we need more African American and Puerto Rican and other kinds of people teaching in the schools. Because their sense of ownership and identity with the children changed as the demographics of the teaching staff changed. I'm positive of that. (H. Kohl, interviews with author, April 4, June 6, 1997)

There were no African Americans in Herb's classes, and by junior high, practically no non-Jews. He was put in a special class in which students completed seventh, eighth, and ninth grades in 2 years. But the school was almost as violent as any urban school today, except there were no guns, just knives. People were mugged in the halls; extortion occurred on a regular basis; everybody learned to fight at least a little bit (H. Kohl, interviews with author, April 4, June 6, 1997).

During Herb's late elementary school years, he extended his childhood fantasy life, developing a fantasy companion and teacher he called the Masked Rider. After a bedtime ritual, the Masked Rider would come to him, and they would go off together on adventures in which they rescued young children, nurtured them for their own sake, and left them to grow up strong. This fantasy had a dreamlike quality in which Herb was deeply involved, yet at the same time he could watch and analyze what took place. By the age of 12 or 13 he realized that he dreamed of being a teacher of young children, with the gift of helping them imagine ways in which the world could be different, ways of transcending their ghetto or other economic or political circumstances (Kohl, 1994).

As a freshman in high school, Kohl had his first opportunity to act on his dream, when he was asked by his chemistry teacher to teach his son to read. This son, Kohl discovered, already knew how to read, but because he had severe cerebral palsy, could not share his knowledge with others. Kohl learned to communicate with him and watched the child's confidence grow in response. Kohl experienced firsthand that people can strengthen one another and felt that continuing this experience would be a wonderful way to live his life.

During early adolescence, Kohl also began to dream of becoming a writer. In the seventh grade, by chance, in the school library he picked up a copy of Howard Pease's *The Tatooed Man: A Tale of Strange Adventures Befalling Tod Moran, Mess Boy of the Tramp Steamer "Araby," upon His First Voyage from San Francisco to Geneva, via the Panama Canal*. Late at night, Kohl imagined traveling with Tod Moran to San Francisco,

> a city smothered in mist, listening with him to "the distant clang of cable cars, the hoar crys [sic] of newsboys, the dull rumble of trucks and drays passing in the gloom like ghosts." That sentence stopped me. I read it over, then over again, and spoke it out loud, quietly so my parents and brother couldn't hear. It conjured up a picture in my mind that was more intense than most of my dreams. Howard Pease's words created a world; they were magic and set me on fire with a burning desire to become a writer. Since that night the necessity of writing has never left me. (Kohl, 1994, p. 35)

Kohl's parents felt that writing would be a good hobby, but that Herb should study hard and learn a profession, which they hoped would protect him from future economic depressions. Despite their parents' strong prolabor loyalties, Herb's parents expected their children to rise out of the working-class circumstances of their lives.

The years during World War II were difficult in Kohl's neighborhood. It was a time of misery and anxiety as people waited to hear news about who had died in concentration camps, who was in displaced-persons camps. People were also talking about the possibility of fighting to establish a Jewish state in Palestine. Kohl's next-door neighbor returned from combat in Europe only to leave a few months later for Palestine, where he died fighting. Gradually, as the anticommunist Red-baiting started in the late 1940s, the fear filtered through to Kohl that the United States might abandon its own Jews just as it had abandoned the Jews in Europe during the 1930s (Kohl, 1994).

Kohl attended Bronx High School of Science, but he didn't yet realize that he was smart, because he never met his parents' standards of excellence. Already, as a sophomore in 1953–1954, he was involved in struggles over the rights of students and getting all kinds of people's voices heard. He based his friendships on affection, deep affinities, and mutual interests, so they tended to cross boundaries and barriers (H. Kohl, interviews with author, April 4, June 6, 1997).

When he was a senior, Kohl represented Bronx High on the Inter-GO Council, the citywide assembly of student organizations. Each high school sent two delegates for a total of 172; those delegates elected their officers, and Kohl was chosen as president in his senior year. Bob Maynard, an African American from Boys' High, who later would become owner of the *Oakland Tribune,* was elected vice president that year. Herb and Bob and their friends hung out together in jazz clubs and other crossover places where people mixed and ignored respectable boundaries. They visited such venues as Birdland and Jimmy Ryans and the Village Vanguard. They were interested in the larger world, in being on the cutting edge, in being committed to justice (H. Kohl, interviews with author, April 4, June 6, 1997).

Kohl's parents would not allow him to bring African American friends home. As a teenager, Kohl decided to accept being in conflict with family members and the community in which he grew up. Kohl calls this race suicide, similar to the class suicide of middle-class people who devote themselves to serving the poor. He experienced not being invited to certain places, people being afraid of what he was going to say and not confiding in him—being excluded from the private rituals of family and culture. It was the price he learned to pay early on for his moral commitment (H. Kohl, interviews with author, April 4, June 6, 1997).

Kohl's years of high school coincided with the period of Joe McCarthy's greatest influence, 1950 to 1954:

> It wasn't as if we were inventing the issue of justice and the right to speak out. If you came from a socialist background in those days, you knew that your people were being opposed, your mother and father, your grandparents, your parents' friends. So we were in the middle of a war; that is to say, society was making war on us. Not only was it making war on black people, but it was making war on progressive people. . . . This was all part of what you had to do to be a decent person, but also to defend your grandparents and your parents and your right to live the kind of life you wanted to live. We weren't hurting anybody, and those people would come here trying to hurt you. Trying to prevent you from being able to work. Trying to get you to betray people. Trying to frighten and intimidate you. . . . My mother was intimidated, without any question. Her family wasn't, but she was damaged for life by those McCarthy people, by oppression within a democracy. It was a big lesson to me, and something very important to know about. This is a very cruel society. It can be cruel to people who did nothing in particular but try and be decent. (H. Kohl, interviews with author, April 4, June 6, 1997)

From 1954 to 1958, Kohl studied at Harvard University, against the wishes of his parents, who wanted him to attend Princeton, from where he could return home for weekends. But Kohl wanted to leave home, to reach out to the larger world. He chose Harvard for its reputation for academic excellence, and he found an atmosphere of intellectual giddiness. The brilliance of the teaching met his eagerness to learn; he studied mathematics, philosophy, fine arts, and literature, trying to absorb everything the university had to offer.

At the same time, Kohl felt socially displaced. He had to figure out how to deal with wealthy Anglo-Saxon Protestants, whom he often found to have a false self-confidence that masked all kinds of chaos and disillusion. He was filled with rage that they could shun him and that nothing he could do would change them. He received his first heavy dose of anti-Semitism at Harvard, as his family had expected. His peers elected him president of the Signet Society, an organization of intellectuals founded by William and Henry James and George Santayana, among others. Kohl was the first Jewish president, and some of the old-time Protestant, Anglo-Saxon faculty boycotted Signet after he was elected. Although they had been regulars at lunch, they stopped coming during his tenure. With Jonathan Kozol and a few other classmates, Kohl tried unsuccessfully to challenge the bigotry of Signet Society (H. Kohl, interviews with author, April 4, June 6, 1997).

As a sophomore, Kohl read an essay by George Santayana, who, he remembers, suggested that if you want to be a philosopher, get a job and do philosophy on the side, but don't become a professor of philosophy. That rang a bell with Kohl, who realized that he wanted to write and think about philosophy—while he was teaching kids. When he told his Harvard tutor that he wanted to be an elementary school teacher, the tutor responded, "Oh, no, you don't. Harvard men don't do things like that."

"Oh, but I'm not a Harvard man," replied Kohl. "I [go] to Harvard and [pay] my dues, but I'm from the Bronx." Kohl had no desire to be wealthy. He was proud to do his work among ordinary people, since he felt all people were ordinary. But he wanted to be certain that wealthy people could not control his life (H. Kohl, interviews with author, April 4, June 6, 1997).

Kohl graduated from Harvard magna cum laude in 1958, and won two postgraduate fellowships: a Henry fellowship to study at Oxford University in 1958–1959 and a Woodrow Wilson fellowship for 1959–1960. He spent part of the time in Paris, listening to the philosophical discussions about the writers Jean-Paul Sartre, Albert Camus, Simone de Beauvoir, and Maurice Merleau-Ponty; in these discussions he encountered existentialist ideas and found them useful for their explanatory power.

His encounter with existentialism had a permanent effect on Kohl's thinking. To this day he refers to existentialist ideas, especially the assertion that being is not fixed—becoming is more important. People have the capacity to transform both themselves and the world. Individuals must take responsibility for their actions, for creating their own selves, because people are not born with set, determined character and destiny. If one refuses to take responsibility for choice, one lives in bad faith with oneself and as a hypocrite in the world. One must struggle to live in good faith with oneself and others, acting consistently with one's best and most fundamental beliefs. These ideas guided his search for the person he wanted to be (Kohl, 1992; interviews with author, April 5, August 30, 2000).

After returning from Europe in 1960, Kohl taught for 6 months in a private school for severely disturbed children. He then decided that he preferred to teach in the public schools, where the challenge came from students who were angry and defiant, rather than suffering from severe psychiatric illnesses. To acquire the needed teaching credential, he enrolled at Teachers College, Columbia University, in special education, because there were scholarships for that (Kohl, 1974).

For his student teaching, Kohl was assigned to PS 41 on the Lower East Side near Peter Cooper Village and Stuyvesant Town. Most of the students were white; his class had six Puerto Rican and black students. He took them for reading lessons to a small room, where he got to know them well. One of them, Stanley, half Puerto Rican and half Jewish, the school considered a problem, because he was dark and spoke with a Spanish accent. But Kohl found him gentle, smart, and extremely artistic.

Already in this early teaching, Kohl's special characteristics emerged—the joy he took in doing interesting things with kids and recognizing their talents, in the opening of possibilities without constraint. For his demonstration lesson to the whole class, Kohl decided to present the cathedral at Chartres, with Stanley assisting by drawing to scale, in chalk on the board, the entire floor plan of Chartres.

On the day of the presentation, Kohl and Stanley came to class early so that Stanley could make the drawing. Unknown to them, the regular teacher was absent; a substitute walked in before the students arrived and ordered Stanley to erase his drawing from the board.

Kohl explained to the substitute that the drawing was part of the lesson he was planning to give, but she repeated to Stanley, "Erase that because I've got some exercises for the kids to do; you can do your lesson later." After repeated exchanges, Kohl interposed himself, saying, "He won't erase it. I'm going to teach this lesson, and we're going to do it this way. I'm sorry, but you can't do this."

The substitute walked out, and Kohl's lesson went smoothly. But when the morning was over, everything had been taken out of his locker. The principal handed it to him in a paper bag and told him: "You are gone. You can never come back to this school."

Kohl had 2 more weeks to complete student teaching. His college supervisor, an older, progressive woman, said, "Well, I figured this would happen to you." She assigned him to Walden School, a private progressive school, where he finished his student teaching and received his credential. But he didn't enjoy the students at Walden as much; they were smart in school but not as intelligent in life, and much too quiet. He preferred the working-class kids of public school (H. Kohl, interviews with author, April 4, June 6, 1997).

TEACHING IN NEW YORK CITY, 1962–1967

When Kohl began his teaching career in January 1962, 7½ years after the *Brown* decision, hope still abounded in the United States that somehow white people would stop being racists, or that enough nonracist white people could join with African American people to heal the wounds of society. But in New York City, no comprehensive effort to desegregate the schools ever materialized (H. Kohl, interviews with author, April 4, June 6, 1997).

For his first job in the New York public schools, Kohl was assigned to PS 145, on the Upper West Side of Manhattan, near Central Park, the neighborhood of the musical *West Side Story*. Most of the children were Puerto Rican, and a few were Irish, Haitian and Dominican.

On his first job Kohl felt good about himself as an independent adult working in a way consistent with his beliefs about social and economic justice for everybody. But he was also stunned by what he found.

> I plunged right into the middle of what were fundamentally racist systems in which the racism was overt, clear, unambiguous in terms of what people said about the kids and their parents. . . . People were calling kids "animals" and using the so-called "N" word. I was shocked, just shocked. In that sense I was innocent. I'm not innocent about too many things, but I was really innocent about the way in which the kids were treated and therefore the almost unambiguous failure that would have to be a consequence of that kind of treatment—what it would take to succeed when you're considered to be incapable of learning. (H. Kohl, interviews with author, April 4, June 6, 1997)

When Kohl found that it was against the rules of the New York Board of Education for students to speak Spanish, he defied the rules, because he believed that they were unjust. He encouraged his students to become bilingual in ways that built on the strengths they already had in their home language. He worked with the few African American students, protecting them from the racism of the school's administrators. But this involved questioning the principal and being insubordinate; after 6 months Kohl found himself being involuntarily transferred to a school in Harlem that had 90% African American students and a 45% turnover in staff every year. This was a common strategy in New York City for getting rid of troublesome teachers.

It is significant that Kohl did not go to Harlem in order to teach black kids; he was involuntarily assigned there by the school administration: "I am not a do-gooder and did not go to Harlem to save anybody. I went to teach. I'm a teacher. I'm an educator. I'll educate anybody's kids. . . . My goals are as unambiguously serious for any kids I teach. . . . If teaching means having to fight alongside a community for what is right and just, that is part of teaching. I mean, teaching is a moral profession" (H. Kohl, interviews with author, April 4, June 6, 1997).

During 1962, Kohl received a master's degree in Special Education, and in September he began teaching in Harlem at PS 103, the same school his mother had attended sometime between 1915 and 1925, when the community had been Jewish and Italian. He rejected the idea, then in fashion, that these students were culturally disadvantaged or in need of remediation. He had taught them before and knew them to be as intelligent as any other children in the world. He did what he always did as an educator; he gave them everything he knew or could provide or could discover.

> I was lucky coming from a working-class immigrant family. . . . It's come a little easier for me than for other very good-willed people who just don't have the advantage of having grown up in communities that other people look down upon. I mean, once you understand that attitude, you realize it's not your problem, it's their problem. Now I've never been focused on trying to change the rich. My role has been to empower those people who are brilliant but victimized. (H. Kohl, interviews with author, April 4, June 6, 1997)

Kohl got the top-level sixth-grade class, designated 601. He had 36 children; the bottom-level classes had only about 24 students. In Kohl's class perhaps six students could read at sixth-grade level in the fall when he started with them. He began using the available textbook, *How We Became Modern America*, which was filled with "stories about family fun in a Model T Ford, the first wireless radio in town, and the joys of wealth and progress." The stories contained such statements as "The Industrial Revolution was a benefit to all" and "Modern America is a place of freedom for all." Kohl couldn't bear these insults to the students; he told them he didn't like the textbook, because it was filled with lies about how things are. He believes that he made his connection with his students when he was able to respond honestly regarding the textbook; from this, they realized that their teacher was really on their side (Kohl, 1967, 1968).

Late in October, Kohl asked his students to write descriptions of the city block where they lived and followed by asking them to describe how they would change their block if they could. What they wrote opened his eyes to their lives:

> How could the children get some saving perspective on the mad chaotic world they existed in, some sense of the universality of struggle, the possibility of revolution and change, and the strength to persist? That, if anything, was my challenge as a teacher; it was spelled out before me unambiguously. Could I find anything in human history and the human soul that would strengthen the children and save them from despair? (Kohl, 1967, p. 52)

As soon as the year was under way, Kohl began visiting with the parents of his students in their homes. He created friendships with them, cared about them as people, and engaged himself in their lives with their children. His students knew him as a guest in their homes and a participant in their community. This dimension of his work seems to him essential; teachers who can't do it, he is confident, can't succeed in the way in which he did (M. Kohl, interview with author, August 18, 1998).

On Halloween, when the streets in Harlem were wild with celebration, Kohl met Judith Murdock, who was just moving into a first-floor apartment below his fifth-floor one, where he lived two miles down from

Harlem. They talked well into the night, Kohl able to articulate the contradictions of his classroom for the first time and, with Murdock, begin to formulate a response to what the children were teaching him. Murdock, raised in California and just returning from several years in Europe, was soon working as a substitute in the New York City schools. On March 22, 1963, 5 months after meeting, they were married, with the full support of the 36 children in 601 (Kohl, 1967).

Kohl responded to his students' writing about what they would do to change their block by creating a curriculum for them that focused on the creation of culture and society brought about by the early Egyptians, Mesopotamians, and Greeks. By studying how these early peoples created culture, he engaged his students in considering how the civil rights movement, and they, could remake culture into one in which everyone contributed to making the world better. His students flowered, developing their own personalities and talents, transformed from the suspicious, indifferent beings they had been in the opening weeks of school. By the end of the year, most were reading at 6th-grade level, and one had reached 12th-grade level (Kohl, 1967).

The following year, Kohl taught the bottom-level sixth-grade class, and again found that he could support his students in rapid growth and creativity, this time focusing directly on contemporary events in the United States. That September, white racists killed four African American girls in Birmingham, and in November President Kennedy was assassinated. Malcolm X was preaching on the streets a few blocks away. Kohl's frustration with the administration of the school led him to approach community leaders in Harlem.

> I told them it was criminal that the principal didn't get books when kids are entitled to books, that there's a lie about the kids' achievement and what actually happens in the school. It's the kids' lives at stake; they actually don't survive. I told the community organizations the only way I could see of doing anything was to have parents come in and insist that the teachers become accountable to the parents, as in most suburban schools. (Kohl, 1968, 1998a)

During this year, Kohl listened to an African American colleague at his school, Joshua Robbins, who told Kohl that his curriculum, based on Greek, Latin, and western European culture, was not enough for his students. They needed black history, an Afrocentric curriculum, if they were to gain enough strength to resist racism. Pushed by these conversations, Kohl learned to integrate cultural studies into every aspect of his sixth-grade curriculum (Kohl, 1998a).

Kohl also carried out his plan of writing philosophy while he was teaching. In April of his year with 36 children, a month after his marriage, he began to write and continued the following year, while teaching his second class of sixth graders. By the end of the summer of 1964 he had finished his first book, a collection of contemporary philosophical writings called *The Age of Complexity*. He wrote an introduction in which he developed the idea that "the world is complex, and don't try to simplify that complexity. Don't try to find one underlying principle . . . or two major principles. Don't try to marginalize any of that; face and live with it in that complexity" (H. Kohl, interviews with author, April 4, June 6, 1997).

After 2 years of teaching sixth grade, Kohl faced difficult questions: What would happen to his students in junior high? He felt as though he were preparing lambs for the slaughter. Was it possible to function usefully within the existing school system? Must one get out and agitate to change the system? Or can one stay enclosed in a "successful" classroom, ignoring everything that subsequently happens to one's pupils? If he stayed, Kohl wanted to teach kindergarten, but New York City regulations prohibited male teachers in kindergarten. Racial tensions were increasing in Harlem; white people were becoming less welcome (Kohl, 1967, 1998a).

The Kohls decided to take a year's leave from teaching, from August 1964 to August 1965, to live simply in the Catalan area of Spain. They moved to a remote mountain village called Martinet, and during that year Herb drafted a novel and made the decision to continue working with children, but on the margins of the public system, attempting to reform the system from the periphery. Kohl was, and has remained, committed to public schools, not as they existed then or now, but rather as he dreamed they could become.

The Kohls returned to New York City, where Judy taught at the Manhattan School for the Severely Disturbed and Herb enrolled for a doctorate at Teachers College, Columbia University. He secured a scholarship that supported his work in Harlem. He arranged to teach a class for some of his former students and attached it to Teachers College. He was looking for an effective way to be involved with New York City schools from the outside, and in 1966 the opportunity began to develop. Kohl was invited to a national conference on the teaching of writing, funded by the U.S. Office of Science and Technology. He insisted that other teachers, not just college professors, be present, and he wrote his first essay, "Teaching the 'Unteachable,'" about what he and other teachers had learned from their students, about how listening to their voices opened the way for them to improve and learn. At the conference, teachers read some of their students' work, followed by established writers—Denise Levertov, Grace Paley, Muriel Rukeyser, and Anne Sexton—reading their own work. Their writing opened a new world to Kohl, who began to imagine how writers and teachers could work together.

After that pivotal conference, Kohl wrote a $1.2 million proposal to the U.S. Office of Education for the establishment of Teachers and Writers Collaborative, whose mission would be to change throughout the nation the way writing was taught in public schools. Writers would work in classrooms to find ways of putting creative expression at the center of the curriculum. When $82,000 of grant money came through, Kohl cut short his graduate work to become the founding director of the collaborative, characteristically more attracted to this than to the university milieu. As director, Kohl worked with a group of teachers and writers who, by focusing on the voices of children and the process of imaginative writing, pioneered the various writing projects that have led to reforms in public school writing instruction over the past 20 years. Teachers and Writers Collaborative grew and flourished as an organization, celebrating its 30th anniversary in 1997. It has supplied writers from diverse cultural backgrounds to the schools, now serving more than 10,000 students a year, and has published some of the most exciting books available about teaching language and writing (Kohl, 1998a; Teachers and Writers Collaborative, 1990; H. Kohl, interview with author, February 27, 1978).

Just before the funding for Teachers and Writers Collaborative began to come through, in late 1966, Kohl was hit in an intersection by a speeding car. His left femur was shattered, but a surgeon with experience in World War II was able to piece it together using a metal plate.

Kohl used his time in a wheelchair to finish his first book about teaching, *Thirty-six Children,* which appeared in 1967. It received enthusiastic critical acclaim, along with a book called *Death at an Early Age,* by Kohl's Harvard classmate Jonathan Kozol. Both books attacked the racism of the North that sabotaged the education of African American children, Kohl by describing education in New York City and Kozol that in Boston. Kohl chose to focus, not on the grim realities of the school system, but on the joyous creativity of the children, whose work pervades his book. By bringing resources to the students and giving them the freedom to follow their imagination, Kohl demonstrated the possibilities of what could be done, even in classrooms of 36 children. He provided abundant evidence that the difficulties lay, not with Harlem's children, but with the system of education and with teachers' attitudes. His book has been in print continuously for 35 years (Kohl, 1998a).

Thirty-six Children is still read today, because it is more than a teacher's tale from the classroom. It is an attack on the thesis that black children can't learn, an argument that was widely made in the 1960s in the intellectual and academic community and in the general media. Kohl wrote five drafts of the book, seeking a genre that would reach an audience beyond a narrow academic one. He chose to seem more naive than he was in order to reach a wide audience. He imagined his ideal audience as his Aunt Addy, rather than a tiny academic circle (H. Kohl, interviews with author, April 5, August 30, 2000).

By the late 1960s, integration had not yet come to New York City; its dense and separate neighborhoods made integration particularly difficult to implement. One integrated school was being planned in Harlem, near the Triborough Bridge, at PS 201, but the plan quickly became a community-control struggle in which black and Puerto Rican leaders decided that they should take over the school, that white people simply could not educate their children. Kohl supported these leaders in what turned out to be a major event in his life. When the United Federation of Teachers threw a picket line around the school to protest the community's takeover, Kohl had to decide whether to cross the line. Loyal to his grandfather's principles, Kohl had been an active union member. But this time he choose to fight racism rather than support the union; to support the black and Puerto Rican leaders, he relinquished his grandfather's most dearly held principle (Kohl, 1998a; interviews with author, April 4, June 6, 1997, August 18, 1998).

> If I was clear about anything after my first six years of being a teacher and an educational activist, it was that my first priority had to be the children. Loyalty to any idea, institution, or organization was secondary. If the children are nurtured, are learning, are treated with dignity and affection; if their voices are honored and their thoughts respected; if their culture and language are welcomed; and if they are acquiring skills and learning about the world and themselves, then I am willing to be loyal to the learning community. A teachers' union has to be judged on the quality of its members' work. When the union tries to blame children, parents—anything but its members—for failure, I refuse to go along. If humiliation, incompetence, and dread of learning characterize an institution, then I oppose it and am willing to take the consequences of speaking out against it. (Kohl, 1998a, p. 174)

In this battle over community control of schools, the community suffered a defeat at the hands of Albert Shanker and the teachers' union, and Kohl experienced the defeat of a cause he supported. He understood that in fighting for something, you may lose, but that does not mean the cause is wrong; you simply have to keep fighting (H. Kohl, interviews with author, April 5, August 30, 2000).

Meanwhile, living in New York City was becoming more difficult for the Kohls. Their first child, Antonia, had been born in July 1967, in the middle of the community schools battle. Herb was suffering from asthma, exacerbated by the pollution. When in spring 1968, Kohl was invited to be visiting lecturer in both the English department and the School of Education at the University of California–Berkeley, the Kohls accepted the chance to leave New York City for a period of rest (Kohl, 1998a).

BERKELEY, 1968–1977

Kohl was not intrigued by his new students, who seemed to him more concerned with figuring out what the professor wanted from them than with learning what they wanted to know. During this time, Kohl finished *The Open Classroom,* subtitled *A Practical Guide to a New Way of Teaching.* Continuing the explorations introduced in *Thirty-six Children* of how a teacher finds his way to alter how he teaches, it includes many practical suggestions that demonstrate Kohl's skill in the classroom. Some teachers and school districts conceived of the "open classroom" in the physical sense, as having flexible partitions; other people perceived it chiefly as antiauthoritarian. But Kohl was exploring the teacher's inner dilemma of how to be emotionally honest, in dialogue with the students, neither authoritarian nor permissive, as he or she strives to connect students' interests to the demands of rigorous learning.

After 6 months at UC–Berkeley, Kohl teamed up with the artist Allan Kaprow and accepted a grant from the Carnegie Corporation to develop a teacher training program affiliated with the Berkeley Unified School District. Called Other Ways, this project, within a year, developed into a public alternative high school, which Kohl directed for another 2 years. During these 3 years the Kohls welcomed the birth of two additional children, Erica and Joshua (Kohl, 1998a).

The first year of Other Ways turned out to be an adventure in group dynamics. Kohl chose six other people to be colleagues, three of them African American. Once a week they held an afternoon open house for teachers in the area and continued meeting as a support group for dinner and the evening. In addition, they worked with young people in nontraditional ways. As a group they wanted to reinvent cultural modes that would overcome hierarchy, racism, and sexism; they succeeded less with sexism than with the other two elements. As a person, Kohl was learning new ways to deal with his peers, more difficult for him than working with children, overcoming his tendencies toward anger and impatience with incompetence and lack of commitment (Kohl, 1974).

In the second 2 years of the grant, 1969–1971, Kohl and his colleagues ran an alternative school for about 70 students who were not fitting well into the regular high school system. About half the students were European American, half children of color. Many had experience with theater and music, and Kohl helped them develop a theater troupe. By the end of the first year, when the school had grown to 80 full-time and 35 part-time students, the school district had rented an old factory for them (Kohl, 1974, 1998a).

Despite the success with the students, the school failed as an institution, for many reasons, among them the temporary funding, which was inadequate and resulted in exhaustion for the faculty and staff. The school district looked on Other Ways as temporary and expected it to vanish with the funding (H. Kohl, interviews with author, April 5, August 30, 2000).

After Other Ways failed to survive, Kohl took a year to write and to care for his own three preschool-age children. Then he turned to a project he had long endorsed—credentialing more people of color to be teachers. The Berkeley school district had hired some Latinos, African Americans, and Asian Americans as "facilitators" in the schools. They were given the responsibilities of teachers, yet they could not remain in their jobs without a teaching credential, which they couldn't earn without resigning from their jobs, because credential programs were not organized for working adults.

To meet the needs of these uncredentialed teachers, Kohl and others set up the Center for Open Learning and Teaching and designed a credential program with classes in the afternoon and evenings. This program became part of the University Without Walls, operated in Berkeley by Westminster College, located in Fulton, Missouri. In seminars and workshops, student teachers explored the complex issues of multicultural education at a time when this notion was new. In a woodworking shop, they constructed multicultural games and materials for their classrooms. Between 1972 and 1975, 45 teachers, two thirds of them people of color, received California credentials through this program (Kohl, 1998a).

During the last 2 years of the program, Kohl set up his own kindergarten–first-grade classroom in a public school and served as master teacher to a succession of credential candidates. At the same time, he was able to keep up a continuous stream of writing. Three of his books about teaching appeared during those years: *Reading: How To* (1973); *Games, Math, and Writing in the Open Classroom* (1973); and *On Teaching* (1976). In addition, from 1968 until 1980, Kohl wrote a column called "Insight" for *Teacher Magazine,* in which he shared his work and inspired progressive teachers nationwide (Kohl, 1998a).

During these high-energy years in Berkeley, Kohl was bothered by his asthma, which seemed triggered even by Berkeley's low levels of pollution. In addition, his previously injured left hip had become increasingly painful, causing him to limp and to avoid lifting heavy objects. He wanted to move to a rural place for the clean air and simpler living, but moving did not seem feasible with his lame hip, until he learned that his hip could be restored. The plate used to hold the femur together while it healed needed to be removed, for it was generating an electric current that caused the pain. A successful operation in the spring of 1977 cleared the way for a move.

Before leaving Berkeley, Kohl wrote an article for a local magazine in which he reflected on his 9 years living in Berkeley and concluded:

Herb Kohl with first-grade boy, Berkeley, California, 1973.
Photo © Elizabeth Crews.

Berkeley, with its liberal gloss, with its radical pretensions, never has come to terms with the racism that pervades much of the life in this community. . . . In some ways, desegregation [begun in September 1969] in Berkeley created a kind of false euphoria, an attempt to believe that deep problems could be solved not only by mechanical means, exclusively in the schools, but would be solved through the children. . . . The exodus from the public schools in Berkeley is no different than in New York, Chicago, Detroit, or Philadelphia. Our enrollment has gone from about 14,500 students to around 11,000. Berkeley, in effect, has become America. . . . Our efforts here haven't been totally without effect, but it's been terribly, terribly hard to change this community. Terribly hard because most radical analysis that I've seen doesn't really understand this community. That is, it doesn't take the community as a whole. It either looks solely at the University or at the oppressed parts of the community. To look at the whole community is to see America again. It brings up the very persistent thought that solutions will emerge only through a re-distribution of the wealth of the community. (Kohl, 1977, pp. 43–46)

POINT ARENA, 1977–1988

In August 1977, the Kohls found their new home, near a small, nontourist town called Point Arena, 3 hours north of San Francisco on the coast. From the sale of their Berkeley house, they were able to buy a house set on 11 acres of land, five miles inland. In addition to the house, there were three cabins and a garage, plus two other outbuildings.

Judy Kohl set up a weaving studio off the garage and used her skill in design and carpentry to renovate the buildings. Together the Kohls set up a learning center and library in one building, and eventually they estab-lished the Coastal Ridge Research and Education Center, which sponsored workshops for parents, teachers, and community leaders.

In October 1977 in Tennessee, the Kohls visited Highlander Research and Education Center, formerly Highlander Folk School, which served as the model for the Coastal Ridge Center. Kohl recognized that Myles Horton shared his deepest values and could be a mentor to him. Eventually Herb and Judy became close friends of Horton and helped him write his auto-biography, *The Long Haul*. At Highlander Kohl also became friends with Septima Clark and, recognizing how significant her story was, arranged the interviews that resulted in her autobiography, *Ready from Within: Septima Clark and the Civil Rights Movement* (H. Kohl, interview with au-thor, October 30, 1977).

As an educator, Kohl always worked for equity and justice. In his teach-ing, he is explicit and unambiguous about this:

I'm not telling my students what to do, but I'm teaching them that unless equity, justice and a deep sense of social responsibility lie at the center of their being, they're missing some very important part of humanity in themselves. . . . [Some resist that], but I tell them it's really up to them to make up their minds. My stu-dents—even ones who fundamentally disagree with me—tend to respect the fact that I respect them.

I do not, by the way, tolerate racist behavior in my class. Period. If that is manifested, I will do anything I possibly can to persuade people to change their attitudes or to keep their mouths shut. . . . My job as an educator is to create a learning community. There's certain kinds of behaviors that disrupt other people's ability to learn. If I call you a "Kike" or a "Spic" or a "Wop" or something like that, then you can't learn that much because you're becoming a self-conscious victim consumed by your rage or are constantly on edge. Therefore, the person who called you that is interfering with your learning. . . . On the other hand, I talk with people after school. I'll spend a lot of time with them. I'll offer everything I can, but I will not tolerate that behavior. (H. Kohl, interviews with author, April 4, June 6, 1997)

In the tradition of his grandparents, Kohl considered himself a socialist and confronted the dilemma of what the role of schools should be in creating a humane socialist system.

In our society "socialism" is a dirtier word than "fuck," and in the schools, using socialism in a positive context is as likely to get you fired as is allowing your students to publish a magazine called "It's Fucked." . . . The question that we have to consider is whether in a non-revolutionary context, being fired or remaining within the system and pushing it to the limits of what is currently possible to do is the better strategy.
    . . . I don't believe a new social order can be built through the schools. I do believe that schools will be an essential part of a new order that is built through the cooperative effort of all of us: teachers, miners, factory workers, professionals—all the people who believe in the social and moral imperative of struggling towards a new order. Thus I find that the crucial question should not be "do the schools have the power to change society?" so much as "what small power can we use in working with others to change society?" And if we do begin to change it, what will be the role of us as teachers in building a lasting new order? (Kohl, 1979, pp. 6, 8)

In the early 1980s, Kohl continued to write at a dizzying rate, sometimes with three or four books appearing in one year. He once explained that he had learned from his contractor father how to keep several projects going simultaneously. Since he had studied math at Harvard and had learned about the beginning of computers, he was able to write two early books about computer games and recreations: *Atari Games and Recreations* (1982) and *Atari PILOT Games and Recreations for Learning* (1983). With Judy, and from their experience living in the country, he wrote two books of ethnography for children, one of which won the National Book Award for Children's Literature: *The View from the Oak: The Private Worlds of Other Creatures* (1977) and *Pack, Band, and Colony* (1983). He wrote books about literary and math puzzles, a curriculum for Amnesty International, a book about parenting, and several more about teaching.

ROVING TEACHER, 1988–PRESENT

By 1988 the Kohls' three children were off to college—Tonia to the Rhode Island School of Design, Erica to Reed College, and Joshua to the New

England Conservatory of Music. This gave Kohl and his wife more flex-
ibility, and he arranged to teach two semesters in St. Paul, Minnesota, at
Hamline College, a predominately working-class Methodist college (Kohl,
1998a).

At Hamline College Kohl discovered that the admissions office selected
for admission some highly gifted minority students and gave scholarships
to minority athletes, with the consequence that some of the white students—
by no means all—felt threatened and manifested their racism. The racial
tolerance of most of the European American students had not been tested
before, since there had been no African Americans or other people of color
in their environment.

> They felt that now all of the students of color were competing with them and were
> going to shove them out of jobs and out of the best grades and out of the right
> roles. So you get some people who will talk about unqualified blacks, but in the
> case of this particular school, people were talking about over-qualified blacks
> coming to their school and pushing them out of what used to be their dominant
> role. So there is a lot of different ways in which racism is manifested. (H. Kohl,
> interviews with author, April 4, June 6, 1997)

Kohl found that college is the place where many white people first
confront the confusions of racism.

Herb and Judy Kohl, Point Arena, California, 1989. Photo © Nicolas King.

It's where the whole thing explodes, and it doesn't necessarily explode well. It's where the kids become problematized, where they end up sometimes more racist than they thought they were. Sometimes they end up alienated from their families. They end up in all kinds of confusion. . . . I find that most kids just desperately want someone to talk to about this. The taboo is you don't talk directly about it. (H. Kohl, interviews with author, April 4, June 6, 1997)

For Kohl, it is important to be aware of the whole continuum of white people's responses to being white, from feelings of being totally superior to having no such feelings.

On the most extreme level you get people who believe [that] this should be a white Christian nation and [that] people who are not both white and Christian are inferior. So you get race theorists, people who take a very, very strong overt position on race, and that would be the extreme of race sentiment. Then you get the Myles Hortons and other people in the world who are not racist. As far as I can tell in all my knowing Myles, he was not racist. He may have been when he grew up. Who knows? I'm sure it was an act of discovery for him. In the middle you get people who are intermittently confused by issues of race, and then you get a predominant number of people who really become racist . . . whenever their security is threatened. It's the fault of blacks. It's the fault of welfare queens. Then you have to separate the people who stir that up—people from the Manhattan Institute and the Lynde and Harry Bradley Foundation in Milwaukee. Some people in the Moral Majority are a little bit more open to a multi-racial Christian nation than others. So I think that any simple fix on why white people are so racist is foolish. It's bound to fail when you want to deal with the issue. You've got to find out where people really are, how they position themselves on issues of race, and how they've encountered those issues. (H. Kohl, interviews with author, April 4, June 6, 1997)

Kohl's sensitivity to the moral choices faced by every person is rooted in his existentialist beliefs:

You don't know what you'll do under severe and extreme personal tests unless those tests confront you. I happen to be an unreconstructed existentialist, i.e. you make decisions in the course of your life, and the authenticity of your life has to do with the responsibility you take for those decisions that you make. Because you are forced to make those decisions. The question becomes not whether you make them or not, because you have to, but the question is how you relate to decisions you've made on a moral ground. That's how you make yourself as a social person and as a person. I do my best to take responsibility for those things. It's not easy. (Kohl, 1998b)

During the years that Kohl taught in Minnesota, he wrote an extended essay about student resistance to learning that is making a significant contribution to reducing the racism of white teachers. In this long essay, titled "I Won't Learn from You: The Role of Assent in Learning" (1994), Kohl explores some of the possible reasons why students refuse to learn. He starts with his own experience of refusing to learn Yiddish from his paternal grandparents because learning it would have entailed excluding his mother, who didn't speak Yiddish, from conversations. Kohl goes on to present stories of African American and Hispanic young people who have their own personal and cultural reasons for not learning certain things.

His essay helps some white teachers, who may assume that students of color don't learn because these students are not capable, rather than because these students are making a choice. A coherence is apparent in Kohl's work, based on the existentialist ideas he is employing. Through this lens, he sees young people as actors in history, not as perpetual victims. If no person is only what they are at the moment, then the realm of possibility becomes the focus of a teacher's work. Believing that people have an abundant capacity for choice enables Kohl to see in students' behavior what others frequently overlook. In the essay, Kohl takes part in an ongoing theoretical discussion being conducted in academic circles about resistance theory, about why people become delinquent. It provoked a round of academic articles in response, demonstrating that Kohl's audience was not limited to a popular one (H. Kohl, interviews with author, April 5, August 30, 2000).

Two years later, in 1993, Kohl published an essay about Rosa Parks that won a national prize for journalism. Kohl had met Parks when she came to Berkeley in 1981 as the honored guest of the East Bay Friends of Highlander, who sponsored a testimonial dinner for her and for her teacher, Septima Clark. In his powerful essay, Kohl shows how stories about Parks written for the elementary classroom usually do not mention the white racism that is essential to understanding the story of what happened. Instead, a myth of "Rosa the Tired" had developed, which never refers to racism or to the fact that the overwhelming majority of white people in Montgomery were capable of being violent and cruel to maintain segregation. The myth portrays Parks as a tired woman who became angry that day in December 1955 and acted completely alone and solely as a result of her psychological state.

After establishing with precision just what the myth of Rosa the Tired is, Kohl demolishes it with additional historical information and insight. He rewrites the story of Rosa Parks for children of elementary school age, acknowledging both the racism of white people and the community context in which Parks worked and made her decisions. Kohl renamed the story "She Would Not Be Moved: The Story of Rosa Parks and the Montgomery Bus Boycott" and revealed how the African American community acted together to achieve the historic victory in Montgomery (Kohl, 1993, 1995).

In composing this essay, Kohl drew from many facets of his experience and beliefs to accurately portray the fullness of the Montgomery experience. He recognized, from his understanding of stereotypes, that the usual account of Parks depicted a stereotype. It couldn't be true, based on what he knew about community struggles, about how smart people are, and about how they make choices and decisions. He wanted to portray what really happened in Montgomery in order to have an example, a weapon, for other community struggles. He made it his business to find out—from Parks, from Myles Horton, from the historical record—how people in Montgomery worked together, and then managed to convey all the complexity in a short account for children. In doing so, Kohl contributed once again to changing white people's perceptions (H. Kohl, interview with author, August 18, 1998).

As he balanced teaching and writing, action and reflection, Kohl developed his instincts for teaching into real virtuosity. He learned while teaching kindergarten and first grade to have an eye in every part of his head, back as well as front. The eyes were not only for locating trouble; he watched all the children individually, to see what they did that they loved. That became the clue he needed, the key to reaching them and igniting their learning. As Kohl explained to a class of graduating teachers:

> If you do not love the people you teach, you shouldn't be there, and to love someone means very deeply to get to know them. Not to get them to conform to what you want necessarily, not to get them to be obedient to the demands of the state and of the system, but to get to know them as people, to look into their eyes, to figure out who they are, to actually have, as deep conviction, that inside each one of them is some dream of being beautiful, some dream of being powerful, some deep sense that I want to do something useful with my life no matter where I came from, no matter what I was gifted with or deprived of, that I would like to be a decent human being and I would like to be a beautiful human being. (Kohl, 2000)

In the early 1990s, as Kohl's mother was nearing the end of her life, he wanted to spend more time with her. His friends in the New York City school system wanted him to consult with them on how to create small, alternative high schools within the system. For several years, he balanced his writing and working with children in Point Arena with consulting in New York City, while completing about one book a year. (Kohl, 1998a)

Kohl does not glorify integration as the sole answer to education for African American children. On the contrary, he is keenly aware of the costs of integration to black children when they encounter the vicious racism of white students and adults. He also acknowledges that there had been some excellent segregated black schools in the years before the Supreme Court decision in the *Brown* case and that to say all-black schools are inherently unequal has racist implications. In the winter of 1996–1997, he published a review in *ReThinking Schools* of two memoirs by black people who had faced white racism while integrating schools in the late 1950s. In one, *Warriors Don't Cry*, Melba Pattillo Beals recounts her experience as one of nine African Americans integrating Central High School in Little Rock, Arkansas, in 1957. The other, *Silver Rights*, tells the story of Mae Bertha and Matthew Carter and 7 of their 13 children, who integrated schools in Drew, Mississippi. In his review of these books, Kohl discussed the price African Americans must pay in going to schools with a dominant white culture and power structure:

> If the problem addressed by the Brown decision were redefined as racism and forced separation instead of integration, remedies would have to confront white privilege and racism. The "inherency" argument avoids this issue. It assumes that white schools are worth becoming part of, rather than institutions that need to be radically transformed as their demographics change.
>
> What kind of schools are African Americans and Latino students being asked to integrate into? And on what terms? What does it mean if we are asking students to integrate into racist institutions? This is not an argument against bringing together children of diverse backgrounds. It is a warning that unless white people take a responsibility to forge anti-racist curriculum and learning environments, we will fail. (Kohl, 1996/1997, pp. 22–23)

Since he stopped teaching at UC–Berkeley, Kohl has depended on his writing for income, together with whatever work he can find or create that is consistent with his values. As his 60th birthday approached, Kohl was sought out by the Open Society Institute, a foundation supported by the Hungarian-American philanthropist George Soros. The institute considered Kohl one of the few educators in the United States who have kept human and civil rights at the center of their work. Kohl found the work of the Open Society Institute sufficiently congruent with his own moral objectives to accept a full-time job as senior fellow, from June 1997 to January 2000. Through this institute Soros wants to support the continuation in the United States of an open society, which he defines as a complex system, with flexible structures and a regulated market economy, that requires all participants to act as autonomous decision-making units. Responsible for advising the foundation on how to give money in the areas of education and children's services, Kohl traveled frequently to New York City from San Francisco and Point Arena, where the Kohls divide their time on the West Coast (Soros, 1991).

One of the most common questions people ask Kohl is whether the schools are worse now than they were when he began teaching. He answers no, they are just about as bad. However, he believes that unfortunately conditions in the world beyond are much harsher; the economic situation of parents has worsened, while society has become more cynical, more willing to demonize young people. The will on the part of adults to change schools seems to have lessened; people tend to be even more obsessed with their own children, to the detriment of other people's (Kohl, 1998a, 1998b).

Kohl's criticism of capitalism remains as thoroughgoing as ever. Times are harder than usual, he believes, with increasing concentration of wealth at the top and increasing misery at the bottom. Global capitalism, the idea that profit is the only thing that counts, seems crazy to him, an iceberg that will melt down and collapse eventually and something new will be born. He cannot understand or tolerate that people can live in a world where their comfort comes at the cost of other people's discomfort, and not care that this is so. Particularly, he does not understand the deep psychology of greed, of people's need to make more money than they can use and their willingness to consume lavishly, never saying, "I have enough" (H. Kohl, interviews with author, April 5, August 30, 2000).

Nevertheless, Kohl believes deeply that most people are, for the most part, decent at their center, that they would prefer to live in a humane society where the needs of all are met. Now that he has been a Californian for 32 years, he references his vision for society to the End Poverty in California Program espoused by the socialist Upton Sinclair when Sinclair lost the race for California governor in 1934. Kohl wants to end poverty—he wants there not to be a single poor child in the United States. He wants the total elimination of racism and ethnic discrimination, completely free education from kindergarten to graduate school for everybody with the skills and capacity to learn, jobs for everyone with a living wage, and decent housing and free health care for all. *Social justice* is a short name for the program outlined here, the components a decent civil society would provide for all its citizens. He has not abandoned his roots, for he believes that there must be a more equitable way than capitalism to distribute wealth, access, property, and opportunity (H. Kohl, interviews with author, April 5, August 30, 2000).

Since the outrageously wealthy will not give up their power easily, Kohl expects struggle. Given the current climate, he does not have the slightest idea how his goals will be achieved. But he expects that they will come about through conscience, especially the conscience of young people, and through a sense that people have that there is a lack of community.

Look at the enormous number of community-based projects that do exist and find ways to help them come together with each other, through the transformation of the expectation in the schools in what people think that kids can do. . . . Through the marshalling of all those people of decency who are doing things, who care about people beyond themselves, to network with each other and begin to create some political and social sense that things can change. There are hundreds of ways to do it, not one large way, not one simple slogan that is going to change all this. (H. Kohl, interviews with author, April 5, August 30, 2000)

Kohl's ability to hope—to envision a better future and hope for it against great odds—underlies his special capacity for teaching. In the late 1990s he looked at his career afresh with the perspective of many decades and came up with the phrase "the discipline of hope" to describe what he had been doing:

What I realized was that for me teaching was, in effect, a discipline of hope— the whole idea that if you cannot find a way to provide hope for your students, you're not going to succeed no matter what skills you teach them. It doesn't make any difference to have skills and have no hope. But the discipline part of it is that you can't just have hope, in a rather romantic and loose manner, with no skills. You'll deceive yourself and then someone will come and take advantage of you. Then you run up against a dead end. . . . In the book [*The Discipline of Hope*] I've tried to encourage people, not in a romantic way but in a truly romantic way. I am still a romantic in the sense that I still believe in kids much more passionately than ever before, but not romantic in the sense of in my lifetime I'm going to see society be decent. I don't think I believe that anymore. I believe that my great-great-great-grandchildren might have an opportunity to see some of the fruits of some of our labor. But I think that the struggle is worth doing and the children are worth doing it for. (Kohl, 1998b)

Specifically, Kohl believes that "schools of hope" are safe, welcoming places for young people where the staff, parents, and community are in accord with the opinion that every child can learn. The faculty are free to innovate, while taking responsibility for their students' achievement. Resources are equalized, and every school has the resources it needs. High standards are appropriate for students and teachers, but not without fiscal equality and equal opportunity. Kohl is uncompromisingly opposed to vouchers, which he sees as an attempt to destroy democratic education. The idea that public money could be used to subsidize private corporations is entirely unacceptable to him. He believes that many of his former students embody in their lives the driving educational ideas of his own life, "that everyone can learn; that you can become the person you want to be and do work that you love; that whatever you do with your life, you can also do things for others; and that being thoughtful and possibly controversial and unpopular can be morally more sensible than being passive and conforming" (Kohl, 1998a).

After he concluded his fellowship at the Open Society Institute, Kohl chose to return once again to teacher education, creating a new credential program called the Center for Teaching Excellence and Social Justice. Launching this new program at the University of San Francisco proved extremely challenging. There was much competition among credential programs for the available candidates going into teaching. The ones who are committed to social justice are seldom able to pay even the tuition, much less the cost of housing in San Francisco, which increased about 25% in the year 1999–2000 alone. But Kohl signed up the necessary candidates, and the program opened in September 2000 (H. Kohl, interviews with author, April 5, August 30, 2000).

Kohl has created a life of unusual complexity and focus. Rooted in his teaching, he has also, through his writing, engaged in serious intellectual issues with a popular audience. All his books combined have sold close to 2 million copies over 35 years. Fifteen to 20 are currently in print, with 4 being reissued in 1999 and 2000. Through an interplay of teaching and writing, he has explored his unambiguous obsession for equity and justice (H. Kohl, interviews with author, April 5, August 30, 2000). He admits:

> I am not a model for anybody's life, I burned out a few times definitely, but there are several ways that I've been able to continue. I've been blessed with a wonderful family. I'm an obsessive worker. I think I inherited from my father and grandfather the inability to relax, to not be working. As I have written, I have taught all kinds of different grade levels. I've moved from high school to kindergarten. . . . I've not stayed in the public school system, working for the system all my life. Nobody was there to drive me crazy. Nobody was there to tell me what I couldn't do. I just refuse to accept the rules, the regulations, the restraints, the constraints, the restrictions that go against my conscience as both a person and as an educator. Sometimes it's been easy, and sometimes it's been very difficult. Sometimes I'm astonished I did survive, quite frankly. The joy of the kids, of teaching—I really love teaching, and I find that a constant source of hope and inspiration. (Kohl, 1998b)

Kohl is still creating himself through the decisions he makes and the risks he takes. He has had the courage to form his own judgments and live by them, consciously maximizing his freedom to be the person he chooses to be. He is a fiercely moral person whose decisions are not, as Virginia Durr's were for her, the only choice he feels he could have made. At every step, Kohl considers his inner questions: Why must I continue? Haven't I done my duty? As a teacher and writer, he sees his life as consisting of small successes, major failures, and continued struggle. A lot of where he thought we would be, in terms of the power of kids and the effectiveness of public schools, has simply not happened. And he never dreamed that the issue of race would be as contentious and terrible as it still is.

Today, Kohl feels, it is not a matter of being a white ally, but of being an ally in the long struggle for equity and justice. Being a white ally is to distance yourself from people you struggle with. "My advice to white people," he says, "is to focus on personhood, to struggle for everybody. Don't be afraid of criticism, defeats, and of making certain sacrifices. Take the joy that comes from solidarity, because it's enormous" (H. Kohl, interviews with author, April 5, August 30, 2000).

Nowadays Kohl thinks often of his father's favorite saying: "If God lived on earth, all His windows would be broken." Kohl restates that as "What kind of person would make a messed-up world if He had the power?" Kohl's life has been filled with a sense of outrage at human suffering in the world and an unending sense of struggle to reduce it.

6

Reflections

I CHERISH THE PEOPLE whose life stories I have told. They rejected the lie of race and gained the strength to control and define themselves. Through their moral imaginations, they reached decisions that shaped their lives and changed their society. Three of the stories portray white southerners who found productive ways to live in southern culture, helping to change it while rejecting its racist assumptions. The final story tells of a white northerner who saw through the complexities of hidden racism and found ways to confront it, when he could easily have dodged the issue. These stories fill me with hope and reassure me that human beings have the power to do what these four people did.

In the Introduction, I called attention to the moral courage that it took to see through the delusion of racial superiority and to act against it, as illustrated in the four stories I have told. Yet these four people did not think of themselves as especially courageous. They were aware that their paths were at times extremely difficult, but their self-identity was so closely aligned with their moral principles that they felt they had no choice. They could not act otherwise and be themselves. In general, they did not agonize over which choices to make; they accepted whatever the consequences would be, because they felt that the choices they made were the only possible ones.

How should the costs to these white allies be evaluated? Clifford and Virginia Durr lost their privileged jobs and home in suburban Washington, D.C., because of Clifford's principled stand against loyalty oaths. Later, he lost white clients in his law practice in Montgomery because he accepted African American clients; the couple lived on an income so low that at times they could not afford an apartment or new clothes for their children.

Waties Waring suffered exile from his hometown and culture, after enduring extreme ostracism from family and friends. But he found other friends and bigger worlds in compensation. Anne Braden's husband served two separate terms in jail, and they lived as social pariahs to a large part of Louisville. Durr, Braden, and Kohl suffered losses of possible income. Most people would consider these significant losses.

Yet these four allies did not feel that they sacrificed anything of great value to themselves. Rather, they felt they were able to work toward achieving that which was of great value to them—a world to live in free of the damage to themselves and to others of racial discrimination. They were aware that they were motivated in part by self-interest; they wanted to avoid the guilt, remorse, denial, projection, and moral confusion that they knew racism inflicted on white supremacists. They knew that what they did to others, they did to themselves. They wanted to live on good terms with humanity. This gain seemed so immense to them that the costs paled in comparison.

Other possible "losses" to consider are those of family connections and of cultural equilibrium, or "cultural disequilibrium," as Young and Rosiek call it in their review quoted in my Introduction. Waties Waring certainly suffered the ostracism and alienation of most of his extended family, but as a mature man, secure in his identity. The other three white allies managed to maintain loving relations with their extended families, despite severe disagreements and conflicts.

I interpret *cultural disequilibrium* as discomfort at dealing with cultures other than one's own, feeling that one's own is diminished or threatened by contact with other cultures. I do not believe that any of the people featured in this book felt this. For the southerners, African American culture was part of their culture, joined and intertwined for generations. Herb Kohl had no ambiguity about his identity as a secular Jew from the Bronx, where he was always in contact with other cultures and refusing to be limited by his own. Possibly this issue is more difficult for European Americans who are living in isolation from other cultures.

Cultural disequilibrium, however, could mean feeling out of balance with one's own culture when one rejected racism, a large piece of it. Certainly all four allies experienced this and dealt with it in their own ways— Waring by moving to New York, Braden by not moving, Durr by her sense of humor.

As I began conceiving this book, I expected to find patterns among the lives of these four allies. After learning about Virginia Durr's life, I imagined that perhaps all white allies had traumatically lost a black mother figure in childhood, as she had. I wanted to find a simplistic answer to what created these daring personalities.

But of course, no simple answer was to be found. I looked for an unusual degree of emotional security in childhood, a sense that the family thought the child was extra special. I believe that the four people portrayed in this book experienced that, yet so did many other people.

No patterns in the sources of morality emerged. For two (Virginia Durr and Anne Braden), the Protestant religion had a significant influence in childhood, but only Anne Braden maintained this connection into adulthood. Waties Waring depended on "the American creed" for his source of morality, while Anne Braden and Herb Kohl found moral resources in secular socialism.

I looked for patterns of support given to these white allies. All of them enjoyed the unwavering loyalty of their spouses, except Judge Waring, who found accord by remarrying. All found ways to create a community of friends and support, even though it meant going far beyond family and traditional friends.

Four significant traits that all four allies certainly shared were these: a high degree of energy with less-than-usual need for sleep, good health, unusual optimism, and a pronounced capacity for independent thinking.

Another trait that the allies seem to share is a relative lack of interest in material possessions and wealth. Judge Waring lived an elite lifestyle in Charleston, but he was able to give it up for a modest apartment in New York City. Virginia Durr enjoyed their sprawling farmhouse in Virginia, but it was not as important to her as her principles, and she was able to live in great simplicity. Anne Braden also does so as a matter of principle, as do Herb and Judy Kohl.

But all these possible generalizations seem oversimplifications. Nothing can be more complex than the way in which human beings develop and sustain their capacity for moral courage. When a person takes responsibility for his or her life, the process is unique for each person. These four white allies understood that they had the freedom to act differently from their friends and relatives. They could imagine a society without racial discrimination, and they let no excuse prevent them from acting to create that possibility. Above all, their lives show us how much more freedom we have than we usually care to admit, if we dare to take full responsibility for ourselves.

Three of these four stories highlight a dimension often hidden—the way in which anticommunist forces were arrayed against antiracist forces. As the stories of Virginia Durr, Anne Braden, and Herb Kohl vividly reveal, from 1945 through the 1970s people working for racial justice were usually charged with being Communist. This intimidated many white people who otherwise might have supported racial justice, and it doubled the courage required from white allies. In addition, at least two of these four white allies—Braden and

Kohl—were working for full social and economic justice, not merely for basic civil rights. For them, racial equality was a precondition to social and economic justice for everyone; their courage in fighting racial discrimination was sustained by this even larger commitment.

The stories of Anne Braden and Herb Kohl bring us up to the present, since they are still working vigorously to achieve social change and racial justice. Where in the long march toward racial justice are we now and what remains to be done?

It is always difficult to evaluate the present. Focusing on African Americans, an excellent case can be made that the circumstances of many, especially those in the middle and upper classes, have improved tremendously in the past 30 years (see Stephan Thernstrom and Abigail Thernstrom, *America in Black and White: One Nation Indivisible*). An equally strong case can be made that the two separate societies predicted by the Kerner Report in 1968 have come true (see Andrew Hacker, *Two Nations: Black and White, Separate, Hostile, and Unequal* and the sequel to the Kerner Report, *Locked in the Poorhouse: Cities, Race and Poverty in the United States*, edited by Fred R. Harris and Lynn A. Curtis).

I believe that we do not have to choose between these assessments; both seem to be valid simultaneously—social reality is complex. Data can be found to corroborate opposite hypotheses. We are immersed in a complicated historical process that cannot be calibrated exactly. The long march toward racial justice greatly accelerated about 50 years ago. Are we halfway to our goal of democratic, antiracist multiculturalism, or further or less far along? We don't know.

It is important to take hope from the the successes of the past half century that racial discrimination can be addressed. Much progress has been made since World War II, a social transformation in my lifetime, and that can be celebrated without concluding that racial justice has been achieved.

What remains to be done? What evidence suggests that racial justice still far eludes us?

Residential segregation has not lessened, on the whole, since 1968. It has decreased in certain cities, but increased in others, fueled by middle-class flight to the suburbs. The circumstances for many African Americans in the eight northern cities with the most extreme segregation—Buffalo, Chicago, Cleveland, Detroit, Gary, Milwaukee, New York, and Newark—are cause for despair. Many European Americans seem as unconcerned now about taking action to combat residential segregation as they were in 1945 (Massey & Denton, 1993, pp. 234–236).

Polls say that European Americans now support equal racial rights to a high degree. One poll in 1996 claimed to reveal that 84% of European Americans believed that the effect of the civil rights movement has been positive. A study in 1994 showed that 73% of European Americans considered at least one African American as a good friend, up from 9% in 1975 (Thernstrom & Thernstrom, 1997, pp. 520–521).

Yet as Rosa Parks says, "All those laws against segregation have been passed, and all that progress has been made. But a whole lot of white people's hearts have not been changed" (Parks, 1992, p. 187).

People of color report frequent discrimination in everyday life, hard-to-document events such as physicians' failing to recommend aggressive procedures or police officers' stopping proportionately more automobile drivers of color. These are the subtle indicators of attitude and belief. The blatant examples are the popularity of a racist book, Herrnstein and Murray's *The Bell Curve: Intelligence and Class Structure in American Life* (1994) and the rise in membership and activity of neo-Nazi and neo-Confederate hate groups. The Southern Poverty Law Center added two new hate groups to its list in the years 1999 and 2000: the Council of Conservative Citizens, with 15,000 members in 44 chapters in 20 states; and the League of the South, with 9,000 members in 96 chapters in 20 states (Southern Poverty Law Center, 2000, p. 26).

From 1977 to 1988 the incomes of the richest 1% in the United States increased by 120%, while the incomes of the poorest 20% fell by 10%, during a policy of supply-side tax breaks for the wealthy. Working-class people also got poorer, while the income of middle-class people stayed about the same, hence losing ground in relation to the rich (Harris & Curtis, 1999, pp. 35–40, 131).

Children, in particular, suffered from declining incomes. By 1995, about 36% of U.S. children were living in poverty, defined as the cost of a minimum diet multiplied by 3 and adjusted for the age of the household head and the number of persons in the family. This average conceals the ethnic disparities—41.5% of African American children live in poverty, compared with 15.5% of European American children (Harris & Curtis, 1999, chap. 3).

Further, the situation in American prisons is shocking. In 1993 44.9% of prisoners in local jails were African American, and 48.2% of those in state or federal penitentiaries were African American. In 1995, one third of the male African American male population aged 20 to 29 was either behind bars or on parole. Racial bias in arrests, convictions, and sentencing occur, but are difficult to pinpoint because African Americans commit proportionately more violent crimes than other groups. Being black in the United States is closely correlated with being poor, suffering from high unemployment, and having low levels of education. Most scholars of criminal justice believe that these are the reasons, together with the contextual discrimination that occurs, that the African American community has relatively high crime rates (Hacker, 1995, pp. 187, 204; Thernstrom & Thernstrom, 1997, pp. 264–268; Harris & Curtis, 1999, p. 131; Southern Poverty Law Center, 2000, p. 37; Walker, Spohn, & Delone, 2000).

States now spend more per year on prisons than on higher education, whereas 10 years ago spending priorities were just the reverse. During the 1980s and 1990s, the number of prison cells tripled, while housing appropriations for the poor were reduced by more than 80% (Harris & Curtis, 1999, p. 131).

But underlying all the other issues is the K–12 education of children of color. The struggle against school segregation succeeded in reducing it in the South during the 1970s. Since 1980, however, the overall national pattern has remained unchanged. Many European Americans have fled the public schools, either to the suburbs or to private schools. In Boston, Detroit, Los Angeles, Houston, and San Francisco, there are only a third as many European American children in public schools as their share of the population would indicate. In Washington, D.C., and San Antonio there are only a sixth (Thernstrom & Thernstrom, 1997, pp. 338, 341).

Now that so few European Americans remain in urban public schools, school desegregation has become a moot issue. The federal courts are backing off and leaving local school districts to work out whatever solutions they can (Thernstrom & Thernstrom, 1997, pp. 343–347).

The most nearly accurate information available about how students of color are doing academically comes from the National Assessment of Educational Progress (NAEP), which sponsors national tests, on a sampling basis, that measure specific cognitive skills, not innate abilities. The first tests administered in 1971 to 17-year-olds revealed wide gaps between African Americans and European American students, almost 6 years in reading, 4.3 years in math, 4.7 in science, and 3.1 in writing. These gaps narrowed by the late 1980s but began widening again in the early 1990s (Thernstrom & Thernstrom, 1997, p. 355). The federal and state initiatives to institute standards-based curricula and testing have not yet had time to demonstrate whether standards can reverse this widening gap of scores or what other consequences standards-based testing will have.

Teachers, together with parents and community, are the key determiners of outcome. Their salaries need to keep up with those of other professionals in order to attract the talent needed. More teachers of color must be attracted, which can only occur on a small scale until there are more college graduates of color. In 1993, African Americans constituted 6.2% of those with bachelor's degrees, and they represented 7.4% of teachers in the nation's public schools. This was well below the proportion of African American students in elementary and secondary schools—16.6%—but suggests that slightly more African American college graduates went into elementary and secondary teaching than into other fields requiring college degrees (Thernstrom & Thernstrom, 1997, p. 374).

In California in 1997–1998, only 23% of teachers were people of color, while 70% of the students were, with the number of students of color rising much faster than the number of teachers of color (Keleher, Piana, & Fata, 1999, pp. 15–16). Nationally, the proportion of students of color reached 30% in 1990 and 34% in 1994, and will grow to 40% or more by 2010. Teachers in public schools were 90% white in 1993, a figure predicted to remain high or grow higher in the next decades (Howard, 1999, p. 2).

What is a white ally to do in the present situation? There is no single answer to this question. I find that a useful guide for analyzing how to go about being a white ally is Paul Kivel, in *Uprooting Racism: How White People Can Work for Racial Justice* (1996). In this book Kivel says:

> There is no one correct way to be an ally. Each of us is different. We have different relationships to social organizations, political procedures and economic structures. We are more or less powerful because of such factors as our gender, class, work situation, family and community participation. Being an ally to people of color is an ongoing strategic process in which we look at our personal and social resources, evaluate the environment we have helped to create and decide what needs to be done. (p. 86)

To move from being a "guilty white" to being a "white ally," in Beverly Tatum's model, European American people have to overcome the guilt, shame, and remorse that arise once we acknowledge our whiteness and become aware of the historic racism that we have benefited from and the current racism that we continue to benefit from. Louise Derman-Sparks and Carol Brunson Phillips have written, in *Teaching/Learning Anti-Racism: A Developmental Approach* (1997), a powerful description of that journey, as they analyze their work over 15 years with students at Pacific Oaks College in Pasadena, California. They confirm what the four allies herein demonstrated—that taking specific action in everyday life according to one's own analysis is the way to avoid remaining mired in guilt.

What are the costs of being white allies now? Certainly, my four stories of white allies reveal that, as a result of their actions, they suffered significant consequences, which most people would perceive as negative, even though these white allies felt the long-range benefits outweighed the sacrifices, and even though eventually they were honored by their society. I believe that it is significant that Herb Kohl suffered fewer serious consequences than the others, presumably because during his adult life more European American people were becoming less racist.

Today the cost of being a white ally varies greatly from place to place and circumstance to circumstance. My own experience, in my living in

Oakland, California, and working at a private liberal arts university in Marin County, has been basically positive. I have found many European American people resistant to change, of course, but my Kentucky family has been supportive, and I have suffered no challenge to my life or career. Over 2 decades, I have had the fulfilling experience of seeing a deep shift toward antiracism in the attitudes and experiences of my mostly European American student teachers. The opportunity to be friends with African Americans and people of many cultures has been one of the chief joys of my life.

But for my friend Francie Kendall, who lives nearby in the Bay Area, and makes her living addressing institutional change and white privilege, the emotional costs have been great, including having to choose between her family in Texas and working against racism. For her, becoming a white ally was a life-altering decision. While it is not one about which she has any regrets, she thinks it is important to be honest that there are real risks to employment and relationships when one chooses to go against those who seem most like you.

In Philadelphia, Bonnie Jonhari and her daughter, who are fair-housing activists, have been pursued by white supremacists affiliated with the Ku Klux Klan. The Jonharis sued Ryan Wilson, head of a neo-Nazi group called Alpha HQ, for postings on the Internet in which he called Bonnie Jonhari a "race traitor" who should be hanged. A federal administrative law judge, on July 20, 2000, ordered Ryan to pay $1.1 million in damages to mother and daughter (*San Francisco Chronicle,* July 21, 2000).

At least currently, the majority of those in the courts, the federal government, and most local governments are antiracist. The time to fight is now. The costs could be much greater in the future if we do not achieve a democratic, multicultural society based on mutual respect and the general satisfaction of all groups involved. African Americans acted decisively in the 1950s and 1960s. Now it is time for European Americans to act decisively.

Fighting racism remains exquisitely difficult and painful for many European Americans. Yet there is much cause for hope. More European Americans are taking the lead against racism. Many colleges and universities are now teaching unambiguously against the destructiveness of racism. Preschool, elementary, and secondary teachers are developing real strength and resources for teaching against bias and discrimination and for taking delight in diversity. A growing proportion of young people are experiencing positive multicultural interactions in everyday life. "White" people are embracing the "black" side of their families, as exemplified in Edward Ball's *Slaves in the Family* (1998). European Americans in the South who attended segregated schools are inviting their African American contemporaries to their high school reunions. A United Methodist congregation in rural Belmond, Iowa, is rejoicing in its female African American pastor, Celestyne DeVance, who has hopes that her flock will someday loosen up enough to say "Amen" loudly and repeatedly (*San Francisco Chronicle*, June 21, 1999, p. A3).

Herb Kohl points the way when he says that we don't need to be just white allies, we need to be allies. Each of us, of every background, can enlarge our identity so that it encompasses all humanity. The heritage of every one of us can be traced back to the same place, the beautiful Great Rift Valley of Africa, and beyond that, to the original Big Bang. When we allow this awareness to clear our minds, the variations in our skin tones are mere dapples in the terrifying beauty of the universe.

European American people are recovering from a social disease of the mind. For 500 years we have taken land, wealth, labor, and other resources from people of color. We must acknowledge our complicity in racism and take responsibility for moving the process of reconciliation forward. It took several hundred years to construct the idea of race and the rationale for the distribution of benefits by race; it will certainly take multiple generations to root these out. European Americans cannot expect this to happen by itself. We must each reach into our hearts and, inspired by the long line of white allies before us and with us, find our own ways to eradicate racism. We must act boldly and learn that action brings its own courage, energy, and rewards.

Appendix
More White Allies

John Marshall Harlan (1833–1911)

John Marshall Harlan was a Kentucky gentleman and former slave owner. He served in the Union Army and after the Civil War converted to Republicanism and the cause of black rights. Eventually he became a justice of the Supreme Court, where he was the lone dissenter in the case of *Plessy v. Ferguson* (1896), in which segregation was ruled constitutional. In his dissent he wrote, "The destinies of the two races, in this country, are indissolubly linked together, and the interests of both require that the common government of all shall not permit the seeds of race hate to be planted under sanction of law."

Robert Gould Shaw (1837–1863)

Robert Gould Shaw, an abolitionist, chose to lead the 54th Massachusetts, the first regiment of African American soldiers in the Civil War. The governor of Massachusetts, also an abolitionist, took the initiative in organizing this group of about 600 men; Frederick Douglass helped by recruiting a hundred of them himself, including two of his own sons. The 25-year-old Shaw rode at the head of his men on May 28, 1863, through Beacon Street in Boston, where 20,000 people gathered to see them off, among them Shaw's parents, sister, and wife of one month.

Two months later, the 54th led the assault on Fort Wagner, which defended Charleston, South Carolina. At the top of the parapet, shouting, "Forward, 54th!" Shaw was shot in the chest. Two other white officers and 62 black soldiers died with him. The Confederates, outraged that a white man would led black troops, tore his uniform from his body and threw it in a common trench with his soldiers.

Now, in the Boston Commons opposite the Massachusetts State Capitol, stands a monument to Colonel Shaw created by Augustus Saint-Gaudens, unveiled in 1897. It shows Shaw on his horse; a few inches behind him, in bas-relief, march four files of infantrymen. The monument inspired the movie *Glory*, a feature film in 1989 that told the story of the 54th.

John Prentiss Matthews (1840–1883)

John Matthews was born near Hazlehunt, Mississippi, to wealthy parents, who owned 33 slaves. Nevertheless, he was a Unionist during the Civil War, and afterward ran a general store. The interracial Republican coalition that governed Mississippi during Reconstruction elected him county sheriff.

When white Democrats took over again in 1875, Matthews organized the Independent Party, of black and white farmers, in his county. The Democrats began night riding to threaten African Americans with death if they voted for the Independent Party. In the election of 1883, white leaders of Hazlehunt delivered a written ultimatum to Matthews, ordering him not to vote. When he persisted, the precinct captain, a white farmer, reached inside a wooden box for a double barreled shotgun and killed Matthews instantly.

Matthews's son, John Prentiss Matthews, Jr., just 15 when his father was shot, carried on his principles and became a leader in Republican politics. He was appointed postmaster in Carrollton, 130 miles to the north. White Democrats nicknamed him "Coon" and on Christmas Day, 1890, when he was 22, they shot him dead on the streets of Carrollton.

Lucy Randolph Mason (1882–1959)

Lucy Randolph Mason was born in 1882 near Alexandria, Virginia, a descendant of John Marshall, Robert E. Lee, and George Mason, one of the few members of the Constitutional Convention of 1787 who refused to sign the new constitution, in part because it failed to abolish slavery. The daughter of an Episcopalian minister, Mason worked for the Richmond, Virginia, YWCA and for the National Consumer League before becoming, in 1937, the public relations representative for the CIO in the South. Based in Atlanta, she fought for fair wages and good working conditions for working people and for an end to segregation. She served on the board of directors of Highlander from 1939 to 1953 and proved to be one of its most assiduous fundraisers. She helped found the South Conference for Human Welfare in 1938 and was active in it until 1947. She was a southerner who tried to move the South toward more democracy for both blacks and whites.

Harold LeClaire Ickes (1874–1952)

A Chicago journalist and lawyer, Harold LeClaire Ickes served as a president of Chicago's NAACP. Appointed secretary of interior under FDR, he directed the Public Works Administration (PWA). Ickes promoted self-government of Native Americans and land conservation. He did more than any other New Deal cabinet member to bring black Americans and liberal white Southerners into government.

Branch Rickey (1882–1965)

Raised on an Ohio farm with a pious Methodist upbringing, Branch Rickey graduated near the top of his law school class at the University of Michigan before deciding to devote his career to baseball. He served as general manager of the St. Louis Cardinals nearly 25 years before becoming the manager of the Brooklyn Dodgers in 1942. Wanting to break the color bar in sports and sensing that the time was right, he handpicked Jackie Robinson to be the first black player in the major leagues; Robinson opened his career with the Dodgers in 1947. Rickey, an unconventional character, was variously known as "Deacon," "Professor of Baseball," and "Mahatma."

Eleanor Roosevelt (1884–1962)

Eleanor Roosevelt was taught by her upper-class family to give service. She worked in a New York City settlement house in her teens. When she went to Washington, D.C., she made friends with Negro educator Mary McLeod Bethune, and she was photographed regularly with black Americans. Roosevelt worked closely with the national president of the NAACP from 1934 to 1940 to secure a federal antilynching bill, in vain. Black leaders turned to her when they could not gain access to President Roosevelt. In 1939, she resigned from the Daughters of the American Revolution, because they refused to allow Marian Anderson to sing in Constitution Hall. Eleanor Roosevelt sought opportunities for black Americans in defense industries and an end to discrimination in the military. She visited black troops. She served on the board of directors of the NAACP from 1945 for a decade. However, she had her limits. As a member of the U.S. delegation to the United Nations, she refused to introduce the NAACP's 1947 "Appeal to the World." Prepared by W. E. B. DuBois, it was a strong indictment of U.S. race relations that requested UN monitoring of racial injustices. Roosevelt felt that it would damage the international reputation of the U.S. She died in November 1962 of bone marrow failure.

Aubrey Willis Williams (1890–1965)

Aubrey Willis Williams grew up in meager circumstances outside Birmingham, Alabama, the descendant of an Alabama family that had lost its land and wealth during the Civil War. He finished a degree in social work and worked for 10 years as executive secretary of the Wisconsin Conference of Social Work. He went to Washington, D.C., to serve as assistant to Harry Hopkins in the WPA and later as head of the National Youth Administration. He was also active in the Southern Conference for Human Welfare, which probably caused the Senate not to ratify his appointment to the Rural Electrification Administration. With financial backing from Chicago retail merchant Marshall Field, Williams returned to Montgomery to publish *Southern Farm and Home,* which supported farmers' unions and integration. Williams was also an officer of the Southern Conference Education Fund.

Joseph Gelders (1891–1950)

Joseph Gelders was born in Birmingham, Alabama, into a prosperous and assimilated German-Jewish family who ran a fine downtown restaurant. He was teaching physics at the University of Alabama when the Depression came. When he saw starving people in Tuscaloosa, he started reading works on economics. When he talked about how he thought capitalism had caused the Depression, he was fired from the university. After a few months of working for the National Committee for the Defense of Political Prisoners, he was beaten by a captain in the National Guard and left for dead. He recovered to meet with President Roosevelt, help organize the Southern Conference for Human Welfare, and serve in World War II. He never broke with Communist ideology, but refused to return to Alabama, as the party wished. Instead, he went to the University of California–Berkeley for a Ph.D. in physics. He died of a heart attack at 58.

Lillian Smith (1897–1966)

Lillian Smith, born in Florida, was educated at George Peabody Conservatory. She traveled to China, then directed Laurel Falls Camp for girls in the north Georgia Mountains from 1924 to 1948. She also edited and published for 10 years a literary journal called *South Today*. In 1942 she appealed to her readers to bring about nonsegregation quickly, producing the first southern appeal in print in favor of abolishing the Jim Crow laws. In 1948 she published one of the first U.S. novels of interracial love, *Strange Fruit,* and followed it a year later with a critique of southern white culture, including sexual aspects, called *Killers of the Dream.* This book is still in print and speaks to the present time as deeply and presciently as it did to the late 1940s. Smith wrote about her lesbianism and lived an open life with her partner, Paula Snelling. In the late 1940s, she withdrew from the Southern Conference Education Fund, because she feared that it sheltered Communists. She supported the *Brown* decision in 1954, writing *Now Is the Time* (1955). She died of cancer in 1966.

John Minor Wisdom (1905–1999)

John Minor Wisdom was born in New Orleans to an aristocratic family; his father was a prominent cotton broker and insurance executive. Wisdom is known as the last surviving judge of the federal appeals court that forced the Deep South to give up segregation. That court was the U.S. Court of Appeals for the Fifth Circuit, located in New Orleans. Judge Wisdom and three fellow members were known as "The Four" by those who felt that the judges had destroyed the South. The other three were Elbert Tuttle of Atlanta, John Brown of Houston, and Richard Rives of Montgomery, Alabama. Together they issued landmark decisions that opened the University of Mississippi to James Meredith; struck down discrimination in voting, jury selection, and employment; and provided legal ground for what is known as affirmative action. "I think the Fifth Circuit prevented a second civil war," Judge Wisdom once said. "If we hadn't made people obey the laws of this country, there would have been a lot more people killed, a lot more people hurt" (Obituary, *San Francisco Chronicle*, May 17, 1999). Judge Wisdom received the Presidential Medal of Freedom in 1993 and died in New Orleans at age 94.

Myles Falls Horton (1905–1990)

Myles Falls Horton grew up in south-central Tennessee, the eldest son of parents who were teachers, until professional requirements were increased and they had to take whatever jobs they could find, including sharecropping. Horton was raised Presbyterian; his parents interpreted religion as love and service to one's neighbors. By high school Horton had stood up for black people to the point of being expelled, briefly, from school.

Horton graduated from Cumberland University in Lebanon, Tennessee, certain that he would not let himself fit into the prevailing social and economic system. He went to work for the YMCA, one of the earliest southern organizations in favor of racial justice. He attended Union Theological Seminary and the University of Chicago, than traveled to Denmark to study adult schools, before returning in 1932 to the mountains near Knoxville to set up Highlander Folk School, to provide interracial, residential workshops for empowering poor people.

Horton, and Highlander, focused first on union organizing as a mechanism for achieving social justice. In the late 1930s, when the CIO wanted to organize both white and black workers, Highlander was able to offer the needed contacts and soon became the official CIO training center in the South. These efforts were defeated by Red-baiting after 1948; in the 1950s, the CIO merged back into the American Federation of Labor (AFL). Horton, and Highlander, then focused specifically on overcoming segregation, with workshops for blacks and whites to plan local action and to prepare for court-ordered desegregation. In 1955, Rosa Parks attended a Highlander workshop, 4 months before her refusal to move on the Montgomery bus. During the Montgomery bus boycott, Horton introduced Parks to Eleanor Roosevelt in New York City as "the first lady of the South."

Together with local black leaders, Horton planned and carried out a literacy program on Johns Island that became a model "Citizenship School" for the deep South. By the late 1950s, Highlander had become so effective in fighting segregation that in 1959 the state of Tennessee sued it for being a Communist training school; when the state could not prove that in court, it confiscated Highlander's property on charges of selling beer without a license. Highlander reopened in Chattanooga. In 1971, when Horton stepped down as director, Highlander was relocated back to a farm near Knoxville, where Horton lived and from where he traveled widely to visit literacy campaigns and social-action projects inspired by his work. He died of cancer at age 85 with a clear conscience; he had never bowed to the racist system.

Lyndon Baines Johnson (1908–1973)

Lyndon Baines Johnson served in Washington from 1932 and was majority leader of the Senate from 1953 to 1960. By the late 1950s, he was the key figure in transforming Congress from a citadel of white supremacy to a functioning institution of American government. When he won election in 1964 as president of the United States, he was committed to ending racial injustice and poverty with legislative accomplishments known as the Great Society. He sponsored the Civil Rights Act of 1964 and the Voting Rights Act of 1965, knowing that they might cause the majority of white voters in the southern states to leave the Democratic Party, which they did. But the proportion of registered black Americans in the South rose from one quarter to two thirds.

Lawrence D. Duke, Sr. (1913–1999)

As a young attorney in Georgia, Lawrence D. Duke, Sr., in the early 1940s successfully prosecuted several Klansmen for the murder of a black man whipped to death. As an assistant state attorney general, in 1946 he won the state's case for revocation of the Georgia Klan's charter of incorporation. He became a state judge and lived to see the New South.

Frank Wilkinson (born 1914)

Frank Wilkinson grew up in Beverly Hills, California, in a conservative family. He graduated from the University of California, Los Angeles in 1936. In 1938 he worked for the Catholic Citizens Housing Council when the first housing projects were built, keeping ethnic groups separate. In 1942 the city of Los Angeles hired him to manage the first integrated housing project in Watts. Simultaneously the FBI opened a file on him that matured into a 132,000-page dossier. He refused to sign loyalty oaths and in 1952 was fired. In 1954 he set up the Citizens Committee to Preserve American Freedom in Los Angeles to help people called before HUAC. In 1957, he joined the national ACLU in the fight against HUAC. In 1960, he helped found the National Committee to Abolish HUAC, for which he worked until they achieved their goal in 1975. He spent most of 1961 in jail for refusing to testify before HUAC. In 1981, he sued the FBI and won.

Frank M. Johnson, Jr. (1918–1999)

Frank M. Johnson, Jr., was the judge of the U.S. District Court who ruled in favor of Rosa Parks. He was born in Winston County, the northwest county of Alabama that seceded from the state at the outbreak of the Civil War to become the pro-Union Free State of Winston. His family was Republican from tradition, dating from then. He earned his law degree at the University of Alabama and practiced law in a small town until appointed U.S. attorney for the Northern District of Alabama in 1952. He was appointed federal judge by President Eisenhower in November 1955, just in time for him to hear the case of Rosa Parks and to rule, in 1956, that segregation on buses was unconstitutional. He also ruled in 1961 against Montgomery and the KKK, in a case filed by the Freedom Riders. In 1963, he ordered the desegregation of Tuskegee High School, and in 1965 he permitted the Selma marchers to protest denial of black voting rights. During his tenure, his court invalidated segregation and other forms of racial discrimination in Alabama's transportation facilities, voter registration processes, schools and colleges, administrative agencies, system of jury selection, prisons, mental institutions, museums, recreational centers, political parties, and government grant programs. He and his family were subjected to ostracism, threats, and vitriolic editorial and verbal abuse, the latter most notably from George Wallace, his law school classmate. Johnson lived in Montgomery and played golf at the Air Force base, shunned at the local country club.

Marge Gelders Franz (born 1922)

Marge Gelders Franz was born in Birmingham in 1922, daughter of Joseph Gelders (see above). Marge joined the Young Communists League at age 13 and the American Communist Party at 15, in which she continued her membership until 1956. When she was 17, she was arrested by Bull Connor for handing out pamphlets that challenged a local ordinance that enabled police to pick up and hold anyone for 72 hours, without permitting a phone call. From 1944 to 1946, she edited the *Southern Patriot*, the newsletter of the Southern Conference Education Fund. In 1947 Gelders moved to Berkeley, married, raised four children, returned to college at age 48, received her Ph.D. in American Studies, and from 1974 to 2001 taught at University of California Santa Cruz. In 1996, she organized 23 women's organizations in Santa Cruz County to oppose the removal of affirmative action by Proposition 209, which won despite her efforts.

Viola Gregg Liuzzo (1925–1965)

Viola Gregg Liuzzo lived most of her early years in Georgia and Tennessee. Her family moved frequently, eventually to Michigan. Viola finished only ninth grade and had two early marriages and two children. At the age of 25 she married Jim Liuzzo, a business agent for the local Teamsters Union. They had three more children. A year before her death, she enrolled in Wayne State University in Detroit to qualify for a bachelor's degree.

Liuzzo became familiar with civil rights issues through her friend and housekeeper, Sarah Evans, and became one of the few white members of the local NAACP. The Episcopal chaplain at Wayne state, the Rev. Malcolm Boyd, had been to the South to help demonstrate, and talking with him made Liuzzo do a lot of thinking. In March 1965 Rev. Martin Luther King, Jr., leading marchers from Selma to Montgomery, sent out a plea for ministers of all races and religions to come to Selma. Unitarian minister Rev. James Reeb from Boston was one who responded. Two days later he was dead from a blow to the head by a white man. Four days later, President Johnson delivered a voting rights bill to Congress.

A few days after that, Liuzzo decided, despite her husband's concerns, to drive the family car directly to Selma. When Liuzzo reached there, she was put up in the apartment of Mrs. Willie Lee Jackson in the federal housing project. For 6 days Liuzzo chauffeured people between Selma and Montgomery for the 5-day march from Selma to Montgomery, which ended on the steps of the capitol. After ceremonies there, Liuzzo and a young African American, LeRoy Moton, drove marchers back to Selma and decided to return to Montgomery for another carload. About halfway there, on a lonely stretch of road in Lowndes County, a car that had been trailing them drew alongside, its occupants opened fire, and a bullet to her head killed Liuzzo instantly.

Four Alabama Klansmen were indicted for the murder. One, Gary Rowe, turned out to be a longtime undercover FBI plant within the Klan; he had not been able to dissuade the killers from the shooting. His testimony gave the state a strong case against the other three. The first jury was hung; the second found the Klansmen not guilty. The U.S. Department of Justice moved to bring federal charges, and the three Klansmen were convicted in the federal court of Judge Frank M. Johnson, Jr., and given a maximum sentence of 10 years. A survey in *Ladies Home Journal* showed that only 26% of readers approved of Mrs. Liuzzo's mission in Selma.

Lois Mark Stalvey (born 1925)

Lois Mark Stalvey grew up in Milwaukee, Wisconsin, the daughter of a Protestant mother and a Catholic father. The city was so segregated that Lois had no contact with African American people until she interviewed Duke Ellington as the editor of her high school newspaper. She ran an advertising agency for 8 years, then married and settled down in Omaha, Nebraska. There she discovered racial discrimination, joined the Urban League, and tried in vain to help an African American family buy a house. After moving to Philadelphia in 1961, the Stalveys chose to live in the integrated Mount Airy section of town. There Stalvey organized a Panel of American Women (Negro, Catholic, Jewish, and Protestant) and wrote articles for national women's magazines promoting tolerance. Eventually she wrote two books that laid out her experience in fighting racism: *The Education of a WASP* (University of Wisconsin Press, 1970) and *Getting Ready: The Education of a White Family in Inner City Schools* (University of Wisconsin Press, 1974). In 1997 the University of Wisconsin Press reissued *Getting Ready* as *Three to Get Ready*; its relevance seemed undiminished. Stalvey retired to Sedona, Arizona.

Charles Morgan, Jr. (born 1930)

Charles Morgan, Jr., was a Birmingham lawyer who, after the bombing of a black church and death of four children on September 15, 1963, spoke at the Young Men's Business Club to deplore the harm done and say that all of Birmingham's white people shared in the guilt. Within 3 weeks he had to move out of town and later wrote his story in *A Time to Speak* (Harper and Row, 1964).

Morris Dees (born 1936)

In a family originally from Scotland, Dees grew up Baptist in a town of 400 people outside Montgomery, Alabama. He finished law school at the University of Alabama, but went into the mail order business with great success. At age 32 he sold his businesses to become a civil rights lawyer. Initially, he sued the Montgomery YMCA summer camp for racial discrimination. In 1971 he cofounded, with Joe Levin, the Southern Poverty Law Center in Montgomery, with Julian Bond as president of the board. In 1980 he started Klanwatch, bringing suits against state and national Ku Klux Klan leaders, in 1987 winning damages of $7 million against the United Klans of America. In 1983, three members of the KKK burned down the building of the Southern Poverty Law Center; in 1985, it was replaced, complete with high-tech surveillance and platoons of guards. An endowment was raised, and a new project added, Teaching Tolerance, which holds workshops for teachers and has distributed $4 million worth of teaching aids. During the 1990s, Dees brought suits against white terrorists, such as the White Aryan Resistance, against which he won $12.5 million in damages. Dees has written his autobiography, *Season of Justice* (Charles Scribner's, 1991), and, with James Corcoran, *Gathering Storm: America's Militia Threat* (Harper, 1997). In 2000 Dees joined with Rosa Parks to launch the National Campaign for Tolerance to counter the rising tide of intolerance.

Louise Derman-Sparks (born 1940)

Louise Derman-Sparks grew up in Brooklyn and Manhattan in a working-class Jewish family. Continuing her mother's activism, she became a preschool teacher for low-income African American children in Ypsilanti, Michigan. She moved to Los Angeles to direct a community-based child care center, then taught full-time at Pacific Oaks College. Through doing research on the development of young children's racial identity, she worked with teachers at Pacific Oaks Children's Schools to produce *Anti-Bias Curriculum: Tools for Empowering Young Children* (NAEYC, 1989). Derman-Sparks travels widely, giving speeches and workshops. She set up leadership-development groups in three cities, coauthoring *Teaching/Learning Racism: A Developmental Approach* (Teachers College Press, 1997). "What has sustained me is my sense of being part of a long, connected historic process. Those who have gone before me inspired and influenced what I do; what I create will hopefully move others to take the work up and bring it to new places and heights."

Mab Segrest (born 1949)

Mab Segrest grew up in Tuskegee, Alabama, where she took part in the struggle to overcome segregation, against her parents' efforts to set up white private schools. Segrest received her doctorate in English from Duke University in 1979 and continues to reside in Durham, North Carolina. She is a cofounder of *Feminary: A Lesbian-Feminist Journal for the South* and has written two significant books: *My Mama's Dead Squirrel* (Firebrand, 1985) and *Memoir of a Race Traitor* (South End Press, 1994). She also coedited *The Third Wave: Feminist Essays on Racism* (Kitchen Table: Women of Color Press, 1997). She illuminates the ways homophobia and racism are linked and insists that the choice is not for race but for humanity, for our whole organism. Segrest coordinated for 6 years the work of North Carolinians Against Racist and Religious Violence; she has served as a board member of the Center for Democratic Renewal (Atlanta) and as coordinator of the U.S. Urban-Rural Mission of the World Council of Churches.

Francie Kendall (born 1947)

Francie Kendall is an upper-middle-class southern woman who grew up in Waco, Texas. Through her experiences in the National Student YWCA she began her life-long work on white privilege and organizational change for social justice. She has continued that work for more than 30 years as a consultant to colleges and universities, corporations, government agencies, and not-for-profits that are working to create hospitable and equitable workplaces. She is the author of *Diversity in the Classroom* (Teachers College Press, 1983 and 1996) and is currently writing a book on white privilege. She lives in the San Francisco Bay Area.

Paul Kivel (born 1948)

Kivel grew up in a white Jewish upper-middle-class suburb of Los Angeles. In 1979 he cofounded the Oakland Men's Project, a nonprofit community program focused on preventing male violence and on issues of social justice. He has conducted hundreds of workshops around the nation for teens and adults on racism, violence prevention, and gender and economic issues, focusing on how people can work together for institutional and organization change. His books include *Uprooting Racism: How White People Can Work for Racial Justice* (New Society, 1996), which won a Gustavus Myers Award for Outstanding Book for Human Rights in 1996, as well as *Men's Work* (Hazelden, 1998), and *Boys Will Be Men* (New Society, 1999). His newest book is *I Can Make My World a Safer Place: A Kid's Book about Stopping Violence* (Hunter House, 2000). Kivel makes his home in Oakland, California, and can be reached at www.paulkivel.com.

References

Adams, F. (1992). *James A. Dombrowski: An American heretic, 1897–1983*. Knoxsville: University of Tennessee Press.

Allen, J., Als, H., Lewis, J., & Litwack, L. (2000). *Without sanctuary: Lynching photography in America*. Sante Fe, NM: Twin Palms.

Angier, N. (2000, June 27). A pearl and a hodgepodge: Human DNA. *New York Times*, pp. A1, 21.

Aptheker, H. (1992). *Anti-racism in U.S. history: The first two hundred years*. Westport, CT: Greenwood Press.

Ball, E. (1998). *Slaves in the family*. New York: Farrar, Straus, & Giroux.

Banton, M. & Harwood, J. (1975). *The race concept*. New York: Praeger.

Barkan, E. (1992). *Retreat of scientific racism: Changing concepts of race in Britain and the United States between the world wars*. Cambridge, England: Cambridge University Press.

Bean, R. B. (1935). *Races of man*. New York: The University Society.

Bell, D. (Ed.). (1980). *Shades of brown: New perspectives on school desegregation*. New York: Teachers College Press.

Blaut, J. M. (1993). *The colonizer's model of the world: Geographical diffusionism and Eurocentric history*. New York: Guilford Press.

Braden, A. (1964). *House Un-American Activities Committee: Bulwark of segregation*. Los Angeles: National Committee to Abolish HUAC.

Braden, A. (1977, Winter). A second open letter to southern white women. *Southern Exposure, 4*, 50–53.

Braden, A. (1979, July). Reminiscences of Anne Braden. Columbia University Oral History Research Office Collection, New York.

Braden, A. (1981, April). Interview with Anne Braden. Conducted by Sue Thrasher. Highlander Research and Education Center.

Braden, A. (1984, November/December). You can't be neutral: An interview by Sue Thrasher and Eliot Wigginton. *Southern Exposure, 12*, 79–85.

Braden, A. (1999). *The wall between*. Knoxville: University of Tennessee Press. (Original work published 1958)

Braden, C., & Braden, A. (1928–1972). Papers. Wisconsin Historical Society, Madison, WI.

Branch, T. (1988). *Parting the waters: America in the King years 1954–1963.* New York: Simon & Schuster.

Burns, S. (Ed.). (1997). *Daybreak of freedom: The Montgomery bus boycott.* Chapel Hill: University of North Carolina Press.

Cannon, P. (1956). *A gentle knight: My husband, Walter White.* New York: Rinehart.

Cash, W. J. (1941). *The mind of the South.* New York: Alfred Knopf.

Chappell, D. L. (1994). *Inside agitators: White southerners in the civil rights movement.* Baltimore: Johns Hopkins University Press.

Clark, S. (1986). *Ready from within: Septima Clark and the civil rights movement.* Navarro, CA: Wild Trees Press.

Clayton, B. (1987). A southern modernist: The mind of W. J. Cash. In B. Clayton & J. A. Salmond (Eds.), *The South is another land: Essays on the twentieth century South* (pp. 171–185). Contributions in American History, no. 124. New York: Greenwood Press.

Colby, A., & Damon, W. (1992). *Some do care: Contemporary lives of moral commitment.* New York: Free Press.

Cook, B. W. (1999). *Eleanor Roosevelt: The definitive years.* Vol. 2, 1933–1938. New York: Penguin.

Coon, C. S. (1962). *The origin of the races.* New York: Alfred Knopf.

Coon, C. S. (1965). *The living races of man.* New York: Alfred Knopf.

Derman-Sparks, L., & Phillips, C. B. (1997). *Teaching/learning anti-racism: A developmental approach.* New York: Teachers College Press.

Diamond, L. K. (1980). The story of our blood groups. In M. M. Wintrobe, *Blood, pure and eloquent: A story of discovery, of people, and of ideas* (chap. 2). New York: McGraw Hill.

Durr, V. (1985). *Outside the magic circle: The autobiography of Virginia Foster Durr* (H. F. Barnard, Ed.). Tuscaloosa, AL: University of Alabama Press.

Dyson, M. E. (2000). *"I may not get there with you:" The true Martin Luther King, Jr.* New York: New Press.

Egerton, J. (1994). *Speak now against the day: The generation before the civil rights movement in the South.* Chapel Hill: University of North Carolina Press.

Formisano, R. P. (1991). *Boston against busing.* Chapel Hill: University of North Carolina Press.

Fosl, C. (1999, Fall). "There was no middle ground": Anne Braden and the southern social justice movement. *National Women's Studies Association Journal, 11,* 24–48.

Foster, M. (1997). *Black teachers on teaching.* New York: New Press.

Glen, J. M. (1988). *Highlander: No ordinary school, 1932–1962.* Lexington, KY: University Press of Kentucky.

Goldcomb, G. S. (1993). *From swastika to Jim Crow: Refugee scholars at black colleges.* Malabar, FL: Krieger.

Goodwin, D. K. (1994). *No ordinary time: Franklin & Eleanor Roosevelt: The home front in World War II.* New York: Simon & Schuster.

Gould, S. J. (1981). *The mismeasure of man.* New York: W. W. Norton.

Grafton, S. (1950, April 29). The lonesomest man in town. *Collier's,* 20–21.

Green, C. M. (1967). *The secret city: A history of race relations in the nation's capital.* Princeton: Princeton University Press.

Hacker, A. (1995). *Two nations: Black and white, separate, hostile, unequal.* Rev. ed. New York: Ballantine.

Hall, J. D. (1979). *Revolt against chivalry: Jesse Daniel Ames and the women's campaign against lynching.* New York: Columbia University Press.

Hannaford, I. (1996). *Race: The history of an idea in the West.* Washington, DC, & Baltimore: Woodrow Wilson Center Press and Johns Hopkins University Press.

Harris, F., & Curtis, L. (Eds.) (1999). *Locked in the poorhouse: Cities, race, and poverty in the United States.* Lanham, MD: Rowman and Littlefield.

Herrnstein, R. J., & Murray, C. (1994). *The bell curve: Intelligence and class structure in American life.* New York: Free Press.

Highlander Research and Education Center. Papers. Wisconsin Historical Society, Madison, WI.

hooks, b. (2000). *Where we stand: Class matters.* New York: Routledge.

Howard, G. R. (1999). *We can't teach what we don't know: White teachers, multiracial schools.* New York: Teachers College Press.

Ignatiev, N., and Garvey, J. (Eds.) (1996) *Race traitor.* New York and London: Routledge.

Jordan, W. D. (1974). *The white man's burden: Historical origins of racism in the United States.* London: Oxford University Press.

Keleher, T., Piana, L. D., & Fata, M. (1999 August). *Creating crisis: How California teaching policies aggravate racial inequality in public schools* [on-line]. Available: erase@arc.org.

Kellogg, C. F. (1967). *NAACP: A history of the National Association for the Advancement of Colored People; Vol. 1. 1909–1920.* Baltimore, MD: Johns Hopkins University Press.

Kelley, R. D. G. (1990). *Hammer and hoe: Alabama Communists during the Great Depression.* Chapel Hill: University of North Carolina Press.

Kincheloe, J. L., Steinberg, S. R., Rodriguez, N. M., & Chennault, R. E. (Eds.). (1998). *White reign: Deploying whiteness in America.* New York: St. Martin's Press.

King, J. C. (1971). *The biology of race.* New York: Harcourt Brace Javanovitch. (Reprinted 1981. Berkeley, CA: University of California Press)

Kivel, P. (1996). *Uprooting racism: How white people can work for racial justice.* Gabriola Island, British Columbia: New Society.

Klibaner, I. (1989). *Conscience of a troubled South: The Southern Conference Educational Fund 1946–1966.* New York: Carlson.

Kluger, R. (1975). *Simple justice: The history of* Brown v. Board of Education *and black America's struggle for equality.* New York: Vintage.

Kohl, H. (1967). *Thirty-six children.* New York: New American Library.

Kohl, H. (1968). Public schools in the ghetto: A conversation conducted by R. Croney (Cassette recording). University of California–Berkeley Media Center.

Kohl, H. (1974). *Half the house.* New York: Dutton.

Kohl, H. (1977, Spring). Reflections on nine years in Berkeley. *City Miner, 15,* 43–46.

Kohl, H. (1978). *Growing with your children.* Boston: Little, Brown.

Kohl, H. (1979, November). Can the schools build a new social order? *Debate, 1,* 6–11.

Kohl, H. (1992). *From archetype to zeitgeist: Powerful ideas for powerful thinking.* Boston: Little, Brown.

Kohl, H. (1993, Fall). The myth of "Rosa Parks the Tired." *Multicultural Education, 1,* 6–10.

Kohl, H. (1994). *I won't learn from you and other thoughts on creative maladjustment.* New York: New Press.

Kohl, H. (1995). *Should we burn Babar? Essays on children's literature and the power of stories.* New York: New Press.

Kohl, H. (1996/1997, Winter). Tender warriors: The dilemma of "inherent" inequality and the personal toll of integration [Review of the books *Warriors don't cry* and *Silver rights*]. *ReThinking Schools,* 22–23.

Kohl, H. (1998a). *The discipline of hope: Learning from a lifetime of teaching.* New York: Simon & Schuster.

Kohl, H. (1998b, March 31). Talk at Cody's Book Store. [Cassette]

Kohl, H. (2000, June 3). Speech to Graduates of Dominican University of California, School of Education.{Cassette]

Korstad, R., & Lichtenstein, N. (1988). Opportunities lost and found: Labor, radicals, and the early civil rights movement. *Journal of American History, 75,* 786–811.

Loewen, J. W. (1995). *Lies my teacher told me: Everything your American history textbook got wrong.* New York: Viking Press.

Lewontin, R. C., Rose, S., & Kamin, L. J. (1984). *Not in our genes: Biology, ideology, and human nature.* New York: Pantheon.

Love, S. (1996). *One blood: The death and resurrection of Charles R. Drew.* Chapel Hill, NC: University of North Carolina Press.

Massey, D. S., & Denton, N. A. (1993). *American apartheid: Segregation and the making of the underclass.* Cambridge, MA: Harvard University Press.

McWhorter, D. (2001). *Carry me home.* New York: Simon & Schuster.

Meltzer, M. (1993). *Slavery: A world history.* Updated ed. New York: Da Capo Press.

Mills, C. W. (1997). *The racial contract.* Ithaca, NY: Cornell University Press.

Mitford, J. (1960). *Daughters and rebels.* Boston: Houghton Mifflin.

Mitford, J. (1977). *A fine old conflict.* New York: Alfred Knopf.

Moore, R. B., & Banfield, B. (1983). *Reconstruction: The promise and betrayal of democracy.* New York: Council on Interracial Books for Children.

Myrdal, G. (1962). *An American dilemma: The Negro problem and American democracy.* New York: Pantheon. (Original work published 1944)

Norton, M. B., Katzman, D. M., Escott, P. D., Chudacoff, H. P., Paterson, T. G., & Tuttle, W. M., Jr. (1990). *A people & a nation: A history of the United States.* (3rd ed.). Boston: Houghton Mifflin.

O'Reilly, K. (1983). *Hoover and the un-Americans: The FBI, HUAC, and the Red menace.* Philadelphia: Temple University Press.

O'Reilly, K. (1989). *Racial matters: The FBI's secret file on Black America, 1960–1972.* New York: Free Press.

Parks, R., with Haskins, J.(1992). *Rosa Parks: My story.* New York: Dial Books.

Record, W. (1964). *Race and radicalism: The NAACP and the Communist Party in conflict.* Ithaca, NY: Cornell University Press.

Relethford, J. (1994). *The human species: An introduction to biological anthropology.* (2nd ed.). Mount View, CA: Mayfield.

Roosevelt, E. (1949). *This I remember.* New York: Harper Brothers.

Rosen, R. N. (1982). *A short history of Charleston.* San Francisco: LEXIKOS.

Rowan, C. (1952). *South of freedom.* New York: Alfred A. Knopf.

Salmon, C., Cartron, J-P., & Rouger, P. (1984). *The human blood groups.* New York: Masson.

Salmond, J. A. (1990). *The conscience of a lawyer: Clifford Durr and American civil liberties, 1899–1975.* Tuscaloosa: University of Alabama Press.

Schrecker, E. (1998). *Many are the crimes: McCarthyism in America.* Boston: Little, Brown.

Shanklin, E. (1994). *Anthropology and race.* Belmont, CA: Wadsworth.

Sipress, J. M. (1997, February). Relearning race: Teaching race as a cultural construction. *The History Teacher, 30,* 175–185.

Smedley, A. (1993). *Race in North America: Origin and evolution of a worldview.* Boulder, CO: Westview Press.

Soros, G. (1991). *Underwriting democracy.* New York: New Press.

Southern Poverty Law Center. (2000, Summer). *Intelligence Report,* 99.

Staples, B. (1999, October 3). A prayer for the dead. *New York Review of Books.*

Stearns, P. N., Adas, M., & Schwartz, S. B. (1992). *World civilizations: The global experience.* Vol. 1, *Beginnings to 1750.* New York: HarperCollins.

Sullivan, P. (1996). *Days of hope: Race and democracy in the New Deal era.* Chapel Hill: University of North Carolina Press.

Tatum, B. D. (1994, Summer). Teaching white students about racism: The search for white allies and the restoration of hope. *Teachers College Record, 95,* 463–476.

Teachers and Writers Collaborative. (1990). *A tribute to Herbert Kohl, June Jordan, and Flora Arnstein: Selections from Teachers and Writers Magazine, 1966–1977.* New York: Teachers and Writers Collaborative.

Terkel, S. (1973, June 8). "Conversation with Rosa Parks, Myles Horton, and E. D. Nixon" [Radio broadcast]. Transcript available from Highlander Research and Education Center, 1959 Highlander Way, New Market, TN 37820.

Thernstrom, S., & Thernstrom, A. (1997). *America in black and white: One nation, indivisible.* New York: Simon & Schuster.

Walker, S., Spohn, C., & Delone, M. (2000). *The color of justice: Race, ethnicity and crime in America.* (2nd ed.) Belmont, CA: Wadsworth.

Waring, J. W. (1955–1957). Reminiscences of Waties Waring. Columbia University Oral History Research Office Collection, New York.

Williams, V. J. (1989). *From a caste to a minority: Changing attitudes of American sociologists toward Afro-Americans 1896–1945.* New York: Greenwood Press.

Williams, V. J. (1996). *Rethinking race: Franz Boas and his contemporaries.* Lexington, KY: University Press of Kentucky.

Wood, P. H. (1996). *Strange new land: African Americans 1617–1776*. Young Oxford History of African Americans, vol. 2. New York: Oxford University Press.

Woodward, C. Van (1966). *The strange career of Jim Crow*. (2nd rev. ed.) New York: Oxford University Press.

Yarbrough, T. E. (1987). *A passion for justice: J. Waties Waring and civil rights*. New York: Oxford University Press.

Young, M. D., & Rosiek, J. (2000, March). Interrogating whiteness [Review of the book *White Reign: Deploying Whiteness in America*]. *Educational Researcher*, 39–44.

Index

About the Author

Cʏɴᴛʜɪᴀ Sᴛᴏᴋᴇꜱ Bʀᴏᴡɴ is a professor emerita of education at Dominican University of California in San Rafael, California, where she was previously director of the Secondary Credential Program. She received her Ph.D. in history of education from Johns Hopkins University in 1964. Her previous books include *Alexander Meiklejohn: Teacher of Freedom*; *Ready from Within: Septima Clark and the Civil Rights Movement*, which won the 1987 American Book Award; *Like It Was: A Complete Guide to Writing Oral History*; *New Faces in Our Schools: Student-Generated Solutions to Ethnic Conflict* (with Karen Jorgensen); and *Connecting with the Past: History Workshop in Middle and High Schools*.